HERMENEUTICS AS CRITIQUE

NEW DIRECTIONS IN CRITICAL THEORY

NEW DIRECTIONS IN CRITICAL THEORY

AMY ALLEN, GENERAL EDITOR

New Directions in Critical Theory presents outstanding classic and contemporary texts in the tradition of critical social theory, broadly construed. The series aims to renew and advance the program of critical social theory, with a particular focus on theorizing contemporary struggles around gender, race, sexuality, class, and globalization and their complex interconnections.

For a complete list of titles, see page 237

HERMENEUTICS AS CRITIQUE

SCIENCE, POLITICS, RACE, AND CULTURE

LORENZO C. SIMPSON

Columbia University Press *New York*

Columbia University Press
Publishers Since 1893
New York   Chichester, West Sussex
cup.columbia.edu
Copyright © 2021 Columbia University Press
All rights reserved

Library of Congress Cataloging-in-Publication Data
Names: Simpson, Lorenzo Charles, author.
Title: Hermeneutics as critique : science, politics, race and culture /
Lorenzo C. Simpson.
Description: New York : Columbia University Press, [2021] |
Includes bibliographical references and index. |
Identifiers: LCCN 2020034143 (print) | LCCN 2020034144 (ebook) |
ISBN 9780231196840 (hardback) | ISBN 9780231196857
(trade paperback) | ISBN 9780231551854 (ebook)
Subjects: LCSH: Hermeneutics.
Classification: LCC BD241 .S582 2021 (print) |
LCC BD241 (ebook) | DDC 121/.686—dc23
LC record available at https://lccn.loc.gov/2020034143
LC ebook record available at https://lccn.loc.gov/2020034144

For My Parents

Lorenzo, Sr. and Bessie—without whom, nothing . . .

CONTENTS

Preface and Acknowledgments ix

Introduction 1

1 Twin Earth and Its Horizons: On Hermeneutics, Reference, and Scientific Theory Choice 24

2 Critical Fusions: Toward a Genuine "Hermeneutics of Suspicion" 54

3 Agency, the "Politics of Memory," and Reparative Justice: Hermeneutics and the Politics of Development 81

4 Toward a Hermeneutics of Race: Biology, Race, Ethnicity, and Culture 103

5 Concluding Reflections: Toward a New Reconciliation of Hermeneutics and Critical Theory, or Notes Toward a Hermeneutic Democracy 142

Appendix: Toward a Hermeneutics of the Ethical Response 155
Notes 165
Bibliography 207
Index 219

PREFACE AND ACKNOWLEDGMENTS

The aim of this book is to move the tradition of philosophical hermeneutics in new directions by developing a hermeneutics with critical intent. In doing so, I extend my earlier attempts to move us beyond the unproductive binary opposition of an imperialistic model of rationality to a normless relativism, an opposition that suffuses so much contemporary thought. In seeking to chart a course between this Scylla and Charybdis by insisting on the salience of the hermeneutic question to all forms of knowing, I highlight the relevance of hermeneutic approaches to matters that are far beyond the field of literary and textual analysis to which, with few exceptions, hermeneutic strategies have traditionally been restricted. Science, politics, race, and culture, along with their various intersections, figure prominently among the matters on which hermeneutics can shed new light. In putting hermeneutics to work within such wide-ranging fields of application, I hope both to demonstrate the distinctive contribution that it can make and to show how it can allow us to avoid many of the dilemmas and aporetics that have plagued other analyses within these fields.

I elaborate a hermeneutic account of linguistic meaning and of progress that allows us to understand the evolution of scientific knowledge as a progressive learning process, thus refuting claims to the effect that hermeneutic analyses are necessarily relativistic or critically impotent. I deploy hermeneutic accounts of cultural identity and of rationality to develop modalities of engagement that will sustain critical dialogues about questionable, although culturally endorsed, practices—practices such as female excision—without invidious ethnocentrism. Forging modalities for dialogues that would bridge the gap between a merely culturally bound interpretation and a respectful transcultural criticism seems to me to be one of the central challenges facing us now. I develop a hermeneutic analysis of racial classification that challenges recent attempts to use current research in population genetics to shore up the view that race as it is commonly understood has a biological basis. And, in thus reaffirming the view that race is a social kind rather than a natural kind, I highlight the ways in which the concept of race is implicated in a variety of social agendas and practices. Furthermore, by providing hermeneutically informed analyses of agency and of racial identity, I highlight hermeneutics' potential to make contributions to ongoing conversations about issues that continue to plague us and topics with which we continue to wrestle—issues such as global justice, poverty, inequality, cultural racism, epistemic injustice, adaptive preferences, and so on.

By developing a critical hermeneutics that addresses issues of scientific progress and cross-cultural understanding as well as fraught issues at their intersections such as that of race, I hope to expand our knowledge and insights about both philosophical hermeneutics and the topics of investigation that I treat. And, in so doing, I hope to offer a distinctive strategy for reconciling

Critical Theory's concern with emancipatory reflection with the imperatives of hermeneutical reflection.

I have read portions of this book in a number of places. Earlier versions of chapters 1 and 4 were first presented in the Faculty Colloquium luncheon series of the Department of Philosophy at Yale University. I am grateful for the helpful discussions that ensued. The earliest version of chapter 2 was presented as the keynote address at the seventh annual meeting of the North American Society for Philosophical Hermeneutics at the University of California, Riverside. I am grateful for that invitation and for the discussion that followed and also for the conversation that followed my presentation of some material from chapter 3 in the Stony Brook University philosophy department's work-in–progress series.

I am indebted to the late Ruth Barcan Marcus and to Jürgen Habermas for helpful conversations about theories of meaning and their implications, the subject matter of Chapter 1. Professor Habermas was kind enough to read and comment in detail on an earlier draft of that text. The final version of chapter 4, devoted to the concept of race, was the beneficiary of careful reading at an earlier stage by the biologist David Ratner, the biostatistician Sean L. Simpson, who also made helpful comments on an earlier version of chapter 3, and the philosopher Robert Gooding-Williams. I am grateful to many others for illuminating conversations about the range of topics taken up in this book: to my colleagues Edward Casey and Harvey Cormier with whom I discussed the general idea of the book; to Kenneth Baynes who, over the course of many conversations, encouraged me to think more carefully about the idea of agential autonomy, an idea that I deploy in chapters 2 and 3; and to Verity Harte and Thomas Schmid for helpful discussions about Gadamer's relation to Plato. Thanks as well to the anonymous reviewers for Columbia University Press. Although we have not communicated directly about this book's contents, a comment by Thomas McCarthy was instrumental in inspiring this study. Well over a decade ago, he said to me something to the effect that I always seemed to manage to find a "hermeneutic angle" on a range of issues that are pertinent to Critical Theory. In some ways, the seeds for this book were sown by that comment. During much of the writing of this book, I have had as a virtual interlocutor the late Richard M. Rorty, a thinker with whom I conversed frequently and disagreed often while we were both teaching in Virginia, a thinker whom I found to be an ecumenical conversational partner of great generosity.

I would like to express my gratitude toward a number of graduate students at Stony Brook who provided research assistance over the course of this book's production: Eun Ah Lee, Nathifa Greene, Alyssa Adamson, and Giada Mangiameli, who also compiled the bibliography. Needless to say, without them this project would have taken much longer to see the light of day. And I am also grateful to Wendy Lochner, philosophy editor at Columbia University Press, for her enthusiasm for this project and for her canny editorial advice. A substantial portion of this book was written while I was a visiting fellow in the Yale philosophy department. I want to express my appreciation to Karsten Harries and to Stephen Darwall for hosting me on those occasions. I would like to thank the College of Arts and Sciences at Stony Brook for research funding that facilitated the completion of this study. And I wish to thank my wife, Marsha, for her forbearance over the course of this book's gestation, for her helpful edits of the final product, and for her aesthetic advice regarding its cover design.

Earlier versions of portions of this book have appeared in print elsewhere and have been revised and expanded for inclusion here: a previous version of chapter 1 appeared as "Twin Earth and Its Horizons: On Hermeneutics, Reference and Scientific Theory Choice," *The Philosophical Forum* 43, no.1 (Spring 2012): 1–25; an earlier version of chapter 2 appeared as "Critical Fusions: Towards a Genuine 'Hermeneutics of Suspicion,'" in *Inheriting Gadamer: New Directions in Philosophical Hermeneutics*, ed. Georgia Warnke (Edinburgh: Edinburgh University Press, 2016), revised as chapter 2; and some portions of chapter 3 appeared in an earlier form as "Epistemic and Political Agency," in *The Routledge Handbook of Epistemic Injustice*, edited by Ian James Kidd, José Medina, and Gaile Pohlhaus Jr. (London: Routledge, 2017).

HERMENEUTICS AS CRITIQUE

INTRODUCTION

Born of a concern to decipher truths jealously guarded by sacred texts, hermeneutics was long loath to traffic in worldly concerns such as those of science, politics, cultural critique, and race. In this book, I steer philosophical hermeneutics along paths that it does not typically tread.[1] I aim to develop a philosophical hermeneutics with critical intent and seek thereby to demonstrate the ongoing relevance of hermeneutic approaches to matters far beyond the field of literary and textual analysis to which, with few exceptions, hermeneutic strategies have traditionally been restricted.

Hermeneutics as a disciplinary practice emerged to meet the demands of textual exegesis, especially of biblical texts. Later, in the nineteenth century, in the hands of thinkers such as Friedrich Schleiermacher and Wilhelm Dilthey, it was developed as an alternative to the explanatory model of the natural sciences for rendering an account of human speech and action. In the mid-twentieth century, in a way that was mediated by post-Hegelian historicism as well as Martin Heidegger's account of understanding (*Verstehen*), Hans-Georg Gadamer developed a general philosophical hermeneutics that emphasized the significant constitutive role that language plays in understanding. As Gadamer put it in his central text, "Man's [sic] relation to the world is absolutely and fundamentally verbal in nature, and hence intelligible. Thus hermeneutics is . . . a *universal aspect of philosophy*, and not just the methodological basis of the so-called human sciences."[2] This approach incorporated Dilthey's analysis of interpretive understanding and the associated idea of the hermeneutic circle (which expresses the reciprocally implicative relationship of whole to part—in the case of a text or text analogue, the relationship of the anticipated meaning of the whole to the meaning of the parts). However, Gadamer rejected what he took to be Schleiermacher's and Dilthey's methodological aspiration to grant to the "human sciences" the sort of "objectivity" presumed of the natural sciences. To do so, Gadamer averred, would be to overlook the ineliminably situated nature of all understanding.[3]

Hermeneutics embraces a distinctive family of approaches to linguistic and nonlinguistic meaning, approaches that grant central importance to the act and context of interpretation. In the case of human agency and its products, hermeneutics' paradigmatic domain, two contexts are at issue: that of the agent to be understood and that of the inquirer. Meaningful understanding of the agent requires that such agents and their actions be situated within their distinctive social and cultural contexts; that is, such understanding must incorporate an acknowledgment of the agent's own self-understanding. The inquirer is similarly situated, for it is only in light of what could be concerns and issues *for the inquirer* that understanding can be achieved. The concerns that constitute a context of interpretation in turn project a corresponding context of salience and an associated matrix of intelligibility. The aim of hermeneutic inquiry is to fuse these two horizons or contexts.

As developed by Gadamer, philosophical hermeneutics has two central claims: first, the conditions of intelligibility, or horizons of meaning, are situated and particular, and second, different conditions or horizons can be brought into relationship with each other in such a way that participants in different horizons can understand one another to be addressing the same topic or to be talking about the same thing, although they may have different ways of addressing that topic or have genuine disagreements about some aspects of it. Bringing horizons into such a relationship forges a sphere of mutual intelligibility subtending the distinct horizons. Gadamer refers to this relationship as a "fusion of horizons," and I have developed this idea in my account of what I have called the "forging of a situated metalanguage."[4]

Gadamer underscores the situated nature of intelligibility by insisting that consciousness is "historically effected," that it is a *wirkungsgeschichtliches Bewusstsein* constituted by the historically forged "prejudices" that span its matrices of intelligibility.[5] These prejudices, or pre-judgments, form the horizons that accrue to the distinctive interests, concerns, and fundamental commitments of particular lifeworlds or forms of life, horizons that are the conditions of the possibility of actions and things showing themselves as the actions and things they are. Therefore, such pre-judgments are conditions of knowledge; they are knowledge-enabling pre-judgments.

Moreover, consciousness so constituted is linguistic. The tradition within which inquiry is situated is borne through language. When Gadamer writes that our relation to the world is in essence verbal in nature, he means that we are intentionally directed to the world under some particular description, where the resources for such a description are drawn from a linguistic reservoir that allows regions of reality (entities) to show up or stand out as distinct things, and to show up *as* the distinct things that they are. What a thing is, i.e., what a distinct thing shows up *as*, is determined by the background of salient distinctions that are articulated in particular languages.[6] So here we are encouraged to think of a language as a particular structure or regime of *intelligibility*, a semantic framework that subtends a particular set of meaningful distinctions and in turn demarcates what sorts of thing can saliently be said to *be* as well as what can intelligibly be predicated of them.

Salience is a contextual matter. Distinctions are salient (or not) within a given teleological or purposive structure. Such structures are generated from the distinctive interests, concerns, and fundamental commitments mentioned previously. From a given context of concern will emerge a project to address that concern, a project that will in turn pro-ject a corresponding context of salience and a corresponding matrix of intelligibility. One of the central forms that the hermeneutic relationship between whole and part assumes is the relationship between, on the one hand, a given purposive context and, on the other, the descriptions and distinctions that are relevant to that context.

Three key elements of Gadamer's formulation of philosophical hermeneutics animate my argument in this book: the idea of a dialogically enabled and endorsed fusion of horizons; the nature of concept formation; and the hermeneutic centrality of the "dialectic of question and answer." Having already commented on the nature of horizonal fusion, I restrict myself here to a few brief remarks on concept formation and on what Gadamer refers to as the logic of the question.

When giving an account of how concepts first emerge in linguistic form, Gadamer invokes Aristotle's account, in his *Posterior Analytics* (100a 11–13), of the acquisition of universal concepts, noting that "out of the flux of appearances a common factor is spied . . . and with this recognition . . . the unity of experience and of the universal concept slowly emerges."[7] It is crucial to note here that, for Gadamer, the commonality that is recognized is not simply an "objective" feature that is intrinsically or inherently present *in* the appearances *in itself*; it is not an *essential* commonality already and independently present, just waiting for us to discern it in such a way that every human culture, if only it saw rightly, would notice the commonalities in the same way. To the contrary, I maintain that everything is both similar to every other thing in some respect and different from every other thing in some respect. The question then is, "What are the relevant or *salient* similarities and differences, and what determines them?" What count as salient similarities and differences are determined by the distinctive practical concerns of different human communities, some of which are shared by all human communities and some of which are not. Such concerns are the basis of the criteria for similarity and difference and thereby also of the various ways in which experience is sorted, configured, or "carved up." The configuration and sorting of experience *culminates*, reaches its completion, in the word (or in the concept, for Aristotle). As Gadamer put it, "The genius of verbal consciousness . . . [and] its fundamental metaphorical nature . . . consists in being able to express these similarities [discerned from the perspective of] their significance for us." And "the articulation of words and things that each language performs in its own way always constitutes a primary natural way of forming concepts . . . one that exclusively follows the human aspect of things, the system of man's needs and interests. What a linguistic community regards as important about a thing can be given the same name as other things that are perhaps of a quite different nature in other respects, so long as they all have the same quality that is important to the community."[8]

It is an important corollary of Gadamer's position that any theory of language that maintains that words are signs that we simply "pick up" to use in indicating an *already configured* world is inadequate.[9] In this sense, Gadamer can be understood to subscribe to a constitutive view of language—one wherein language establishes or institutes beings in the way that they are—for language is the site where the logical spaces within which things can intelligibly appear as one thing as opposed to another come to expression. Language is the presentation of the world in its broadest outlines, "the initial schematization for all our possibilities of knowing."[10]

With regard to the "dialectic of question and answer," Gadamer holds it to be a fundamental axiom of philosophical hermeneutics that "no assertion is possible that cannot be understood as an answer to a question, and assertions can only be understood in this way."[11] No meaningful understanding can float free of such ultimately context-linked questions. An adequate understanding of a claim requires the prior identification of the question to which that claim is put forward as a response. Hermeneutic understanding, then, is informed by a principle of charity requiring the interpreter to discern the question that maximizes the plausibility of the response, to seek to bring adduced question and interpreted response into a sort of reflective equilibrium. It becomes incumbent upon the interpreter, then, to appropriately situate the claim or text in question. Unless we can locate the logical space in which the to-be-understood text or text analogue resides, we cannot understand it. And, because we are constrained to do so from within our distinctive horizon of understanding, we can discern the appropriate context for the text in question only through modeling upon what can be logical spaces or dimensions of experience *for us*. In what can be questionable for us is manifested our historically effected consciousness, a consciousness that sets the *initial* limits on our matrices of intelligibility, limits that can be superseded in the fusion of horizons requisite to adducing the questions that animate alien horizons. As will become apparent, especially in chapters 1 and 4 of this book, such considerations ultimately point to the methodological priority of the question for any mode of inquiry, including those of the natural sciences. The ways in which we take reality to be partitioned, and the metrics of similarity and difference that govern that partitioning, will need to be understood in light of the questions that animate our inquiry.

CONTESTING HERMENEUTICS

Characteristic of hermeneutic approaches is an insistence on taking as a touchstone the meaning or intelligibility of a text, utterance, or action to an agent, be it the agent who seeks to understand or the agent who is to be understood. In the paradigmatic hermeneutic situation of the dialogue, ego and alter seek to forge a common language by "fusing" their respective contextual horizons. Dialogical acknowledgment on the part of the to-be-understood agent is a crucial moment in hermeneutic approaches. That the validity of the result of an act of dialogical understanding is presumed to be so tightly indexed to such an agent or to a community of such agents seems to many to leave no space for rationally challenging the world as those agents know it. Hermeneutics has thus seemed to be unable to critically interrogate the status quo of a given tradition because of its overweening concern with understanding others in their own terms. Furthermore, hermeneutics' emphasis on the contextuality of knowledge claims has just as often led to charges that it is a relativistic enterprise.

Much of my previous work has been devoted to exploring the implications of hermeneutics for addressing the distinctively modern phenomena of technological rationality and the salience of cultural difference.[12] My last book responds to what has increasingly become a fairly widespread cynicism regarding the nature and scope of intercultural understanding. The conception of humanism and of mutual cross-cultural understanding developed in that book arises directly from, on the one hand, the concern to adequately acknowledge social and cultural difference and, on the other, to counter claims that differently situated persons and cultures are thereby ineliminably opaque to each other. I pursue there what one might call the social epistemological problem of determining how genuine, that is, non-invidious, understanding of other cultures is possible, of determining what the conditions and limits of such understanding are. In the course of this investigation, I develop and defend a conception of mutual understanding that avoids the issue of incommensurability by adducing and defending a framework in which differences of cultural viewpoints can be interpreted and understood as *different* perspectives on the *same* range of issues.

In this book, I take the further step of developing a critical hermeneutics, a move that will ultimately require me to develop and supplement the framework we have inherited from Gadamer. The need for such an emendation was first, and perhaps most vividly, brought to the fore in the so-called Habermas-Gadamer debates of the late 1960s and early 1970s.[13] Although the social theorist Jürgen Habermas was quick to acknowledge the significance for the methodology of the social sciences of Gadamer's achievement, Habermas believed that it was a systematically inadequate basis for a critical social theory. In response to what he took to be the overly contextualist account of rationality put forward by Gadamer, Habermas objected to what was for him the consequent critical impotence of philosophical hermeneutics, pointing out that it could not incorporate a non-question-begging critique of a given horizon or regime of intelligibility and, thus, could not allow for a systematic distinction between an ideological regime and a nonideological one.[14] Indeed, in its insistence on the tradition-bound content and context of any putatively "critical" norms, hermeneutics is often understood to be at odds with the tradition of critical social theory. Habermas's own project has undergone considerable development following that initial rejoinder, with Habermas increasingly granting systematic importance to the Heideggerian/Gadamerian conception of the lifeworld, so he has perhaps moved somewhat closer to Gadamer's position in some ways. However, Habermas still opposes a universalist conception of reason to Gadamer's more situated and contextualist account. Gadamer's initial reply to Habermas's objection was that the fact that there cannot be knowledge without prejudices does not entail that any particular prejudice is beyond criticism. In developing this point, Gadamer draws a distinction between "legitimate" and "illegitimate" prejudices and implies that attending to this distinction could serve as an effective stand-in for ideology critique.[15] However, he does not provide a fully satisfactory account of how this distinction is to be applied. Addressing this issue is central to fashioning a critical hermeneutics with emancipatory intent.

Gadamer's claim to hermeneutics' universality has met with an even more generalized resistance. As we have seen, Habermas, whose sympathy toward hermeneutics never waned, partitioned hermeneutics' domain of validity in such a way that its claim to universality rang hollow. For many other thinkers, its usefulness did not extend beyond the cultural sphere, and even for the purposes of historical understanding, the method of *Verstehen*—and the closely allied "agent's reasons" approach of the Canadian philosopher William Dray—was challenged by positivists. And, a fortiori, such thinkers believed that the approach to the natural sciences it would endorse—as well as the relevantly similar approaches of such philosophers and historians of science as Norwood Hanson, Stephen Toulmin, and Thomas Kuhn—would be woefully inadequate. I propose the argument in this book as a contribution toward the redemption of Gadamer's claim that hermeneutics is "a universal aspect of philosophy." When hermeneutics shifts its focus from understanding texts, utterances, and deeds produced in the interpreter's own tradition to coming to terms with those produced within unfamiliar cultures, traditions, and epistemic regimes, it can facilitate an understanding that is critical as well as interpretive.

CHAPTER SUMMARY

To briefly recap, hermeneutics' insistence on the contextuality of intelligibility has encouraged the view that it thereby countenances relativism, critical impotence, or indifference, and even incommensurability. In the domain of social theory, we saw this to be at the heart of Habermas's ambivalent reception of hermeneutics. In the philosophy of science, it is what motivated the positivist's rebuke of hermeneutics-adjacent approaches to the history and philosophy of science. I suggest that not only are such ambivalence and rebuke unwarranted but that hermeneutics can make a distinctive contribution both to social critique and to understanding the nature of scientific inquiry.

In this book, I extend my previous hermeneutic investigations by mounting an explicit defense of hermeneutics' critical potential and by further pursuing hermeneutically informed investigations of theory choice in science, racial politics, and culture. My defense throughout assumes the form of an explicit response to the commonly voiced charges of relativism and critical impotence. I show that a critical understanding does not necessarily require a move beyond hermeneutics; rather, we must go more deeply into it and increase the depth of our hermeneutic analysis. I begin on ground often regarded as the least hospitable to hermeneutics—the natural sciences. Here I respond to the epistemological challenge by demonstrating hermeneutics' ability to do justice to the rationality of theory choice and to the idea of progressive learning processes. I then turn to the practical/ethical domain to display the cogency of hermeneutically informed social critique, to show that hermeneutically informed conversation can be deployed with genuine critical intent. Next, I expand the practical/ethical discussion by developing a hermeneutically informed critical analysis of some consequential policy-informing claims that have been made in recent global development theory and that continue to animate policy with regard to matters of race. Last, I turn to an explicit discussion of race. Here, drawing on both my earlier discussion of the natural sciences and the so-called new biology of race, I first revisit the question of whether the practice of segmenting humanity into what are commonly understood as races has a biological justification. This allows me to lay bare the role of hermeneutic interpretation in ordinary racial classification and, thereby, to highlight the criticizable social strategies enacted in practices of racial classification.

I now turn to an overview of my main arguments. In the next chapter, I defend hermeneutic approaches to the understanding of science—and especially hermeneutic accounts of the meaning of scientific terms—against the charge that they have unavoidably relativistic implications. In so doing, I set the groundwork for a critical extension of hermeneutics by addressing the issue of incommensurability it seems to provoke and by showing how a critical hermeneutics can accommodate the idea of rational theory choice. I point out that the hermeneutic approach to language can be correlated with two theses:

that meaning determines reference, and that the meaning of an expression is determined by the role it plays in the network of which it is an element (semantic holism). When a given expression is circulated in different systems or networks, its meaning and, consequently, its reference change as well. Accordingly, it is said that the hermeneutic account of meaning can do justice neither to the possibility of communication across such networks nor to the critical comparison of competing networks. As a result, hermeneutics is claimed to lack the resources necessary to represent science as a rationally progressive enterprise. It has been claimed that some version of a theory of direct reference is required to address these lacunae. I assess this claim and argue that hermeneutics does indeed possess the requisite resources and, incidentally, that theories of direct reference themselves are unable to escape the hermeneutic circle in that they have an ineliminable hermeneutic moment or dimension.

I argue here that the determination of the referents of scientific terms always takes place within and depends on a taken-for-granted local ontology, a matrix of intelligibility that is contextually indexed. The so-called natural kind terms of science, I argue, refer to entities and classes of entities under descriptions that are—at a given stage in the development of a particular science—believed to be *explanatorily* relevant. Hence such terms should not be understood to refer, as theorists of direct reference would have it, to fully determinate structures that have an independently existing metaphysical status. Natural kind terms refer to the constructs—ultimately to the explanatory primitives—that we take to have the greatest salience at a given stage in the development of a particular science. These structures can enjoy no metaphysical necessity wholly independent of our beliefs. It is apposite, I claim, to think of the scientific community as a community of interpreters that has reached a *revisable* consensus on the meaning of the terms that refer to its fundamental structures. This notwithstanding, I argue that many of the distinctions held to be salient for an account of science as a rational, progressive enterprise can nevertheless be retained in a hermeneutical analysis, if they are suitably reframed. For instance, by attending to the hermeneutic distinction between meanings associated with a shared matrix of intelligibility versus those that are not, we can retain the observational/theoretical term distinction in such a way that we can make it intelligible that observations can be dispositive in adjudicating between competing theoretical claims. This is but one example of hermeneutics' ability to do justice to the idea of scientific change as a rational, progressive development.

In chapter 2, I take up my concern to demonstrate the critical potential inherent in hermeneutic approaches to social and cultural understanding. These approaches signal not only hermeneutics' *relevance* in these domains. In addition, given contemporary concern about questions of global justice and, in particular, the skepticism voiced by some "postcolonialist" and "multiculturalist" thinkers that any ethical regime with cosmopolitan intentions must inevitably founder on the shoals of a Eurocentric ethnocentrism, hermeneutic approaches to social justice may be *uniquely* well positioned simultaneously to do justice to cultural difference and to avoid situations where critique depends for its legitimacy on normative standards developed in and imposed by the West. I begin by highlighting three conditions that allow for internal or "immanent" normative pressure to be brought to bear on social/cultural practices when hermeneutically understood. Among these conditions are the facts that cultures are not monolithic, homogeneous wholes and that cultural identity itself can be understood as a "cluster" concept, whereby certain elements of the set of features that collectively constitute one's social identity may be revised as a result of critical reflection without resulting in the loss of that identity. I further develop my position by arguing for a conception of "second-order rationality," a mode of rationality that has a culturally invariant purchase, and end by elaborating a critical approach to cross-cultural understanding that is informed by what I currently call "counterfactual dialogical critique." In that both appeal to the possible acknowledgment on the part of the to-be-understood agent or agents, these conceptions of rationality and of critique provide a more genuinely *hermeneutic* basis for what Paul Ricoeur has famously dubbed the "hermeneutics of suspicion" than do the critical strategies of those whom Ricoeur cites as the masters of this "suspicious interpretation"; namely, Nietzsche, Marx, and Freud.[16] The self-understanding of Nietzschean, Freudian, and Marxian theory does not unambiguously require that the validity of critique be hostage to its acknowledgment by the agents being critiqued.

"Second-order rationality" refers to the inclination that we are entitled to impute to everyone to alter their ways when their own lack of rationality is pointed out to them in terms they can understand. This species of rationality—which can be deployed to critical effect in scientific experimental design, in the interpretation of sacred texts, as well as in the interpretation of political constitutions—has, I argue, a context-invariant status. My conception of second-order rationality further allows me to demonstrate that hermeneutic accounts of knowledge need not illegitimately conflate the appearance/reality distinction. Without an appeal to anything beyond the standards of rationality or the central vocabulary of any particular epistemic community, my conception allows us nevertheless to mark a distinction between what even everyone in such a community happens to think and what is reasonable *for them* to believe. And I demonstrate that it is this context-invariant form of rationality that hermeneutics can leverage in its application to the various kinds of differences and disagreements that I discuss throughout this book, thus enabling critique and underwriting rational progress.

By "counterfactual dialogical critique," I refer to a conversational modality that can be triggered by an encounter with a social or cultural practice, e.g., female genital cutting, that may seem questionable even when pursued in cultural contexts in which members of the affected group themselves seem to be part of the consensus in its favor. This critical modality is partially informed by the just mentioned ideas that cultural identity is best conceived as a cluster concept and that cultures are not monolithic, that they are always in the process of interpretation and reinterpretation by cultural members themselves. Cultures are, thus, sites of conflicting interpretations of what their identity-defining structures are. Consequently, no *single* narrative purporting to definitively capture a culture's identity should be given carte blanche to function in such a way as to quarantine intracultural practices from discursive view and immunize them from critical examination. In particular, we should be on the lookout for assertions of cultural identity that may operate as cloaks or ideological veils concealing prudential interest-based concerns. And if there is no overt contestation of what may seem to us problematic cultural practices—practices such as female circumcision or genital cutting—the *appearance* of asymmetrical or invidious treatment of identifiable demographic groups can serve to trigger hypotheses about the real interests implicated and about whether or not those interests converge in the way that prevailing cultural identity claims implicitly assert that they do. This way of proceeding allows me to give a nonfoundationalist hermeneutical account of ideology and of ideology critique that avoids standard epistemological criticisms.

The general idea behind this critical method is that cultural agents can be invited to consider social possibilities that, although currently unrealized, might be preferred by them if given the option, social possibilities whose realization is suppressed not because such realization would offend against all intelligible interpretations of their cultural identity but primarily because it would offend against particular vested interests. This would mean we could hypothesize and subsequently confirm—even in the case of an apparent cultural consensus—"suppressed" interests of distinctive classes of cultural agents by conversationally entertaining counterfactually imagined social arrangements. The suspicion of latent social and cultural dissensus that may arise as a result of the hermeneutically informed expectations of a critical participant/observer can also be *hermeneutically* redeemed (or, for that matter, falsified). The reasoning behind the ascription of a potentially hidden interest can, indeed should, be a collaborative dialogical project, one involving those whose interests are in question. As an illustration of the sorts of question that might, whether implicitly or explicitly, underlie such a dialogical engagement, capture its critical intent, and perhaps thereby prompt some of the processes of cultural self-reinterpretation to which I have alluded, I offer the following reflections. For example, when encountering some form of the practice of excision or female genital cutting, a witness (whether sharing cultural membership with the affected women or not) who failed to find the "general" acquiescence to the practice on the part of women to be perspicuously intelligible might, in appropriately "safe" spaces, initiate conversations of a particular sort with them. These conversations would be guided by the following basic question: Armed with the knowledge of the all too likely physical and emotional consequences of the procedure, if the connection between undergoing the procedure (or the procedure in its current form) and your chances for flourishing in your society were virtualized, if that connection could be severed, would you still choose to undergo the procedure? This is the sort of question that could be raised in the conversational modality that I refer to as counterfactual dialogical critique, a modality that, if practiced within a society, suggests the plausibility of non-question-begging, non-invidiously ethnocentric, critical perspectives on cultural formations not our own. To summarize, counterfactual dialogical critique is structured by a series of conversationally executed thought experiments. In its basic interrogative framework, the question is posed: Given the conceived alternatives our discussion has brought to mind, and in light of the hypothesis that the restricted alternatives in terms of which you originally chose were promulgated in the interest, or implicitly served the interests, of some as opposed to others, would you now *endorse* the choices you would have otherwise made?

I show, further, that this dialogical method of critique, which can be regarded as a "critical developmental practice," requires no wholesale opposition to the actual options and choices of action available to, and sustained by, a given culture. It is attuned more to the nature of the *distribution* of those social options and choices. This allows us to split the difference, so to speak, between, and thereby to reconcile, the emancipatory reflection championed by Habermas and others, on the one hand, and a hermeneutically sensitive consciousness, on the other. The position I develop here does not require—as Gadamer occasionally "falsely" alleged against Habermas—that emancipatory reflection dissolve all of the structures of intelligibility intrinsic to the culture in question. Ultimately, I suggest that the hermeneutic distinction between legitimate and illegitimate prejudice—a distinction that Gadamer famously invoked but for which a fully satisfactory account has yet to be provided—is not merely arbitrary. This would be tantamount to a capitulation to the charge of relativism. Instead, I provide an account of this distinction by showing that the criteria for making it depend on the idea of genuinely autonomous consent on the part of the to-be-understood agents. This, of course, will in turn require a non-question-begging account of genuine autonomous agency, an issue I address under the rubric of "situated autonomous agency" at the end of chapter 3.

In chapter 3, I bring hermeneutic considerations to bear on a broader range of issues found under the umbrella of globalization and development debates, particularly those that focus on global and racial justice. Central to a particular strand of thought in these debates is a tendency to view relative poverty and abjectness as a function of social pathologies attributable to members of the "underclass" in so-called developed societies and, more broadly, to society itself in "underdeveloped" nations. I focus on a primary claim made under the aegis of the so-called culture of poverty thesis—the claim that members of such societies suffer from an agency deficit. I understand this agency deficit to have two components: a values deficit and a volitional deficit, which is understood as a species of weakness of will, *akrasia*, lack of discipline, self-control, and so on. On the first component, I argue that values cannot be inferred from behavior in any straightforward sense. Values are thus not observables; to gain access to an agent's values, we must enter the hermeneutic circle. The relationship between values and behavior is mediated by the cognitive representation an agent holds about socially available avenues of action. To understand, therefore, what values are in fact held by an agent, one must gain hermeneutic access to the view of the social world held by the agents in question. It is the failure of such culture of poverty theorists to acknowledge this and their consequent *assumption* (as opposed to hermeneutic demonstration) of such value differentials that underwrite their assertions to the effect that behavior regarded as dysfunctional within the global-capitalist system can be attributed to deficient values.

On the question of volitional deficits, I argue that we should distinguish between agential capacities of the first order, to wit, the capacity to produce an effect or to bring about a state of affairs; and agential capacities of the second order, to wit, the awareness of and the ability to produce, acquire, or to avail oneself of the facilitating conditions of agency in the first-order sense. The second-order capacities are those that condition the exercise of capacities of the first order. Second-order agency can be systematically undermined for some agents due to wholly contingent, structural features of society that are beyond their control. Think of children living in poverty who may well be fully *willing* to apply themselves to their studies but who are unaware of or unable to avail themselves of requisite quiet spaces. Generally speaking, lack of educational opportunity will compromise social agency. It is in this sense that social and economic rights and the material conditions they would procure can be understood to be conditions of first-order agency, say, of civil and political agency.

To fully understand global injustices, I argue that we need a way of making salient the discrepancy between, on the one hand, the historically sedimented conditions that continue to impede agency for some and, on the other hand, the enabling but often hidden or unacknowledged conditions that facilitate agency for others. These are situations in which second-order agential conditions are, respectively, absent and present. I argue that drawing a distinction between first-order agency and second-order agency allows us to illuminate this discrepancy insofar as this distinction disaggregates the volitional and epistemic components of agency. Although the facilitating conditions of first-order agency may be of both a material/structural and an epistemic sort, my interest in developing a hermeneutics of agency leads me to focus primarily on the latter sorts of condition, the epistemic. If persons who suffer under current conditions appear, through their actions or inaction, to be culpable for their own suffering, I argue that we ought to heed the aforementioned distinctions because it may be that we do not yet truly understand their choices. To understand a person's choices will require that we engage in a hermeneutical investigation undertaken under what I call the constraint of narrative representability. That is, we must ask: How do things appear from the first-person perspective within which these choices were made? Understanding such choices in this manner can bring into focus cases in which the agent making the choices is not culpable for the failure to make life-enhancing choices (of course, still leaving open the possibility that in some cases they may be) but where instead an injustice of an epistemic sort is present. By "an injustice of an epistemic sort," I refer to the injustice of failing to acknowledge the agent's epistemic state when that state, or the structural conditions responsible for it, through no fault of their own, unfairly compromises the agent's ability to act. This would be tantamount to the compound injustice of having one's agency compromised by an epistemic limitation for which one bears no culpability and of nevertheless being judged or blamed for that lack of agency.

Diagnosis of both of these putative pathologies, of values and of volition, will require a hermeneutic investigation aimed at construing the web of beliefs that agents actually have regarding the range of social options available to them as real possibilities. The results of such diagnoses, I argue, can underwrite critical social interventions guided by acknowledgment of the manifest injustice of expecting feats of first-order agency from segments of society bereft of conditions that most of us take for granted.

In their explorations of different facets of the relevance of hermeneutics for sociocultural analysis, chapters 2 and 3 are bound by two central "hinges." Insofar as the mechanism of counterfactual dialogical critique outlined in chapter 2 can foreground the ideological nature of particular cultural interpretations, we can view it as addressing an epistemic condition of agency that illuminates the phenomenon of adaptive preference briefly discussed in chapter 3. Second, in chapter 3, I further develop the idea of the importance to social agency of achieving semantic authority for agency-enabling interpretations of social experience.

In chapter 4, I consider what light hermeneutics can shed on the status of racial discourse, racial classification, and the social practices associated with such discourse and classification. The hermeneutic account of the meaning of natural kind terms previously presented challenges the idea that such terms can be unproblematically mapped onto an independently existing determinate reality. My discussion of the ontological status of racial categories is pursued both in light of that account and within the context of recent work in population genetics, genomics, and evolutionary medicine, research that has led to the so-called new biology of race. Given my account of natural kind terms, I argue that, a fortiori, conventional racial categories cannot be understood to be isomorphic to what Plato would refer to as nature's joints. We know that the phenotypic traits conventionally used to demarcate races have neither intrinsic biological significance nor been shown to correlate with characteristics of intrinsic significance, and further, that intraracial diversity is far more pronounced than is interracial diversity. In discussions of race, I argue that we should always inquire after the conditions under which race becomes a salient item of discourse, why it becomes privileged in highlighting or picking out the similarities and differences among us that matter. Any discourse in which race figures will reflect a structured social interpretation or construction, so we need to interrogate the sorts of discourse in which the concept appears, to ask what interests they serve and what social strategies they enact. "Sameness vs. difference," like "kind vs. degree," are sliding signifiers; that is, their application must be understood to be relative to both altitude and *attitude*. In chapter 1, I argue that in science natural kinds are "artifacts" produced or instituted in the service of the epistemic goals of prediction and explanation. Because, as I shall argue, racial categories in themselves have little, if any, predictive or explanatory significance, their status is perhaps doubly artifactual. To this extent, their employment may well betray a social interest that is susceptible to rational critique. In this way, my discussion displays the internal connection between a hermeneutics of race and the concerns of critical race theory.

I conclude with a recapitulation of the implications of my argument for our understanding of the scope and critical/diagnostic significance of hermeneutics. The pursuit of hermeneutical investigations within wide-ranging fields of application, both those of the philosophy of science and of sociocultural politics, serves to demonstrate the distinctive contribution that hermeneutically informed approaches can make and how such approaches can avoid many of the aporetics and dilemmas that have plagued these fields. For instance, my methodological proposal of counterfactual dialogical critique allows us to avoid the dilemmatic portrayal of the cross-cultural critic wherein she can avoid the charge of question-begging and patronizing ethnocentrism only at the price of an uncritical acquiescence to a prevailing cultural narrative that serves to justify the practice in question. As I point out in my concluding remarks, in addition to its theoretical merits, my proposal has the practical advantage of mitigating the potentially compromising ambivalence that such a morally committed agent may face when confronted with differently situated actors. Furthermore, I consider how the constraint of narrative representability developed in chapter 3 can be deployed to deepen discussion of issues of global injustice and inequality by bringing into sharper relief the otherwise hidden structural components of inequality.

In general, I make explicit and elaborate upon the normative claim implicit in my effort to reconcile the concerns of hermeneutics and Critical Theory. It is the claim that a genuinely legitimate sociocultural self-understanding on the part of a society is one that acknowledges the horizons of intelligibility from which its constituent stakeholders speak and act. A self-understanding that occludes any such horizon—except in cases where the horizon in question can itself be demonstrated to be systematically dismissive or intolerant of others—is prima facie a flawed self-understanding. In large measure, it is such a flaw that ensures the ideological status of cultural interpretations that justify such practices as female excision and require so-called adaptive preferences on the part of deprived women; that underpins the misdiagnoses and epistemic injustices that follow from the fallacy of psychologizing the social, i.e., of assigning causal responsibility for the plight of the poor to deficits of agency while overlooking the role played by social and economic structures; and that fails to acknowledge the legitimate claims of those who, from the margins, struggle to have their perception of society acknowledged.

1

TWIN EARTH AND ITS HORIZONS

On Hermeneutics, Reference, and Scientific Theory Choice

PROLOGUE: OF CONTEXTS AND LUMPS

In a galaxy long ago and far away, there lived two strikingly different tribes. When stumbling across an unfamiliar object, members of one tribe—called the Angles—picked it up, squinting in the light, examined it, and tried to determine its intrinsic properties through measurement, weighing, and eventually chemical analysis, and so on, ultimately attempting to develop precise criteria for distinguishing in a univocal way a lump of one kind of stuff from a lump of another kind of stuff and for distinguishing a genuine instance of a particular kind of stuff from a pretender. Over time they developed ever-more precise tools and techniques for doing so. When members of the other tribe—called the Frankendeutschers—happened on an unfamiliar object, they tended to leave it in place, carefully examining its context, connections, relationship to, and lines of affinity with the other stuff in its environment—perhaps attempting to imagine how its appearance would be transformed if its environment were altered. They would try to determine its genealogy, its history, the forces that led to its production, and so on. They might even ask about their own role in comprising its context.

The Frankendeutschers became increasingly subtle in these sorts of investigations. The questions they raised about the objects they encountered would generally take the form of "How does it fit in?" The Angles would more typically ask, "What *kind* of a thing is it?" Both tribes continued in their typical and distinctive ways until they all had to flee their galaxy to escape a great cosmic conflagration.

The lineal descendants of the Angles tribe colonized and settled in England, North America, and Australia, and they bore names like Ayer, Devitt, Donnellan, Kripke, Katz, and Putnam. The descendants of the Frankendeutschers tribe settled in France and Germany, and some in Italy, and they bore names like Heidegger, Sartre, Irigaray, Vattimo, Derrida, Foucault, and Gadamer. With rare exceptions, the descendants of the Angles and the Frankendeutschers were unable to talk to each other about anything of importance until a child of hybrid lineage emerged who, although disowned by both branches of his family, issued Rodney King–like appeals for them to "all just get along." This child, who grew up to be Richard Rorty, dreamed of a grand conversation in which the Angles, so preoccupied with their lumps, and the Frankendeutschers, concerned with their talk of texts and contexts, could face each other as respectful interlocutors. He urged them to try to see themselves as occupying positions on a sliding scale that differed by degree rather than occupying fixed points on different sides of a nonnegotiable divide.[1]

Many, if not most, of the recent attempts to bridge this divide have assumed that the bridge is a one-way thoroughfare—tools imported from the "analytic" side are conveyed to the "continental" side of the divide to repair potholes discovered there. I wish to present a case in which resources indigenous to continental habits of mind may shed light on some analytic roadblocks, namely, on the issue of incommensurability as it has arisen in the philosophy of science and also perhaps on the distinction between attributive and referential uses of descriptive phrases. I use hermeneutics to argue that the embrace of the linguistic turn by postempiricist philosophy of science need not inevitably run afoul of our intuition that scientific change can be rationally motivated and, consequently, that such a metascientific philosophical position does not require the emendations of the so-called new theory of reference. My thesis in this chapter is that once certain crucial distinctions are made, a perfectly respectable account—one avoiding embarrassing incommensurabilities and a disabling relativism—of rational and progressive learning processes can be fashioned using the resources of hermeneutics alone.

The Linguistic Turn in Hermeneutics

In this section, I address some of the consequences, real and imagined, of a distinctive family of views about the relationship between language and the world that animates both hermeneutical philosophy and influential strands of postempiricist philosophy of science. These are views about the nature of linguistic meaning and its relationship to reference. To capture what is salient about these views, one prominent commentator, no doubt inspired by the title of an early collection of Richard Rorty's work, speaks of a "linguistic turn" in hermeneutic philosophy.[2]

The linguistic turn is a turn from what to what? It originated in a critique of the view of philosophy embodied in the so-called philosophy of consciousness. If philosophical practice was dominated by an orientation toward ontology in ancient and medieval thought, then the concern of thinkers from Descartes to

Husserl conspired to effect a "bracketing of Being," one might say, in favor of an epistemological turn to focus on ideas as objects of consciousness. In the philosophies of consciousness, language is relegated to a merely instrumental role; it is conceptualized as a tool for the designation of aspects of the world that are independent of it or for the designation and communication of thoughts that are determinate prior to their being expressed in language. The thinkers collected under the rubric "the linguistic turn" explicitly eschew such a purely designative conception of language. The linguistic turn is therefore a turn away from the philosophy of consciousness and its associated instrumental view of language to one that holds language to be "constitutive" of our relationship to the world in some sense. It is a critique of the view that words are names for independently given ideas, or tags for concepts that have been offered ready-made to the mind's eye. After the linguistic turn, language is seen to segment or carve up the undifferentiated stuff of experience, thus securing both the existence and stability of our concepts. This in turn issues in an emphasis on the world-disclosing function of language, on its capacity to project and express the categories that are constitutive of the world—to *institute* the kinds of thing there are and what can be meaningfully predicated of them.

Through the critique of Kant launched by Hamann, Herder, and Humboldt, the world constituting power of the transcendental ego was vested in language. This new view of language is central to Heidegger's and Hans-Georg Gadamer's hermeneutics. It can be discerned in Heidegger's early discussion of being-in-the-world, where the conviction that meaning determines reference assumes the following form: The being of an entity is determined by what it is understood as; and understanding is itself eminently practical, for it will unavoidably invoke or be informed by the roles that things assume or play in the repertoire of practices that a particular culture, form of life, or lifeworld sustains; referring is effected in virtue of those practices.

This new view appears perhaps most starkly when Heidegger, in *On the Way to Language*, approvingly embraces the poet Stefan George's announcement that "where the word breaks off no thing can be"; when he claims, in "Hölderlin and the Essence of Poetry," that "only where there is language is there world"; or when he famously announces in "The Letter on Humanism" that "language is the house of Being."[3] It is evident again in *Truth and Method* when Gadamer avers that "language is not just one of man's possessions in the world; rather, on it depends the fact that man has a *world* at all."[4]

This linguistic turn has left far-reaching consequences in its wake. Because languages occur in the plural, it has had a detranscendentalizing effect. The fact of the plurality of language games leaves no room for a functional equivalent to "consciousness in general." The common consciousness and objectivity of experience underwritten by Kant's transcendental unity of apperception is dispersed into particular world disclosures or into the particular worldviews that, as Humboldt argued, are embodied in the various historical languages. This has been taken by many to have at least two significant consequences. One is that the assumption of a single objective world of things that are independent of language is revealed to have no basis because of what has been called the incommensurability of world disclosures associated with different languages. Reference and truth must now be taken to be immanent to language. This implication can be articulated in a number of ways, all variations on the theme that meaning is the condition of the possibility of our access to reference. Referential acts can occur only under the descriptions provided by a language. Language determines that to which we can meaningfully refer, for reference is always to an aspect of the world under a description. (This is what can be called the Fregean dimension of the turn; singular terms refer to objects indirectly through the sense that the term has.) Closely associated with the thesis that meaning determines reference is the thesis of meaning holism. Languages are symbolically structured wholes in which expressions derive their meaning from the contexts in which they figure, from the system of differences in which they function, and from their place in and relationships to the entire system of which they are a part. So a second consequence comes to the fore: An uncompromising linguistic turn threatens the intersubjectivity of communication, throwing into question the possibility of agreement or, for that matter, disagreement about the same subject matter and issuing severe restrictions on translatability between languages. Humboldt's assertion that "every language [contains] a peculiar worldview" captures the nature of such a thoroughgoing turn nicely.

Reservations About the Linguistic Turn from Within

This relativistic "fracturing of reason" along linguistic fault lines—although perhaps viewed as liberating in the largely French poststructuralist tradition departing from Nietzsche—is seen within the context of German philosophy as the source of a potential and deeply troubling consequence of the linguistic turn, particularly within the tradition of hermeneutics. Thinkers within this tradition as various as Humboldt, Gadamer, and Habermas have found it important to respond to it in some way. It has been argued that the only way out of this impasse is to adopt a designative or direct theory of meaning, that is, one through which we can understand language to refer directly to objects and not only in ways fabricated by the descriptive resources of a given language. This move to recuperate what Rorty has called the world well lost is predicated on thematizing language's designative, as opposed to world-disclosive or attributive, function. Only with an understanding of language's ability to refer to the world in ways not fatally prejudiced by particular worldviews, it is argued, can we make sense of the way in which language enables the sorts of learning process that Habermas, for example, focuses on, processes that can throw into question the very worldviews from which they arise.

Among the commentators who are both knowledgeable about, and sympathetic to, the hermeneutic tradition, perhaps none is more explicit in attempting to bring this tradition's putative epistemological shortcomings sharply into focus than Cristina Lafont. Over two sustained monograph-length critiques and several shorter articles, she has pointed to what she takes to be the inevitable and untenable relativistic implications of hermeneutics.[5] In addition to the issues to which I have just alluded—namely, skepticism about hermeneutics' ability to do justice to the intersubjectivity of communication across distinct world disclosures and concern about its threat to the "unity" of the objective world—Lafont is especially concerned about what she takes to be a third consequence of the conception of meaning associated with hermeneutics. Having thus abandoned a universalist perspective on the plurality of world disclosures, this conception of meaning, she claims, cannot provide us with the resources to understand the evolution of knowledge as a progressive learning process.[6]

In the course of his celebrated debate with Gadamer and his explicit critiques of Heidegger, Jürgen Habermas has also been quite outspoken in his concern about hermeneutics' inability to extricate itself from a disabling relativism. Lafont refers to

Habermas's critique of Heidegger to convey a sense of what is at stake here. Seeking to address the issue of how we can achieve rational and critical control of the background knowledge that plays an ineliminable role in world constitution, Habermas avers that

> the linguistic world view is a concrete and historical a priori; it fixes interpretative perspectives that are substantive and variable and that cannot be gone behind. This constitutive world-understanding changes independently of what subjects experience concerning conditions in the world interpreted in the light of this preunderstanding, and independently of what they can *learn* from their practical dealings with anything in the world. No matter whether this metahistorical transformation of linguistic world views is conceived of as Being [Heidegger], différance [Derrida], power [Foucault], or imagination, and whether it is endowed with connotations of a mystical experience of salvation, of aesthetic shock, of creaturely pain, or of creative intoxication: What all these concepts have in common is the peculiar uncoupling of the horizon-constituting productivity of language from the consequences of an intramundane practice that is wholly prejudiced by the linguistic system. Any interaction between world-disclosing language and learning processes in the world is excluded.[7]

Habermas here implies that acknowledging and demonstrating the connection between the constitution of meaning, on the one hand, and learning processes, on the other, would allow us to place the constitution of meaning itself under the control of universal validity claims.

But Lafont thinks that as long as Habermas too fails to distance himself from the central assumptions of hermeneutics and, in particular, from the thesis that meaning determines reference, as long as he too fails to reject the idea that speakers need to rely "on identical meanings" (guaranteed by the world disclosure inherent in language) in order to talk about "the same thing"—and he does not do so in her view—he will be unable to demonstrate the plausibility of a rational assessment of the disclosures enabled by background knowledge by connecting those disclosures to learning processes. As Lafont puts it, "if the 'constitution of meaning' inherent in language does have the constitutive character of a world disclosure that determines everything appearing in the world, the possibility of 'intraworldly learning' can only be understood as derived from that prior world disclosure (and hence limited by it)."[8] Furthermore, on this view, we could not make much sense of the idea that the collective social subject had undergone learning processes wherein what was an intractable problem for one research tradition had been solved by another; in order to do so, we would have to be able to identify the same problem across the distinctive traditions. That is, we cannot comparatively assess different complexes of background knowledge in terms of their differential ability to solve problems because each such complex will project its own distinctive set of problems. We will thus be unable to identify problems across such complexes.

Is there anything to this? To lay the groundwork for an adjudication of this matter, let us consider first a hermeneutic account of "talking about." A necessary precondition of a conversation is that interlocutors be in agreement on the topic of conversation. But what is meant by the expression "sameness of topic"? How do we identify and reidentify a topic as being "the same"? Can it be done by a neutral, extralinguistic inspection? A hermeneutic account would reject this possibility, claiming that we are never in a position to have such access to the topic in itself. Consensus on a topic is always a matter of harmonizing interpretations rather than a pure "seeing" that it is so.[9] Agreement on a topic means that something gets described, responded to, or interpreted in the same way, or in sufficiently similar ways, by both parties. So "identity of topic" means identity to the interlocutors, not identity in itself. The expression "same subject matter" then has no meaning apart from the situated descriptions that refer to it. The conversational requirement implies that the interlocutors need sufficiently similar beliefs about the topic to be assured that they are talking about the same thing. If there were *no* overlaps in belief about the topic of conversation, then they would have no basis for assuming they were talking about the same thing. This hermeneutic position would seem to rule out the possibility of our being able to adjudge someone as being *completely* or *entirely* and *systematically* in error about a topic, because any evidence for this would also be evidence that that person was addressing a *different* topic from the one we assumed.

But, it will be objected, if reference is always effected via a detour through a linguistic horizon of meaning with its distinctive set of associated descriptions, then speakers from different hermeneutic horizons will *unavoidably* refer to *different* things and hence will not be in a position to discuss (agree on or disagree on) what may nominally seem to be the same topic. There would seem, then, to be no way to adjudicate incompatible descriptions or accounts of "an object." It would seem more apt to say that we have two possibly correct descriptions of *different* objects. We would not be in a position to say that one of us has an incorrect description of *the same* object of which the other had a correct description. The object would *be* just what is referred to by the sum of the descriptive phrases used about it. And, so the objection goes, if we do achieve sufficient overlap of horizons to identify the same object, there cannot be disagreement about its properties. So the situation that we could not find intelligible is one in which there is *agreement* on the object or topic and an adjudicable *disagreement* about accounts of it. It has been argued by Lafont and others that the only way to make sense of the possibility of an interlocutor being willing to regard her account of a topic as being an *incorrect* account of the *same* topic that is in dispute is to go beyond what the tradition of hermeneutics provides and supplement it with a theory of direct reference that challenges the assumption that reference is effected only through the detour of meaning, a theory that throws into question the Fregean idea that meaning or sense determines reference.[10]

The criticism Lafont raises with respect to hermeneutics is structurally isomorphic to many of the criticisms that have been leveled against the relativism and incommensurability held to be implicit in many postempiricist accounts of science, Kuhn's being perhaps the most prominent among them. So a response to this critique of hermeneutics, important in its own right, has much broader significance. Lafont puts it this way: There follows from the hermeneutic conception of language what she calls a strong incommensurability thesis, namely, the claim that it is impossible "to compare and evaluate different scientific theories with regard to a single standard of objective truth."[11] And this critique seems to get its bite by reference to the empirical scientific examples considered by Heidegger, from which it is concluded that hermeneutics prevents us from understanding the development of science as a learning process.

In postempiricist philosophy of science, a Kuhnian paradigm, or some cognate version thereof, is treated as an analogue to a language. Such paradigms are thought to project distinct physical domains through distinct theoretical languages. Typically, a holistic theory of meaning is also assumed, whereby the meaning of any term, be it theoretical or observational, is influenced by the paradigm's unique theoretical concepts and meanings. In this case, observational terms would have their meaning wholly determined by their context, their relation to the paradigm's theoretical terms and commitments. For example, consider Johannes Kepler and Tycho Brahe gazing toward the eastern horizon in the morning. Kepler was theoretically committed to the view that the Sun was an immovable focus of the solar system about which the Earth, along with the other planets, revolved. Brahe was committed to the Ptolemaic picture in which the Earth stood still and the Sun did the moving. To what extent are they observing the same thing? In an important sense, they are not, insists Norwood Hanson, a major architect of this postempiricist picture of science.[12] Brahe sees the Sun rising from the horizon; Kepler sees the horizon descending as the Earth rotates on its axis. The observation term "sunrise" has differing meanings for them, he would say.

This encourages us to view proponents of rival theoretical paradigms as being imprisoned within their own observational languages and thus as having access only to the unique observational data that are subtended by those distinctive languages (meaning determines reference). Neopositivist philosophers of science such as Dudley Shapere and Israel Scheffler offer typical formulations of this view.[13] Moreover, if competing theories do not share sufficient language or commitments for commonly formulatable data, then they surely lack the common resources for sharing questions about the data. Simply put, proponents of rival paradigms could not converse about the *same* data; they could neither agree nor disagree about it. Neither could be said to offer a better account of the same data. Lacking access to a common language, such paradigms cannot be meaningfully compared, it is argued. Critics such as Shapere and Scheffler trace Kuhn's inability to give an account of science as a rational enterprise to his failure to distinguish sense from reference and to acknowledge that reference can remain stable even as sense or connotation changes.[14]

The Theory of Direct Reference to the Rescue

Theories of direct reference reject Frege's idea that meaning determines reference, at least as far as proper names and so-called natural kind terms are concerned. Natural kind terms are the common nouns that refer to species or substances found in nature, as opposed to artifacts such as tables and chairs. Direct reference theories hold that the meaning of a proper name or of a natural kind term is its reference, not its sense.[15] In an early collection devoted to such theories, it is claimed that they have in common three main features: "proper names are rigid [they designate the same individuals in all possible worlds]; natural kind terms are like proper names in the way that they refer; and reference depends on causal chains."[16] So natural kind terms, they hold, pick out their referents directly. Such a noun, like "water," is used as a tag that directly designates that substance; we now know it to designate H_2O. The meaning of "water" is the substance water. It is as if the thing itself gets marked with, to use Ruth Marcus's original term, a tag or label or brand that identifies it as being the thing that it is and to which we refer when we use the word "water." This is to be distinguished from the indirect route, whereby water would be referred to as that stuff that satisfies the criteria of our conception of water, for example, being a transparent liquid that is potable and so on. As is well known, Hilary Putnam has argued that it is what water really is to which we refer when we use "water," and thus as our knowledge about what water really is improves, as we learn more about it, we can correct the statements in which "water" appears.[17] This, in outline, shows how linguistic acts of referring can, in principle, be connected to learning processes, and they can presumably be so only insofar as we reject the idea that meaning determines reference.

Beyond the Theory of Direct Reference

A. HOW "DIRECT" CAN REFERENCE BE?

Theories of direct reference are still controversial, and many are counterintuitive. As one commentator observes, before it was discovered in the nineteenth century that the chemical composition of water is H_2O, this account suggests that speakers of English did not know what "water" meant. If we train our gaze on the communicative or pragmatic aspects of meaning, however, speakers of English were clearly able to use "water" to communicate in intelligible ways, so they *did* know what it meant.[18]

There are a number of lines of criticism of the most prominent direct reference theories.[19] I concentrate my analysis on those that highlight the vulnerability of such theories to hermeneutic elucidation and their consequent susceptibility to inscription within the framework of hermeneutics. In what is generally conceded to be one of the founding documents of the modern theory of direct reference, or of what has come to be called the "new theory of reference," direct reference is not construed as a "substitute program" for indirect reference but rather has been understood to be a complement to the latter. In "Modalities and Intensional Languages," Ruth Barcan Marcus claims

> that any language must countenance some entities as things would appear to be a precondition for language. But this is not to say that experience is given to us as a collection of things, for

it would appear that there are cultural variations and accompanying linguistic variations as to what sorts of entities are so singled out. It would also appear to be a precondition of language that the singling out of an entity as a thing is accompanied by . . . unique descriptions, for otherwise how would it be singled out?[20]

In Marcus's discussion of what can be called the "reference-fixing descriptions" that do the work of singling out entities as things, she suggests that we assign names to things on the basis of the descriptions we use to single things out. She goes on to speak in terms of "entities being *countenanced as* things *by* [some *particular*] language-culture complex" (emphasis added). What a proper name "tags" is a thing *so picked out*.[21]

Marcus implies that the things we encounter in experience are not neutrally there in a prefabricated mode simply awaiting our encounter. There is no culturally and linguistically neutral prefabricated collection of things of which we can be referentially aware (experience). The objects of reference are singled out by the descriptive phrases that circulate in the variously culturally indexed languages, and such objects are determined with respect to the various semantic differentials that are characteristic of those languages. This would suggest that, even for Marcus, it is the *sense* of a definite description that singles out entities, that originally fixes the direct referent of a name. So, sameness of reference, for her, is guaranteed by, and can only be guaranteed by, sharing a descriptive language, a shared descriptive language. The direct referring of the name would seem to be, in this sense, parasitic on the singling out and fixing procured by definite descriptions.

From Marcus's account, I would hazard to draw the following three conclusions. First, in the "originary" singling out of entities as things, the denoting is presumably effected via the detour of the *sense* of the definite descriptions, so it makes no sense for us to entertain the idea of an "angelic" or extralinguistic and ready-made inventory of things themselves. Second, language "institutes" the realm of things (it does not create them but confers on entities a particular status, namely, that of being a thing). So tagging, it seems, is predicated on something being made publicly salient and perspicuous prior to tagging or naming. Otherwise, how is it clear what is being tagged? I grant that this will not in every instance require that a unique description of the to-be-tagged item be available prior to the tagging—one can imagine scenarios in which one can simply point and tag, for instance. However, third, it does seem to be the case that tagging is, in general, parasitic on a thing being picked out against the background of an *already assumed* ontology (a set of commonplace beliefs about what kinds of thing there are). The thing to be tagged must stand out as a definite and individuatable item as opposed to other possible such items in the local ontology corresponding to a particular language/culture complex.

Now compare this to Heidegger's distinction between assertion (*Aussage*) and interpretation. For Heidegger, meaning—that which can be articulated in an interpretation—is a matter of taking something *as* something; "meaning" refers to the "existential phenomenon . . . in which the formal framework of what can be disclosed in understanding and [a]rticulated in interpretation becomes visible":

> The pointing-out [of something, or referring to something, or predicating some property of something] which assertion does is performed on the basis of what has already been disclosed in understanding or discovered circumspectively. Assertion is not a free-floating kind of behavior which, in its own right, might be capable of disclosing entities in general in a primary way: on

the contrary it always maintains itself on the basis of Being-in-the world ... Any assertion requires a fore-having of whatever has been disclosed.[22]

So for Heidegger, too, nomination is founded on disclosure.

In *Being and Time*, Heidegger does not make language per se an explicit theme until after his discussion of assertion and interpretation. And when he does so, his focus is on what he takes to be language's constitutive ground, in his words, its "existential-ontological foundation." And that foundation, which he calls discourse or talk (*Rede*), is taken by him to be the enabling condition of the articulation of meaning. Thus discourse grounds the hermeneutical "as-structure" of interpretation, which in turn grounds the apophantic "as" of assertion. Discourse, understood as the "articulated whole of significance," is the world-disclosing vocabulary that first supplies "linguistic beings" with the requisite intelligibility to enact interpretations and make assertions.[23] Discourse names the condition that intelligibility is *publically communicable*. Think of discourse then as the condition of being or the capacity for being a participant in a system of *intersubjectively shared* resources for intelligibility. Dialogue can take place only on the basis of a shared world disclosure. Here the pragmatic dimension arises; there is an internal connection between the pragmatic or communicative dimension of discourse and its semantic or world-disclosive aspect. The disclosures that discourse constitutes are public disclosures. In attaching a publicly disclosed predicate to a publicly disclosed subject (what is talked about) discourse communicates and an intersubjectively shared world is invoked and articulated. The articulation of intelligibility has the imprimatur of publicity.

There is no reason to think that hermeneutics must deny the distinction between names used as tags and descriptions.

In Heidegger's case, for instance, a thing is encountered as the thing that it is against the backdrop of, or within the context of, our practices, practices that ground meaningful descriptions. Entities are *revealed* as such and such. We can *then* go on to make statements about those things as tagged (the apophantic "as" of propositional discourse). But clearly, for Heidegger, the apophantic "as" is parasitic on the hermeneutic "as."

With these considerations in mind, when reading Putnam's account, particularly his famous "twin earth" scenario, in the course of which he declares that the referent of "water" is H_2O, we might find ourselves fighting the urge to say, "yes, but that is merely *our* settled view" (where "merely" is not intended to have invidious force because we have no reason to think that anyone will have any *reason* to doubt its truth, although questions might be raised about its success in mirroring "nature's joints"). As we shall presently see, we should be forgiven this urge and shall find our predilection vindicated—even in Putnam's own eyes—by the course of subsequent discussion.

The theory of direct reference, motivated in the first instance to render an account of proper names, must be extended to natural kinds to be relevant to scientific description. But when so extended, such theories have a more problematic standing. As John Dupré points out, that status rests on the strong ontological presuppositions that there are real natural kinds out there, cutting nature at its joints, that natural kind terms pick out.[24] The kinds are taken to be demarcated by a real *essence*, a property thought to be both necessary and sufficient for an entity to be a member of the kind.[25] Kind terms then are taken to designate structures that are essential features of the referents. It is currently believed that molecular structure is the touchstone for the demarcation criteria and identity criteria of physical substances.

Furthermore, the Kripke-Putnam position holds that ordinary language use involves the *intention* to refer to natural kinds, such as water and gold, so that a large class of ordinary language kind terms actually map onto the requisite natural kind. But many distinctions circulated in ordinary language having to do with flora and fauna, for instance, divide scientific classifications in ways that have little or no biological significance.[26] This is to be expected because the distinctions codified in ordinary language emerge from the concerns of ordinary, practical life and may well be at cross purposes with the distinctions that serve the interest of scientific classification. The way in which ordinary language organizes the world is dependent on the projects in which a particular culture is engaged. Practice determines what are relevant similarities and differences, and language stabilizes them and makes them stand. The similarities and differences that ordinary language expresses are thus grounded in the relationship of things to our needs and interests. Accordingly, there may be several words for a given thing as scientifically characterized, depending on the relationships in which it stands to the interests of a given community or on the importance to those interests of making finer and finer distinctions. Conversely, there may be a single term for a number of otherwise quite different things as long as they all possess the same significance for a given community.

Well, we might here say, "so much the worse for prescientific, ordinary language." But how does the theory of direct reference fare when applied to scientific accounts of natural essences? The paradigm examples in such discussions are drawn from biology and chemistry. In biology, the species is the usual candidate for being a natural kind. The philosopher of biology David Hull has claimed, for example, that species are individuals. But whether species constitute natural kinds is a matter of more than a little controversy among biologists, and the species concept itself is notoriously rife with ambiguity. What criterion determines species membership: interbreeding capacity, morphological similarity, or phylogenetic affinity? The widely used criterion of capacity to interbreed and produce fertile offspring, for example, fails to meet the benchmark of essentialism required by the theory because it is simply not true that it holds between all and only members of a given species.[27] Here hermeneutics would seem to have a distinct advantage over direct reference theories because it need make no such essentialist, ontological assumptions.

Putnam's celebrated division of linguistic labor—between that of the expert and that of the "stereotype"-entertaining layperson—is a distinction that can be understood to hold *within* the context of an essentially Fregean view. That is, it can be maintained that the distinction between what is internal—what a term means to a speaker who uses it—and what is external—what is actually referred to by the term—is not an absolute or categorical distinction but is rather a relative one. "Internal" refers to criteria of application that agents implicitly appeal to in their usage; "external" ultimately refers to the criteria that we, or some relevant group of experts that we endorse, use for determining the extension of the term, and the latter is, of course, internal relative to us or to the relevant group of experts. Putnam seemed to want to make categorical use of this distinction, but as Rorty puts it, "our *present* views about nature are our only guide in talking about the relation between nature and our words" (emphasis added).[28]

Putnam and others believed that we would have to resort to a wholesale overthrow of Fregean semantics, replacing it with a nonintentionalist, causal theory of reference to render it intelligible that we can intend to pick out objects about which many of our beliefs are false (these are the counterexamples that Donnellan discusses in opposition to the Searle-Strawson criterion of reference[29]). But our assessment of how language hooks up with the world can only take place within the ambit of our present theory of the rest of the world. So our referring acts can have no "transcendental" guarantee because, as Rorty puts it, they would be underwritten by the circularity of our using part of our current theory to underwrite the rest of it.[30] In recanting his "metaphysical realism," Putnam himself came to realize the force of this[31] because it is not at all clear where the Archimedean point could be from which we could, as Rorty again puts it, "inspect the relations between [our present] representations and their object." It will inevitably turn out to be situated within our present set of representations. And they can change.

In the final analysis, I would argue that the significance of natural kinds—be they held to be substances or properties—lies in the role they play in our explanatory practices. Natural kind terms refer to the ontological primitives that are governed by the laws of nature; natural kinds are the things that are taken to be subject to the regularities imposed by nomological necessity. It is their role in *explanatory* accounts, their explanatory value, that gives them their purchase. Natural kind terms pick out the basic structured constructs that we take to have the most explanatory salience at a given time. The idea of natural kinds as real essences stands or falls with the presumed metaphysical necessity of the explanatory primitives posited in a given explanatory paradigm, and what is explanatorily primitive can change.[32]

Putnam and Kripke assumed that the salient properties of natural kinds, namely, those that determine the most explanatorily primitive factors for a given kind (for example, being constituted as H_2O for water) enjoy a metaphysical necessity that is wholly independent of our beliefs, theories, and attempts at classification. But what if, for example, it turns out that the primitive microstructure of water that has the greatest explanatory value is not its molecular structure but something else, perhaps a more fundamental primitive "ontology" within a deeper theory? Would a theorist committed to the direct reference view be willing to concede that our current scientists were mistaken about the referent of "water"? Such a fundamental change in scientific sorting categories would force theorists of the Kripke-Putnam persuasion to embrace their fallibilism—no shame in that. But if, in acknowledging the defeasibility of natural kind claims, its adherents nevertheless persist in insisting that there *are* such kinds with criteria rigidly referred to, even though we do not know yet what they are, such an insistence can get to the point of being gratuitous and ultimately question-begging. It would seem that a Quinean position of being committed to no more ontology than is required for our science to carry out its explanatory mission would be sufficient here.

We shall never get outside our system of *beliefs* about reference. Or, as Putnam himself later came to see, the attempt to adduce nonintentional, causal relations will always be vitiated by the fact that those relationships are simply threads from which the current theory of the world is woven.[33] There are no context-free descriptions of reality. Or, as Rorty puts it in summing up Putnam's revised view, nonintentional relations are as theory laden as are intentional relations.[34] So the theory of direct reference may be no less susceptible to relativistic scenarios than is the hermeneutic theory that it would rescue. Indeed, the view that Putnam felt compelled to embrace as a replacement for his earlier view, what he calls internal realism, bears significant elective affinities with hermeneutics.[35] The community of scientists that is responsible for determining the extension of a term is itself a community wherein a consensus on identity of meaning has been achieved. So, in this sense, a hermeneutic dimension is unwittingly presupposed even by the theory of direct reference; such theories cannot escape the hermeneutic circle.

B. AN ALTERNATIVE ACCOUNT

As salutary as is Rorty's pragmatist response to the idea of direct reference, I think Rorty nonetheless evinces a tendency to remain captive to the set of alternatives depicted in the Kripke-Putnam picture. That picture implies that we can have intentionalism, on the one hand, *or* sameness of reference and the possibility of disagreeing about the (same) referent, on the other hand, but not both. When approaching this fork in the road, Rorty follows the path not taken by Putnam and Kripke. But the point of my argument is to reject this picture and its false dichotomy by holding out for intentionalism *and* sameness of reference. Putnam's response to Paul Feyerabend's notion of radical meaning variance was motivated by the insistence that we retain the conceptual space for leveling the charge of committing the redefinist fallacy, that is, of redefining the things talked about in such a way as to *guarantee* that what is said about them is true.[36] My point here is that this imperative can be accommodated within hermeneutics. We can distinguish the thing meant from competing claims about the thing meant.

The issue is not simply to be, in some global sense, "in the same world" but to have sufficient consensus on the referents to have reason to expect *mutual* acknowledgment of a *mistaken* predication. This is at bottom the concern of the theorists of direct reference and why they propose it as a bulwark against relativism, skepticism, and incommensurability. I will argue that hermeneutics can make this possibility intelligible as well, and without the metaphysical baggage.

Now, as I noted in an earlier section, it does seem to be the case that the hermeneutic position, for conceptual reasons, will never license our being in a position to say that our interlocutor is *completely* wrong about a given topic, but it seems perfectly able to make intelligible all sorts of adjudicable disagreement short of that. When Gadamer insists that "every conversation presupposes a common language, or, [it] creates a common language," he means that a common way of identifying the topic of conversation must either be at hand or must be created, a description of the topic that is shared, a way of referring to it in descriptive phrases having virtually the same *sense*.[37] One of the problems that will concern us here is to what degree does a common language for the discussion of a topic restrict the scope of possible disagreement about the topic. That is, to what extent can such a common language countenance a *genuine* conversation? Does the common *meaning* necessary to establish the *referent* leave room for the contestation of the referent's attributes? Can we intelligibly distinguish between agreement on meaning and agreement in belief? In part, as a way of accommodating the possibility of such contestation and such a distinction, I have argued, *pace* Gadamer, that we should analytically distinguish two stages or two levels at which dialogue operates: the construction of the common language itself and the dialogical interaction that makes use of, or is enabled by, the ongoing processes of metalanguage construction.[38] The scope of reference that is determined by the necessary agreement on meaning is *narrower* than that of the common referent plus what is additionally predicated of it. Assuming that interlocutors begin with sufficient descriptive overlap to assure themselves that they are indeed addressing the same topic, it is certainly possible that they may *disagree* about further properties of the thing they are talking about.

And we need not stop here; we can go on to develop inferential consequences of the *disputed* predications for an area of experience on which there is *agreement* in order to attempt to adjudicate the dispute. So I would respond to the critique of hermeneutics that we are here considering by pointing out that the linguistic disclosure of the world, or the thesis that meaning determines reference, does not necessarily mean that adjudicable disagreement about the *same thing* is unintelligible.

I propose the following account of critical learning processes that accepts the idea that meaning determines reference, that is, that our referring is always an indicating under some description or other. First, assume that the dispute in question is occasioned by two distinct theoretical paradigms (analogous to distinct complexes of background knowledge) that can be understood to project distinct and characteristic objects of reference. Insofar as we look only at the area in which these complexes of meaning fail to intersect, we cannot perform a critical comparison of them—they are simply "talking past each other," and a certain species of relativism or of incommensurability could be understood to follow. Second, insofar as there is a field of commonly projected referents, a world on which they agree, there can be a *common* touchstone for disagreement and comparison. Rival paradigms can share commonly formulatable observational data. For instance, when asked to describe the motion of Mercury as it traversed its solar orbit, adherents of both Newton's celestial mechanics and of Einstein's general theory of relativity would issue similar if not identical observation reports, even though the former would interpret its motion as anomalous and the latter would not. And, as I indicate below, this is typically the case. So my insistence that there can be no linguistically innocent experience by no means implies that there cannot be paradigm-invariant experience.

Third, look for logical implications of claims about the *distinctive* referents for the field of *common* referents. And, fourth, this then allows us to connect the theoretical world disclosures to learning processes undergone with respect to the field of common referents without giving up the idea that meaning determines reference. So, we ask, what are the *differential* consequences for the field of common referents of the distinctive sets of background assumptions associated with the competing theoretical paradigms? What are the inferential claims about the common field made by paradigm T1 that are disputed by, or are in conflict with, the claims about that field that are derived from T2? My claim that some such disputed assertions can be *generally* recognized as warranting acceptance whereas their rivals do not is something that can be acknowledged by proponents of both T1 and T2. I see nothing that would in principle block such mediated comparisons. The wider in scope is the field of common referents about which they make conflicting claims, the better. Thus, for example, when the fossil record and other evidence support the claim that humans and other mammals share an ancestor, this should be dispositive for proponents of both pre-Darwinian natural history and evolutionary theory. That is, it should be dispositive independently of the fact that pre-Darwinians and post-Darwinians do not use the term "species" in such a way that it refers to the same entity.

Insofar as meaning is construed holistically, a full account of the meanings of things in the *shared* realm may exhibit some differences, but there is no reason to doubt that there may still be enough overlap at the core to make this picture plausible. We just need to assume that the overlap is sufficiently robust to guarantee that the entailments of the rival theories for the domain of overlap could be viewed as dispositive for both sides. The domain of overlap must subtend referents of *mutually acknowledged salience*.

How plausible is this scenario, given the thesis of meaning holism? Let us indicate the region of overlap by R_M. Holism would imply that we can draw no absolute distinction between the "observation language" in which R_M is articulated and the relevant "theoretical vocabularies," and the relevant theoretical vocabularies are, by hypothesis, distinct. At the level of R_M, the region of overlap, one can argue, as I have elsewhere, that this domain can be described with predicates with cross-contextual purchase.[39] *Or* it can be argued that one can *always* get down to a R_M that does have cross-contextual purchase even if it is somewhat differently modulated in each context. For example, even though evolutionary theorists and their opponents may use "species" in different ways, where it is holistically defined in terms of their respective and competing "theories," both groups can nevertheless refer to a R_M that is understood more neutrally to be a collection of distinctive varieties or kinds about whose nature or definition they could agree. Furthermore, although they would *meaningfully* disagree on what gave rise to them, both sides could even acknowledge that new kinds have arisen over time.[40] Although I do not yet claim to have fully settled convictions about the best way to accommodate holism in a systematic fashion, at least two ways of approaching the issue seem promising to me. Either approach would do justice both to the account that I am proposing and to a conception of holism that explains Gadamer's impatient interjection: "What sort of folly is it to say that a child speaks a 'first' word?"[41]

A thoroughgoing, unmitigated global holism *might* place us in danger of landing on the thresholds of incommensurability and nonintertranslatability. But one consideration is that a modified holism that maintains that the meaning of an expression is not dependent on, and only on, the *totality* of the expressions in a language but rather is a function of a relevant *region* of expressions—particularly perhaps a region associated with a particular dimension of experience, for example, color—would, I think, be a plausible candidate. Here relevance would be determined by the purposes that are pursued in the use of an expression or by the nature of the practices in which it is invoked (although I have doubts that *principles* can always be specified for demarcating regions of relevance). In this case, expressions located in regions that are treated as being external to the region of relevance could still contribute "overtones" or nuances to the meaning of the expression in question, but they would not be determinative. This bears some similarity to the molecularism of Dummett, but largely because of my doubts about being able to specify demarcation criteria in advance it should be distinguished from that position.

As for the second alternative, I pursue in the next chapter what I have elsewhere discussed as the concept of social identity as a cluster concept, whereby a particular set of features is understood to constitute one's social identity, the elements of the set functioning collectively in such a way that any particular element of the set could be contested or revised without resulting in the loss of that particular identity. Few, if any, of those elements, taken singly, would be essential to one's having that identity.[42] It has come to my attention that John Searle deploys a linguistic analogue to this idea that is quite useful: We refer in our use of "X" to whatever object would make most of our central beliefs about X true.[43] On this view, interlocutors would not need perfect agreement but only a sufficiently overlapping agreement on the sense of terms in order for them to be treated as coreferring. Happily, this also harmonizes well with what I have said about agreement on a topic. If this conception of meaning, which does not make sameness versus difference of meaning an absolute distinction but rather tolerates our thinking in terms of degrees of *similarity* of meaning, is combined with holism, then problems of commensuration and translation would be mitigated.[44]

One can adduce Davidsonian arguments to underwrite the conviction that there is a level R_M whereby scientists from differing research traditions inhabit the same world as long as each has reason to think that the other is engaged in rational linguistic activity of a certain sort. Or one can acknowledge the contingent fact that scientists are part of a tradition, a historical nexus of continuity wherein new theories are acquired with reference to the observational correlates of the previous theories from which they develop or with respect to which rival theories are rivals.[45] I would say further that when "we" get down to this level R_M, then and only then do we get a structure of attribution or a "taking as" that is (for the time being, at least) unrevisable on the basis of empirical discovery, and it would be so because the framework articulated as R_M would constitute what could *be* empirical experience. This is what I call a form of "transcendental intersubjectivism."[46]

Lafont says that from Heidegger's hermeneutic view "it follows that there is no absolute truth across incommensurable understandings of being. They are unrevisable from within and inaccessible (meaningless) from without."[47] Although I might well concede that the account of language provided by Heidegger—insofar as he does not thematize the "strong" intersubjectivism invoked in my account of the mutual forging of vocabularies requisite for what I called topic identification, or what Gadamer considered horizontal fusion—is not adequate for an acceptable philosophy of science, I would have to reply that we can, however, infer from Gadamer's hermeneutics, from the resources of hermeneutics itself, that there is no clear, bright line demarcating the inside of a horizon from its outside, a line that serves as a nonarbitrary boundary between horizons.[48] And we need something like this in order to get a strong incommensurability thesis off the ground.[49]

If, with Bas van Fraassen and others, we employ the idiom of a generalized model-based picture of scientific theories, in which models provide an interpretive framework for talking about theories and are ultimately understood to subtend empirical substructures, my proposal can be put somewhat differently. If models are understood to satisfy the principles of a theory and to preserve their truth value, then each model can be understood as a structure that offers an interpretation of the theory that will include substructures that are candidates for the direct representation of observable phenomena.[50] (The generalized model-based picture can be formulated in a way that is indifferent to one's position on the realism/antirealism spectrum regarding the status of scientific theories and to whether one holds that the difference between so-called theoretical vocabularies, on the one hand, and observational vocabularies, on the other, is one of degree or kind.[51]) In general, scientific theories can be satisfied by a number of distinct models, so each theory can be associated with a distinctive class of models. Whenever models of distinct theories overlap, we can treat the intersection as referring to the world common to the theories (R_M), and then proceed as I suggested previously. The area of intersection is the *topos* in which the *distinctive* theories are making claims about the *same* range of phenomena.

To conclude, we do not need a distinction between indirect reference and direct reference, or as some philosophers of science would put it, between theory-dependent meaning and theory-independent meaning, to get out of this relativistic conundrum. *All we need is a distinction between meaning that depends on a distinctive theory (that is a theory or horizon that is not shared between interlocutors) and meaning that depends on a shared theory or language.* Hence it is not at all clear that we need to depart from the ambit of hermeneutics to address this problem.[52]

2

CRITICAL FUSIONS

Toward a Genuine "Hermeneutics of Suspicion"

One of the questions facing global multicultural societies is how we should negotiate judiciously the criteria that will guide us in determining what should command our recognition as participants in cultural and political communities and what should not. The dilemma lies in discerning how to pursue such a negotiation in a way that does not beg questions against the yet-to-be included or against what is taken to have established its credentials for recognition. Central among the concerns of democratic and democratizing societies the world over is the challenge to find principled ways to acknowledge the claims of the distinct cultural groups comprising them. Forging a language for such a negotiation seems to me to be one of the central challenges facing us now.

Any conception of intercultural understanding that will be politically credible at our current juncture must also be a *critical* conception. As hermeneutically informed conceptions exhort us to fuse horizons, to pursue an open-minded and nonparochial inclusiveness, in a sense, to expand the circle of the "we," they must also have the resources to challenge those practices and social formations that thwart or undermine human flourishing. In this chapter, I outline what can be characterized as a critical hermeneutics, and I do so by way of an elaboration and extension of what I have elsewhere referred to as a dialogical or postmetaphysical humanism.[1] Humanism, properly conceived for our times, must be informed by a conception of critical pluralism, a nonrelativistic but hermeneutic version of critical rationality.

Throughout this book, my case for a critical hermeneutics takes the form of an extensive response to commonly voiced charges of relativism and critical impotence. In chapter 1, I responded to the epistemological challenge posed by the thorny issue of theory choice in the natural sciences by demonstrating hermeneutics' ability to do justice to the *rationality* of scientific theory choice and to the idea of progressive learning processes. In this chapter, I turn to the practical/ethical domain to display the cogency of hermeneutically informed social and cultural critique, showing that hermeneutically informed conversation can be deployed with genuine critical intent. Here hermeneutics as traditionally understood presents distinctive challenges. When hermeneutics shifts its focus from the understanding of texts, utterances, and deeds produced in the interpreter's own tradition to coming to terms with other competing cultures, traditions, and epistemic regimes, the question of its ability to provide an understanding that is simultaneously both noninvidious and genuinely critical arises. Indeed, in its insistence on the tradition-bound content and context of any putatively "critical" norms, hermeneutics is often understood to be opposed to the tradition of critical social theory, in particular, to the form that social theory assumes in the work of Jürgen Habermas.

I urge that hermeneutics can be a critical philosophical enterprise as much as it is an interpretive one. In particular, I want to develop the resources that hermeneutics makes available for social and political theory, more specifically for a critical social theory. By exploiting those resources, I hope to demonstrate a role for hermeneutics in social and political contexts that remains true to the spirit of hermeneutics but nevertheless goes beyond what Gadamer's writings explicitly provide. I have elsewhere pursued at length the potential for self-critique and self-estrangement that is inherent in an adequate conception of hermeneutic understanding, and I do not wish to downplay its importance (indeed, as I have argued, because of the symmetry inherent in mutual understanding, any fully adequate understanding of another will place the informing assumptions of both self and other at risk).[2] Here, however, I train my focus in a more sustained way on highlighting this understanding's potential for nonparochial questioning of the other.

The form my argument takes is in part a response to a still-influential conception of the nature and scope of intersubjective or mutual understanding. This conception has been pithily articulated by the distinguished German phenomenologist and Levinasian Bernhard Waldenfels, who claims that thinkers who promote and privilege the virtues of mutual understanding ineluctably presuppose a "third-person position," a standpoint that, in allowing for comparability, is itself a moment of convergence, stability, and universality that effaces difference, alterity, and the distinctiveness of the other.[3] In my view, this conception holds out unjustifiably limited prospects for mutual understanding; it is a conception that locates the very idea of reciprocal understanding somewhere between chimeric illusion and imperialist gesture. I argue, here and in the brief excursus on Waldenfels's "ethics of alterity" in the appendix, that this dichotomy between Enlightenment universalism and postmodernist fragmentation and relativism—a dichotomy that informs much of our social and political discourse about difference and identity—is a false one. In addition to underestimating the potential for edifying and self-transformative encounters with cultural others, this "postmodern consensus" has profound implications for our understanding of the nature and scope of practical deliberation. That is, it has profound consequences for our confidence in our ability to frame non-question-begging, critical responses to the manifold cultural practices that populate global society—responses to the treatment of women under Islamic law, for instance—and for our understanding of the scope of community given the salience of matters of "difference" in multicultural societies.

Although I take issue with the "postmodernist" position, it is important to remain informed by postmodernism's salutary critique of essentialism as well as by its sensitivity to matters of social and cultural difference. So my conception of critical hermeneutic understanding arises directly from two concerns: on the one hand, to acknowledge social and cultural difference, and on the other, to counter claims to the effect that persons and cultures are thereby ineliminably opaque to each other, claims that give rise to the relativistic conundrums that are typically taken to follow from this mutual opacity. Accordingly, the position for which I offer a brief here implies that non-question-begging critical perspectives on cultural formations need not entail an objectionable universalism or essentialism, just as an appreciation of matters of difference need not entail a simplistic relativism.

In his influential anatomy of hermeneutics, *Freud and Philosophy*, Paul Ricoeur contrasts two genres of hermeneutics: the hermeneutics of the recovery of meaning, which is associated with Dilthey, Heidegger, and Gadamer; and the hermeneutics of suspicion, whose masters were Marx, Freud, and Nietzsche. In the latter, the "true" or "real" meaning of actions, be they verbal or not, is presumably masked by a surface signification, and the "real" meaning gives the lie to what is manifest. As typically understood, the practice of the hermeneutics of suspicion depends for its legitimacy on what Richard Rorty, following Stanley Fish, called an *illegitimate* "theory hope," a view of the true that is vouchsafed to a *theoria*-like pure seeing, which is itself, Rorty averred, an anachronistic holdover of foundationalist philosophizing.[4] In such foundationalist thinking, the ineliminable role of finitude and of situated horizons from which interpretations of meaning necessarily emanate was overlooked, he claimed. The aspirations betokened by such a putative theory hope have been relentlessly ridiculed by many of the dominant philosophical movements of the twentieth and twenty-first centuries; the "negative dialectics" of Adorno, Heidegger's "destruction of metaphysics," Derrida's so-called deconstruction, as well as by Rorty's own neo-pragmatism. In many ways, this was the central issue that animated the celebrated debates between Habermas and Gadamer. Indeed, in an essay titled "The Hermeneutics of Suspicion," Gadamer dismisses this genre as but another species of foundationalism.[5] Another way of putting this, of course, is to say that the "hermeneutics of suspicion" is not sufficiently *hermeneutical*. On the other hand, because—to my mind at least—he never provided a clear and convincing account of the distinction between legitimate and illegitimate *sociopolitical* prejudices, one might say that hermeneutics, as Gadamer conceived it, was not sufficiently *suspicious*. Indeed, I find Gadamer's claim that his account of this distinction could serve as an effective stand-in for ideology critique to be unconvincing.[6] In the discussion that follows, I address the question, "How can critical suspicion be genuinely hermeneutic?"

CULTURAL IDENTITY, SECOND-ORDER RATIONALITY, AND COUNTERFACTUAL DIALOGICAL CRITIQUE

In our current moment of global modernity, hermeneutics can make a unique contribution to critical social and cultural understanding. Given contemporary concern about questions of global justice and, in particular, the skepticism voiced by some "postcolonialist" and "multiculturalist" thinkers that any ethical regime with cosmopolitan intentions must inevitably founder on the shoals of a Eurocentric ethnocentrism, hermeneutic approaches to social justice may well be the best positioned to simultaneously do justice to cultural difference and avoid situations in which critique depends for its legitimacy on normative standards developed in and imposed by the West. To make this case, I highlight three conditions that allow for immanent or "internal" normative pressure to be brought to bear on social/cultural practices when hermeneutically understood. First are facts about culture and cultural identity. It is widely acknowledged that cultures are not monolithic, homogeneous wholes. Furthermore, cultural identity itself can be understood to be what I would call a "cluster" phenomenon, which means that certain elements of the set of features that collectively constitute one's social identity may be revised as a result of critical reflection without resulting in the loss of that identity. Second, I propose a conception of "second-order rationality," a mode of rationality that has a culturally invariant purchase; and third, I elaborate a critical approach to cross-cultural understanding that is informed by what I currently call "counterfactual dialogical critique." Because these conceptions of rationality and of critique appeal to the possible acknowledgment on the part of the to-be-understood agent or agents, I maintain that they provide a more genuinely *hermeneutic* basis for what Paul Ricoeur has dubbed the "hermeneutics of suspicion" than do the critical strategies of those whom Ricoeur cites as its masters. The self-understanding of Nietzschean, Freudian, and Marxian theory does not unambiguously require that the validity of critique be subject to the acknowledgment of those to whom the critique is addressed.

My proposal for a dialogical method of critique requires no wholesale opposition to the actual options and choices of action available to, and sustained by, a given culture. It allows us to split the difference between, and thereby potentially to reconcile, the emancipatory reflection championed by Habermas and others, on the one hand, and a hermeneutically sensitive consciousness, on the other. And that is because the position that I develop here does not require—as Gadamer occasionally "falsely" alleged against Habermas—that emancipatory reflection dissolve all of the structures of intelligibility intrinsic to the culture in question. Ultimately, I suggest that the hermeneutic distinction between legitimate, or "true," and illegitimate, or "false," prejudice—a distinction Gadamer famously invoked but for which, at least in practical/ethical contexts, a fully satisfactory account has yet to be provided—is not merely arbitrary. To leave it at this would be tantamount to a capitulation to the charge of relativism. On the other hand, the redemption of this distinction does not require an appeal to a discredited foundationalism. To avoid both, I propose criteria for making this distinction by a consideration of what is required for autonomous agency, by a consideration of what is meant by genuinely autonomous consent on the part of to-be-understood agents. In so doing, I offer a modality for bringing to bear critical perspectives that are both sensitive to cultural difference and avoid an indiscriminate relativism.

THE HERMENEUTICS OF INTERCULTURAL UNDERSTANDING

Before pursuing the idea of *critical* understanding, I want first to clarify my conception of understanding itself, in particular, what it means to understand another person or a culture other than one's own. To do so, I briefly address the social-epistemological problem of determining how genuine, that is, noninvidious, understanding of cultural formations not our own is possible and what the conditions and limits of such understanding are. In general, I take the perspicuous *intelligibility* of the other to be a criterial property of an adequate hermeneutic understanding. This involves the production of a perspicuous account of what the other takes her life to be about, that is, of her distinctive and fundamental aims and commitments, of the ways those aims are pursued or addressed, and of the assumptions she holds about the situation—structures or institutions—that provides the setting or context for those pursuits. If we pay adequate attention to these facets of interpersonal or intercultural hermeneutic understanding, we will discover that the potential for meaningful *critique* is an ineliminable *internal* feature of such understanding.

In general, and especially in the case of intercultural encounters, such an account of where the other is "coming from" will emerge from a distinctive kind of dialogue whose vocabulary does not fully precede the dialogue itself. It is rather a dialogue that is enabled by ongoing practices of forging commensurable or mutually enriched vocabularies for identifying and discussing differences, vocabularies that enable a mutually respectful exchange about matters of common concern among people differently situated.[7]

I understand the vocabularies that can emerge from intercultural encounter to be "situated metalanguages." Each distinct cultural vocabulary embodies a distinctive set of responses to the full range of human concerns, and it is the distinctiveness of the responses that distinguishes one culturally indexed vocabulary from another. Put somewhat differently, the criteria of individuation for such vocabularies are furnished by the distinctive classes of shared points of appeal or of shared matrices of intelligibility that provide common reference points for those who are said to share a culture, allowing for the mutual intelligibility of agreement and disagreement within a culture.⁸ Dialogue between such communities of intelligibility is enabled by forging situated metalanguages that facilitate linguistically mediated community formation, a process that can produce a new community of consensus on terms for negotiating and adjudicating differences by expanding the scope of what is mutually intelligible, even if it only yields the mutual acknowledgment and acceptance of the terms in which disagreement or difference is expressed. Such an emergent common language will be the source of an ever-expanding shared vocabulary for discussing and representing, although *not* for standardizing, moral and cultural identity. This negotiated metalanguage—marking an emergent moment of common humanity as it enables the articulation of difference—is a situated metalanguage that is reflexively constituted by difference.

Dialogue between or across communities of intelligibility requires the identification of the *topic* or *Sache* that is being addressed in perhaps contrasting ways by the communities in dialogue. Here I believe we must consider the hermeneutic problem from a somewhat different angle than the one Gadamer was wont to adopt. His tendency was to focus on the tradition that both text and interpreter share, a focus that can occlude the problematic and deeply contested nature of topic identification when one cannot rely on the commonality provided by a shared tradition. By this I mean the problem of identifying the topic that will allow us to maximize the conspicuous intelligibility of a given response. So my concern is first to "rotate" the relationship with which Gadamer is preoccupied, namely, the vertical relationship of an authoritative tradition to an interpreter, so it becomes a horizontal relationship between interlocutors. This will mean that, in general, we will be unable to take for granted a shared tradition and the advantage that it gives us of already being "in" on the cultural conversation and the topics being addressed. In cross-cultural conversation, we may often be able to rely on only our hermeneutic talents and, crucially, the free response of intercultural interlocutors to our proposals. Consequently, the presumption of authority that Gadamer accords tradition, I locate in the reciprocal recognition of interlocutors (although we must, of course, take care to remain sensitive to real asymmetries between dominating and dominated languages[9]).

General methodological constraints condition our access to the fundamental concerns of others. It is in light of what are or could be concerns and issues for us that we are able to understand a form of life other than our own. When we understand, we invoke *Sachen* or dimensions of *our* experience, dimensions such as love, sexuality, religion, power, natality, and an awareness of our mortality. That is, unless we can identify the dimensions of experience that are addressed by the practices that are distinctive of the form of life we seek to understand, and we can do this only through modeling on what can be logical spaces or dimensions of experience *for us*, we cannot understand it. The aim of a nontendentious dialogical understanding of another is to produce an "ordered pair"—consisting of topic and response—that manifests a "reflective equilibrium" that displays the most *compelling connection* between a topic and the correlative response to it.[10] And here, indeed, we would do well to heed Gadamer's advice. In the case of textual interpretation, Gadamer exhorted us to "anticipate completeness," "to interpret to the strongest case that can be made."[11] This will be a connection that, in the *final* analysis, will be viewed as compelling or not *for us*.

I argue that analogy plays a crucial role here.[12] When we seek to identify the topic in question and to make the best case for a response to it, we ask questions such as, What category of phenomena, or what topics, do *we* treat similarly, or address in the way—or in *some* way that can be intelligibly connected by us to the way—that *they are* addressing X? Guided by such questions, we provisionally adduce such a category, say, that of "art," that we then *hypothetically* project on them. We then ask, *Is there, for them*, a category of objects that they treat (both linguistically and nonlinguistically) in the way—or in a way that can be intelligibly connected by us to the way—that *we* treat things we call "art"? In both cases, in the generation of a topic and in its justification, we are relying on analogy. In the first case, we are asking, Which of the topics with which we are familiar is analogous to what they are addressing, so the best case can be made for what they are doing? In the second case, we are asking more generally, *Is* there for them something analogous to our X?[13]

There is thus a sense in which some degree of ethnocentrism is epistemologically unavoidable. To see others as engaged in, say, argumentative practices or in morally relevant practices requires *our* experience with those kinds of practice as a touchstone. And we can be sure, to pick morality, that if another culture's criteria for the application of moral terms demonstrated *no* overlap with ours, we would have no reason to think that they were engaged in moral discourse at all. The interpretation that yields a *Sache* and contrasting approaches to it is, in the last analysis, ours. But I take this to be relatively harmless for two reasons. First, we can distinguish, on the one hand, what I would call the "transcendentally" necessary ethnocentrism of our unavoidable appeal to our notions of rationality and cogency, or to what we deem can be intelligibly related to them, from, on the other, the residue of a contingent, empirical and possibly invidious ethnocentrism. We can combat the latter by acknowledging the crucial importance of dialogue (with cultural others) aimed at mutually acceptable descriptions of the *Sache* and of its correlative contrasting practices. So finding the appropriate topic of concern will require both my interpretive powers, which will by themselves yield only hypotheses, and the confirmational resources of dialogue.

On this account, then, a hermeneutically self-aware ethnocentrist, one who is aware of her transcendental ethnocentrism, would interpret others in accordance with the criteria that her lights reveal, but not in a way that dogmatically precludes the possibility (or desirability) that her standards may change, i.e., that she could learn from others. Indeed, the relativist's refusal to judge can betray a refusal *to be judged*, a refusal both to make claims *on* others and to be claimed *by* those others.

Second, who "we" are is always subject to revision. Our identities are best viewed as being open to nonfatal contestation because certain elements of the set of features that collectively constitute one's social identity may be revised as a result of critical reflection without resulting in the loss of that identity. Such a threat to cultural identity need not be feared if we acknowledge that identity is a cluster phenomenon in the sense that few if any beliefs or professions of value, taken singly, are essential to an identity. Our identities need not be construed as being *identical* to our *prevailing* purposes, goals, and projects. What counts as the proper description of the self is open to contestable interpretation. Thus the modification of one's matrix of intelligibility in response to an interpretive/dialogical challenge need not entail the risk of losing oneself.[14] And, again, this holds for both sides of an intercultural dialogue. The critical renegotiation of identity can take place on both sides of the conversation table.

TOWARD A CRITICAL HERMENEUTICS OF INTERCULTURAL UNDERSTANDING

Given the hermeneutic account of intercultural understanding briefly outlined, what resources does it offer for critical responses to differently cultured others? Or, to invoke a formulation recently used by Habermas, with what success can it mediate between, on the one hand, a "politics of identity" with its tendency to make *collective* rights of different social groups sacrosanct and, on the other, an "Enlightenment fundamentalism" that would in an invidious fashion abstract individuals from their identity-informing sociocultural milieux? To address this challenge, I briefly discuss my account's implications for human rights and show how it licenses a form of immanent critique, and then I consider a conversational modality that takes advantage of the fact that, as my remarks on identity suggest, cultures are not monolithic, homogeneous wholes but rather are sites of contested interpretations, of competing interpretational narratives.

The maxim that I adopt, the assumption that others have distinctive takes on the world that I can learn to respect and from which I can perhaps learn, is a methodological assumption that underlies cross-cultural understanding. However, it is not an indefeasible claim with respect to any particular case; in fact I would insist that there are practices that *defeat* such a presumption. In the last section of *The Unfinished Project*, I briefly consider practices that fall under the sign "human rights violation." I say there that "we would fail to learn from the latter sorts of practice because they arguably violate an 'un-get-overable' criterial property of the good life. I take the recognition of the centrality of the freedom of individuals to assent to or reject propositions put forward by others—propositions purporting to articulate what those individuals would endorse as being of central importance to them—to define the minimalist core of any set of criterial properties of the good life that would meet with reciprocal acknowledgment and survive the test of the conversation of humanity."[15] So, in this minimalist sense, something like an "ethics of human rights"—which places a premium on the freedom of individuals to accept or reject descriptions of themselves or the languages within which those descriptions are couched—is built in and can be viewed to be so either on proceduralist grounds as a presupposition for participation in such a conversation or as a claim about the minimalist core of any product of such a conversation.

There is a second sense in which the model of understanding that I am proposing, emphasizing as it does hermeneutic charity, does not leave us powerless to respond critically to the forms of life that we wish to understand. That it does not promote, or even countenance, a promiscuous relativism can be demonstrated by way of a brief counterargument to a claim that Richard Rorty was wont to make, namely, that the only way to take seriously the distinction between the merely socially or culturally sanctioned, on the one hand, and the valid, on the other, is to adopt a discredited Platonic foundationalism. Lacking such a foundation to provide an "honest broker," there can be no non-question-begging way, Rorty insisted, to critically evaluate or to referee conflicts between sociocultural practices.

Pace Rorty, I believe that there are grounds for critically assessing social practices that are *internal* to the cultural horizons that sustain those practices, grounds that make it unnecessary that critique appeal to anything beyond the standards of rationality or the central vocabulary of a particular cultural group. The intuition that supports my conviction here is fed by the recognition that *we* can sometimes be brought to see that social practices and procedures of epistemic justification that *we* may have heretofore relied on may prove to be unreasonable or untrustworthy, to us. And there is no reason to think that others cannot be brought to see this as well. Consider cases like that of the discovery of an unbalanced scale in an economic transaction, where the outcome of an accepted procedure for assessing relative value will have been *exposed* as having been an artifact of bias in the procedure itself, cases where it has been discovered that the procedures have been "loaded" in such a way as to prejudice their outcome. In such cases, there are *reasons* to modify the procedure that can be acknowledged by *all* who engage in the practice.

My commitment to hermeneutic humanism entails, among other things, a disposition to genuinely respect differently situated others. And this will, I argue, transcendentally demand that we treat differently cultured others as being like us in that they, too, operate with an *ideal* of themselves wherein their actions, if challenged in ways that are understandable to them, can be held accountable to *reasons* that have a nonparochial purchase and that are binding for them. Now, given its identity, every culture implicitly makes the claim that its practices provide the best avenue for *its* flourishing, that they represent the best way for *it* to address the *Sachen*. Even the most insular forms of life can be understood implicitly to make the claim that their practices are the best way for *them* to flourish. This sort of culturally rooted validity claim provides the occasion or basis for a non-question-begging cultural critique informed by the presumption of what I call second-order rationality.

Second-order rationality is quite obviously invoked when an experimental design in the sciences is criticized—for example, when a particular experimental setup is shown to be flawed in such a way that it cannot be dispositive for testing a given hypothesis, that it prejudices its outcome. But this mode of rationality can also be deployed in the interpretation of sacred texts and of political constitutions. The form of rationality that is implicit in my account here is one that I take to have transcultural or cross-cultural or culturally invariant standing. It is a disposition or mode of rationality that we are entitled to impute to everyone—that is, an inclination to reform one's practices in the direction of more rationality when one's lack of rationality is pointed out in terms with which one is conversant.

Therefore, without appealing to anything beyond the matrices of intelligibility, standards of rationality, and central vocabulary of any particular epistemic community or cultural group, we can intelligibly mark a distinction between what even everyone in a particular epistemic community *happens* to believe and what is, by their *own* lights, *reasonable* for them to believe, a distinction, moreover, that should command *their* attention. To *convince* someone of the questionability of their practices is ipso facto to provide them with a *reason* to consider alternatives.

The cross-cultural commitment to second-order rationality implies that social agents must, even if only prereflectively or implicitly, *anticipate* a relationship among their aims, beliefs, and practices whose rational coherence differently situated others (including cultural "outsiders") could also appreciate. (I should emphasize, however, that this exploitation of the transcultural presumption of second-order rationality depends on a prior hermeneutic *understanding* of the cultural context in which the disputed practices are situated; we would need to know what the aims of the disputed practices are, which topics they are addressing. Only such an understanding would allow the sort of critical representation that I have here elaborated.) In so providing members of a particular cultural tradition with an optic for recognizing and acknowledging what could be problems *for them*, the unavoidable presumption of this modality of reason also fully entitles critical outsiders to view "insiders" as being eligible, and in a way that begs no questions, to accept the burden of rational critique. In this sense, social agents, however implicitly, anticipate a dialogical confirmation of their rationality, granting an opening to potential critics.

I conclude my reflections here with a sketch of a third way in which hermeneutically informed approaches to intercultural understanding can allow us to successfully navigate between the

Scylla of arrogant cultural imperialism and the Charybdis of impotent cultural relativism. I wish to make a case for a particular sort of conversational practice that can lay claim to being a genuine "development practice." Like the invocation of second-order rationality, these would be conversational practices whose *internal* normative pressure would perform critical work without the *imposition* of normative standards from cultural "outsiders."[16] I illustrate this conversational modality with primary reference to the practice of female genital cutting or excision in locales—such as those parts of Africa, the Middle East, and Southeast Asia—where women themselves seem to be part of the consensus in its favor. Now, to be sure, although the existence of such a practice is clearly a matter of concern in and of itself, I am not here claiming that the fact of its existence is the main problem to be addressed in these societies. Focusing on it, however, is useful for illustrating how resources for critique can be unearthed when careful attention is paid to the *autonomously* voiced preferences and concerns of those local cultural agents who are affected by such a practice, resources whose critical potential can be redeemed independently of any one-sided imposition of "Western" standards.

I begin with the reminder that cultures are not seamless wholes; in the words of one observer: "since a culture's system of beliefs and practices, the locus of its identity, is constantly contested, subject to change, and does not form a coherent whole, its identity is never settled, static and free of ambiguity."[17] And, as a United Nations report on justice and gender indicates: "the history of internal contestation reinforces [the premise] that cultures are not monolithic, are always in the process of *interpretation* and *re-interpretation*, and never immune to change" (emphasis added).[18] These statements, of course, echo what I earlier referred to as the conception of culture as a cluster concept and the idea that cultures are in general sites of conflicting interpretations. If we further concede, as I have argued elsewhere we must, that the distinction between *intra*cultural hermeneutic dialogue and *inter*cultural hermeneutic dialogue is a matter of degree, not kind, then we should expect to find *within* many cultures traces of the tensions that we are more accustomed to noticing between them.[19] Consistent with this, it can be argued that many intercultural normative disagreements can be productively analyzed as *intracultural* conflicts.[20]

To take but one example, Akeel Bilgrami, a philosopher who is himself Muslim, has argued that being a Muslim is not necessarily to accept the strategic framing of one's identity put forward by some of one's fundamentalist coreligionists;[21] such an identity can be critically reconfigured. He points out that Muslim communities are defined by competing values, of which Islam is one and, furthermore, that Islamic identity is itself negotiable.[22] Given the spectrum of positions actually occupied by members of Muslim communities, he goes on to make the point that critical pressure need not necessarily be viewed as an ethnocentric, imperialistic imposition from the outside but rather that it can be applied from the inside, where there are indigenous resources and aspirations that can fuel *internal* processes of critical response.[23] And, as the political theorist Yael Tamir has argued, "although cultural choices are neither easy nor limitless, cultural memberships and moral identity are not beyond choice," and they can be made the subject matter for a politicized discussion oriented toward bringing these emotional processes to discursive consciousness.[24] I contend that cultural identities are as much forged as found. They are fields of contestation and negotiation, often of struggles to expand existing and socially acknowledged logical spaces to accommodate the intelligibility of styles and forms of group membership that were previously marginalized.[25]

Given that cultures are not monolithic, homogeneous wholes such that none of their component parts—beliefs and practices—can be altered without loss of integrity, it behooves us to be wary of taking at face value any *single* narrative purporting to capture definitively a culture's identity. This suggests that we be attentive to ways in which cultural identity claims may be reified products. Categorically asserted cultural identity claims can be understood to be reified products in at least two ways: they may disingenuously veil strategic orientations, and they may belie the conflict of interpretations that shapes the reception of a culture's identity-defining structures, the fact that cultural identity is best seen as a cluster concept.[26] Cultural identity claims should not then be given carte blanche to function in such a way as to quarantine intracultural practices from discursive view so as to immunize them from critical examination. As I shall presently suggest, the plurivocity of legitimate cultural narratives underwrites the hermeneutic intelligibility of a cultural agent assuming an oppositional stance vis-à-vis elements of her cultural matrix.

The central operative assumption behind the conversational practice that I am here endorsing, "counterfactual dialogical critique," is that cultural agents can be encouraged to consider social possibilities that, although currently unrealized, might actually be *preferred* by them, social possibilities whose realization is suppressed not because such realization would offend against all intelligible interpretations of cultural identity but rather primarily because it would offend against *particular* interpretations, namely, those that may serve particular vested interests. For this reason, then, we should be on the lookout for interpretations of cultural identity that operate as cloaks or ideological veils concealing prudential, interest-based concerns.[27]

The interests that occasion such strategic representations are unlikely, except in unusual cases, to be distributed *uniformly* across individuals and groups within a culture. The *representativeness* of such strategic self-images can then be interrogated through dialogue with a representative variety of such individuals, acknowledging of course that what counts as a representative variety may be itself a matter for interpretive contestation. Nevertheless, it would be reasonable to start with representations parsed out in terms of standard demographic categories such as those of class, ethnicity, and gender.

Now, obvious overt signs would trigger a "hermeneutics of suspicion," signs such as observed conflicts of interest within a society, observed indices of perceived or actual power asymmetries between categories of social membership, and so on.[28] But what if, as is not infrequently the case with female excision, there is no overt contestation of what seem to us problematic cultural practices? Here I should like to note that the *appearance* of asymmetrical or invidious treatment of identifiable demographic groups can serve to trigger *hypotheses* about the real interests implicated and about whether or not the interests of all cultural members converge in the way that prevailing cultural identity claims implicitly assert that they do.

It is useful here to consider a suggestion made by Habermas, indeed, one that I have myself criticized in another context.[29]

> I make the methodological assumption that it is meaningful and possible to reconstruct (even for the normal case of norms recognized without conflict) the *hidden* interest positions of involved individuals or groups by . . . imagining the limit case of a conflict between the involved parties in which they would be forced to consciously perceive their interests and strategically assert them, instead of satisfying basic interests simply by actualizing institutional values as is normally the case.[30] (italics added)

I suggest that we treat Habermas's comments as pertaining to what philosophy of science was wont to call the context of generation, the context within which hypotheses are proposed. Central now is the question, How to "test" these hypotheses concerning hidden or suppressed interests? Habermas makes reference to the possibility of indirect *empirical* confirmation based on predictions about conflict motivations.[31] However, I want to emphasize the extent to which the suspicion of potential dissensus can be *hermeneutically* redeemed (or, for that matter, falsified). We need not restrict ourselves to the social theorist's monologically produced picture of a counterfactually imagined conflict. The justification of the ascription of a potentially hidden interest can, indeed should, be a collaborative, dialogical project, one involving those whose interests are in question. With regard to the question of female excision, this means the affected and potentially affected women, whose perspective would be articulated under conditions that I shall now describe.

As an explicit *stylization* of the sorts of question that might, whether implicitly or explicitly, underlie such a dialogical engagement, capture its critical intent, and perhaps thereby prompt some of the processes of cultural self-reinterpretation alluded to previously, I suggest the following. When encountering some form of the practice of excision or genital cutting, a witness, whether sharing cultural membership with the affected women or not—one who failed to find the "general" acquiescence to the practice on the part of women to be perspicuously intelligible—might initiate conversations of a particular sort with them, conversations guided by the basic question: Armed with the knowledge of the all too likely physical and emotional consequences of the procedure, if the connection between undergoing the procedure (or the procedure in the concrete form that it now assumes) and your chances for flourishing in your society were virtualized, if that connection could be severed, would you still choose to undergo the procedure?[32] This is the sort of question that could be raised in the conversational modality that I refer to as counterfactual dialogical critique, a modality that, if practiced within a society, illustrates the plausibility of non-question-begging, noninvidiously ethnocentric, critical perspectives on practices within cultural formations that are not our own.[33]

Non-question-begging conversations with potentially affected social agents—in "safe" spaces providing immunity from the threat of reprisal—aimed at eliciting fundamental or overriding interests can be initiated.[34] Woven into such a conversation might well be discussions in which the agent is encouraged to engage in an imaginative variation of possible conditions on the realization of those interests, say, the interests in cultural solidarity and social flourishing; these are the virtualizations of counterfactual dialogical critique. This would entail consideration of scenarios in which the linkage between succumbing to the procedure of excision in the form that it currently assumes and being able to realize those interests is gradually severed. These counterfactual narrative scenarios may range from replacing clitoridectomy with lesser forms of mutilation, to a ritualized symbolic circumcision consisting of a small cut on the external genitalia performed under medical supervision and hygienic conditions, all the way to nothing at all.[35] If the agent, on reflection, expresses a genuine *preference* for situations wherein her interests—chances for marriage and other important forms of social recognition, for example—and *forgoing* the procedure were jointly realizable, then this would count as her opting out of the putative "consensus." At the very least, we could say that a discussion that is informed by a consideration of these alternatives is more autonomously pursued—and that a life that is led in an awareness of them is more lucidly lived—than one which is not. This would be a means of conversationally interrogating the reasonableness of sociocultural configurations wherein women are faced with the forced choice between flourishing and bodily integrity, are confronted with the demand to choose "mutilation" or face "social death." It would foreground the possibility that the social forces that sustain this forced choice are a reflection of *one* particular cultural interpretation among others. Its aim is to effect a piercing of the epistemic/cognitive veil by raising the possibility of a way to extricate oneself from bondage to such a dichotomous conception of social options, thus enhancing the scope for autonomous agency.[36] My normative focus here is to deploy in this account some of our intuitions about the criterial conditions for the exercise of genuine autonomous agency, and minimally that involves the agent's *informed endorsement* of what she does.[37] Moreover, the more this endorsement is given in the context of perceived alternatives, many of which can be understood to cohere with valid interpretations of the culture in question, the more *meaningful* that endorsement will be.

It might be objected that this conception of autonomy is too demanding to be of critical use, for none of us chooses all of our choices. Many of them are "thrust" upon us because of the nature of things or in situations that we would uncontroversially regard as "normal conditions." Everyone faces disjunctive situations not of their choosing, e.g., "do your job or lose it." But some face situations of this sort that others do not, and do so for reasons that are more contingent than necessary, more "contrived" than "natural." The critical purchase of the concept of the restriction of autonomy takes as its background, then, what someone would otherwise—that is, absent arbitrary constraint—be capable of doing. The asymmetrical arrangement wherein one determinate group of mature agents must exercise a choice within a dichotomous or disjunctive framework—e.g., one structured by the alternatives of flourish or retain bodily integrity, but not both—while others are exempt from facing such a dilemma may be an arrangement that may well serve the interests of those who are exempt. This, I argue, provides sufficient grounds to question the rational warrant of this arrangement and therefore to suspect the arbitrary, i.e., *unreasonably* limited, and, hence, *criticizable* nature of the framework for choice for those who are constrained by it.

A second plausible objection to this critical deployment of autonomy is to claim that autonomy is but one value among other, perhaps competing, values.[38] Even if this can be persuasively demonstrated, the cultural practices we are considering, if challenged, tend to be defended in one of two ways: they are claimed to be essential to the integrity of the culture in question or it is claimed that they are willingly endorsed by the cultural agents who participate in them. What I have said about the plurivocity of legitimate cultural interpretations addresses the former, and in the case of the latter, the *claim* to autonomous acceptance is precisely what serves to anchor the immanent critique that I have proposed.

It is important to note that this dialogical method of critique requires no *wholesale* opposition to the actual options and choices of action available to, and sustained by, a given culture. It is attuned more to the nature of the *distribution* of those social options and choices. And what about those cases in which, even after such a conversation, some persist in holding to the view that such a ritualized procedure, in its current or traditional form, has an identity-constitutive character that is itself of overriding value? Consistent with the dialogical nature of the enterprise that I am here proposing, such a response may ultimately have to be acknowledged as a "falsifying" event. Prior to such acknowledgment, however, and given the heterogeneous constitution of culture, our questioning can be broadened to press the issue of social *interest*. We might pose these questions:

Given the likely physical and emotional harms of undergoing such a procedure, whose interest is served by the perpetuation of the practice? Given the conceived alternatives that our discussion has brought to mind, and in light of the hypothesis that the restricted alternatives in terms of which you originally chose were promulgated in the interest, or implicitly served the interests, of some as opposed to others, would you now *endorse*, in the sense of voluntarily choose, what you would have chosen before? The conception of autonomy that has informed my discussion is, I contend, a distinctively hermeneutic one in that it is not conceived of as a property of a disembodied, acultural subject but is rather predicated of an agent who is *situated* within a particular concrete matrix of intelligibility.[39]

And that matrix of intelligibility is contingently expandable. This can happen when the semantic resources that would enable alternative legitimate cultural interpretations are enriched by the participation of those whose interests had been marginalized in the interpretive process itself. This expanded "hermeneutic" agency would remediate what was possibly a disguised unequal hermeneutic participation and ideally, at least, level the playing field.[40] I have described this within-group negotiation to expand the stock of generally acknowledged social meanings as a matter of expanding that group's moral horizon by advocating for the semantic authority or interpretive adequacy of alternative descriptions of a shared social world.[41] The exploitation of these newly available semantic resources would allow formerly marginalized agents to "name" and coherently depict the newly suggested options, to name their preferences in a way that they would be intelligible from within their cultural horizons. In the case under discussion, the goal of such a semantic expansion would be to achieve general social recognition for the newly emergent social category "unmutilated female cultural participant," where there had been no semantic space for such a description previously.⁴²

Lest what I have proposed be dismissed as a "mere" armchair philosophical "thought experiment," consider some of the conversations about genital cutting that have recently begun to take place in a number of societies in which it has been traditionally practiced. The conversations are just of the sort that I have proposed. In the African country of Mali, for example, they are pursued under the indigenous auspices of the COFESFA Women's Association and other NGOs. These conversations highlight the physical and emotional consequences of the ritual, the plurivocity of the cultural narratives deployed to justify the practice, and the patriarchal interests that it serves. There are, of course, no guarantees, given that these conversations seek to engage opinion leaders and take place among both men and women in local communities, but they may give rise to proposals that will be candidates for the sort of general social recognition, or what I have called semantic authority, that can foster cultural reinterpretation. It is useful, surely, to think of these conversations as a component of the within-group struggle to expand the group's moral imaginary by persuading members of dominant social groups to acknowledge the semantic authority of claims put forth by others. Indeed, such community-based discussion, sponsored by an NGO in Kenya (the Maendeleo Ya Wanawake Organization), has in some cases led to the implementation of alternative noninvasive rituals marking female rites of passage in local communities.⁴³ Similar developments are occurring in Senegal. It is worth noting in the Senegalese case, where the issue of genital cutting was explicitly raised by Senegalese women themselves, that care was taken in the discussion of this issue to avoid descriptors such as "barbaric" and other potentially question-begging cognates that would invidiously pre-judge the issue.⁴⁴

What lessons can we draw from these examples, highlighting as they do the conversationally underwritten and enhanced agency of local groups? Hermeneutics' emphasis on the conversational negotiation and expansion of interpretive frameworks enables a distinctively illuminating analysis of the pragmatics and intelligibility of such conversational situations. And this evaluative stance is, I believe, an inescapable aspect of intercultural understanding. This serves to underscore the status of my proposal as a model for mutually critical conversation and thus as an exemplar of a genuine hermeneutics of suspicion.

3

AGENCY, THE "POLITICS OF MEMORY," AND REPARATIVE JUSTICE

Hermeneutics and the Politics of Development

Chapter 2, in part, focused on the autonomy of agency; in this chapter, I focus on the nature of agency itself, i.e., on the capacity to engage in effective action. In offering an account of the hermeneutic dimension of agency, facets of this capacity will be brought to light that would otherwise escape our notice. Furthermore, bringing such unacknowledged facets to the fore will enable an exploration of a kind of epistemic injustice that may be implicated in assertions about the agential deficiencies of members of disadvantaged groups as well as the injustice of withholding what I have called semantic authority from the sorts of interpretation of social experience that underwrite the social agency of such persons.

I argue that to fully understand global social injustices we need a way of making salient the discrepancy between, on the one hand, the historically sedimented conditions that continue to *impede* agency for some and, on the other hand, the enabling but often hidden or unacknowledged conditions that *facilitate* agency for others. My claim is that drawing a distinction between what I shall call first-order agency and second-order agency allows us to do this insofar as this distinction disaggregates the volitional and epistemic components of agency. Second-order agency refers to the ability to produce, acquire, or avail oneself of the facilitating conditions of action in the first-order sense. Although those conditions may be both material/structural and epistemic in nature, in this chapter I concentrate primarily on the epistemic conditions. If persons who suffer under current conditions appear, through their actions or inaction, to be culpable for their own suffering, I argue that we ought to heed the aforementioned distinctions because it may be the case that we do not yet truly understand their choices. To understand a person's choices will require that we engage in a hermeneutical investigation undertaken under what I call the constraint of narrative representability. That is, we must ask, How do things appear from the first-person perspective within which these choices were made? Understanding such choices in this manner can bring into focus cases in which the agent making the choices is not culpable for their failure to make life-enhancing choices (of course, still leaving open the possibility that in some cases the agent may be), but where instead an injustice of an epistemic sort has occurred. By "an injustice of an epistemic sort," I refer to the injustice of failing to acknowledge the agent's epistemic state when that state, or the structural conditions responsible for it, unfairly compromise the agent's ability to act. This is the *compound injustice* of having one's agency compromised by an epistemic limitation for which one bears no culpability and of nevertheless being judged or blamed for that lack of agency.

ON AGENCY, THE POLITICS OF MEMORY, AND EPISTEMIC INJUSTICE

Thomas McCarthy provides a wide-ranging treatment of matters of global justice from the perspective of Critical Theory.[1] Central among his themes is the claim that global justice requires sustained attention to the repair of the "harmful effects of past injustice." In matters of race—despite a scientific consensus that dismisses the biological significance of race[2] and the formal legal protections afforded by the civil rights movement—the persistence of perniciously systematic racial stratification in the United States is instructively on display, for instance, in *pre*-Katrina New Orleans. Well before the levees broke, New Orleans was paradigmatically illustrative of the kinds of social practice that reproduce racial formations in a way that fully warrants McCarthy's application of the term "neo-racism." A lawyer I encountered soon after the storm, who had lived in the "Big Easy" for twenty years until departing just before the storm, helped me to connect the dots. He informed me of an astonishing set of conditions, a set of conditions obtaining in a twenty-first-century American city. (And as an African American who grew to adolescence in the segregated South, I am not inclined to be easily shocked by instances of racial injustice.) Among those conditions were the mutually reinforcing relationships between public educational expectations (and delivery), the predominance of low-wage service sector employment opportunities for unskilled workers, and the "homestead exemption" tax policy. The latter exempts a designated class of real estate owners from having to pay property taxes that, of course, fund the public schools.

This lawyer went on to speak of young African American children who were his legal wards and who seldom went to school and whose high levels of truancy were hardly an aberration within the New Orleans public school population. Worse yet, their *teachers* showed up only infrequently. This too was apparently unexceptional. And it did not seem to matter. Or rather it worked out "all too well" because the predominance of jobs open to the New Orleans poor were in the service sector of the tourist industry. Too much education would be dysfunctional in this system. In many ways, and almost 150 years after the *legal* end of slavery in the United States, New Orleans still seemed a virtual "plantation" society where the inertial effects of that past wound maintained their viselike grip on the present.

One way of pursuing what McCarthy aptly calls the "politics of public memory,"[3] a politics in which a critical theory of global development must engage, is to address the hysteretic effects of both racial discrimination at home and colonialism abroad. I adopt the expression "hysteretic effect" from physics, where it refers to the inability of a disturbed system to return to its original state when the external cause of the disturbance has been removed, to effects that persist in the absence of initiating causes. Because past states of systems remain present in this way, hysteretic effects are those in which systems retain a "memory" that haunts the present, or in the recent words of Barack Obama, where "past injustices continue to shape the present."[4] A typical formulation of the refusal to address these effects, and one that is symptomatic of our public amnesia regarding matters of race, is the neoconservatives' well-known "culture of poverty thesis" and, in the global arena, the invocation of the "dysfunctional cultural values" of "underdeveloped" societies.[5] In challenging the claim of the neoracists and other like-minded commentators that the social pathology of the poor is the independent variable in accounting for their social wretchedness, McCarthy suggests instead that social structures and processes, on the one hand, and psychological and cultural patterns, on the other, should be understood as being reciprocally related.[6] I endorse this view—with the emendation that structural disparities will often have as their corollaries epistemic disparities, an unfair distribution of epistemic resources—and would like here to develop it a bit further.

The expression "culture of poverty" is a signifier for a weakness of culture and character that manifests itself as an agency deficit, a deficit conceived of either as a values deficit or as a species of weakness of will, *akrasia*, lack of discipline, self-control, and so on. In the latter case, the agent is taken to be *culpably* unable—for want of will or discipline—to make good choices. I argue here that the invocation of the culture of poverty thesis may well instantiate a fallacy that some have dubbed "psychologizing the structural."[7] This refers to the false assumption that a particular population's failure to flourish is caused primarily by psychological deficits rather than by that population's structural environment. Such a verdict fails to take into account the agents' conceptions of socially available courses of action. Only a hermeneutic investigation will enable us to know whether or not such a fallacy has been committed. Central to such an investigation is the acknowledgment that an agent's knowledge of the social world is essentially interpretive, that is, it is knowledge of that object domain *under a particular description*.[8] Structuring any such interpretation will be beliefs about what socially available options there are, beliefs about what can intelligibly be done. Moreover, only such a hermeneutically informed diagnosis can point us in the direction of appropriate remedies.

I first briefly address the thesis of value deficit. Perhaps the deepest conceptual flaw in neoconservative thinking about values is a related fallacy, what might be called the fallacy of "reading off" values from behavior itself. In "The Moral Quandary of the Black Community," a once prominent spokesperson for this view deployed the formulation "values, social norms and personal behavior *observed* among the poorest members of the black community" (emphasis added).[9] A more recent formulation of this view can be found in the work of *New York Times* writer/journalist David Brooks who, in his call for a renewed emphasis on the social psychology of the poor, writes that "the real barriers to mobility are matters of social psychology, the quality of relationships in a home and a neighborhood that either encourage or discourage responsibility, future-oriented thinking, and practical ambition."[10] Unlike behavior, however, values are not observable in any straightforward sense. To gain access to them we must enter the hermeneutic circle of beliefs, desires/values, and actions. The relationship between one's values and one's behavior is mediated by one's beliefs and, relevant here, by one's general conception of the social world or milieu in which one is embedded. Values are held within some cognitive or epistemic scheme or other and emerge in behavior in a mediated way. One might conveniently speak of valuation as being inscribed in an interpretive context, a context in which conceptions of "social space" serve as interpretive frameworks or matrices of intelligibility. Part of any such conception will be beliefs about what socially available options there are. In order, therefore, to understand what sort of valuing is going on, one must gain access to the view of the social world held by the agents in question. In other words, one must seek an answer to the question, What do they take themselves to be doing?

What is at issue here is how to determine appropriate act-descriptions. Such descriptions must make an appeal to relevant intentions and beliefs in order to discern the meaning that informs action. An action description is a description of behavior in terms of its intended end, purpose, or point. In an earlier work, I have given an account of the ineliminably hermeneutic nature of this determination.[11] In brief, it is a matter of proffering a description that most adequately renders the behavior *understandable-in-context*, an act-description that exhibits the most compelling connection between behavior and the agent's situation-interpretation.

Acknowledging the importance of seeking appropriate act-descriptions might lead us to question, for example, social-psychological studies that purport to establish differential attitudes toward immediate gratification exhibited by poor Black children as compared to whites. Is the unwillingness of the poor Black children to forego a prize in the present in order to receive one of somewhat greater value in a specified future testimony to a culture of hedonism? Or is it an instance of pragmatic behavior predicated on the rationally acquired belief that the system cannot be trusted to deliver, predicated on the absence of a basis for hope? As I have argued elsewhere, it is the failure of neoconservative thinkers to acknowledge this and to *assume*, as opposed to hermeneutically demonstrate, such value differentials that underwrites their assertions to the effect that behavior regarded as dysfunctional within the global-capitalist system can be attributed to deficient values.

This situation is analogous to a standard issue in ethical theory. To make good the claim of so-called descriptive ethical relativism—namely, the claim that different persons or cultures have different values or adhere to different moral principles—one must first demonstrate that the persons or cultures in question have the same or relevantly similar notions of what the facts of the matter are and, second, that, this similarity notwithstanding, they nevertheless go on to evaluate differently. For example, people who believe in an afterlife and, further, that one's eternal condition will be a function of one's physical condition at the time of death might, in good conscience and presumably with their consent, put healthy parents to death while subscribing to the very *same* moral principle as those from a more skeptical culture who might stand aghast at such a practice. Both might hold fast to and be guided by one and the same moral conviction, e.g., one ought do what secures one's parents' long-run interests: belief in an afterlife conditioned in a certain way might support parricide; the lack of such a belief would encourage radically different behaviors.

A more explicitly political example can be usefully deployed to show that behavior per se cannot be taken to be a reliable guide to aims, values, and goals. Is a disruptive protest demonstration an attempt to get a hearing, to redress humiliation, to recover a sense of dignity, a bargaining gambit, or merely an expression of blind anger?[12] If we consider the recent "Occupy Wall Street" movement within the unquestioned matrix of interpretation that Charles Taylor dubs "the civilization of work," then the descriptors that are most readily available for characterizing the activity of members of the movement are that they are either bargaining gambits or expressions of madness. However, neither description is adequate to the nature of the movement.

I have so far concentrated on situations in which, without justification, we may think, based on their behavior, that others are beholden to values that we do not share. There are other cases in which nonstandard behavior is assessed in terms of the values to which we do subscribe and is accordingly found wanting. These are cases in which we simply presume that our aims are *shared*. This has special relevance in the context of assessing "developmental advance." Our assessment of claims about developmental advance, or the lack thereof, should be informed by the concerns I have raised here because such a claim typically presupposes that practices in other cultures are to be judged by the extent to which they exhibit "a more or less deficient mastery of our competencies rather than as expressing mastery of a different set of skills altogether."[13] But we should be wary of the tendency to assume the cultural invariance of the identification of salient problems or that such problems are self-announcing across cultural horizons. For example, if one assumes, as did Habermas at one point, that certain mythical narratives were attempts to *explain* natural phenomena, then one gets a "contrast" between mythical narratives and scientific narratives.[14] Indeed, one will have produced an invidious contrast because mythical narratives must then be viewed as failed or outmoded *scientific* narratives. But this may well be a *false* contrast because mythical narratives may be addressed to an entirely different concern or topic, e.g., to the issue of identity. Such mythical narratives may be a symbolic or expressive means of recovering a people's sense of important and sustaining meanings. We should then properly look to contrasting ways of addressing *this* concern. Or, as the philosopher Peter Winch has pointed out, it is a mistake to see the Zande magical rites made famous by Evans-Pritchard as irrational *technological* practices, as Sir James Frazer would, rather than as something more like the prayers of supplication that the West, too, takes seriously. The concerns I have been raising suggest rather that we should guard against faulting *them* for not doing *our* tricks well, for such claims may well be question-begging. In short, we should be hesitant to assume that the cultural practices under scrutiny are addressing the same type of problem.[15]

In addressing the first form of agency deficit, I have concentrated on cases in which problematic assumptions have been made about actors' aims and values. I now turn to cases in which the source of concern, and of opprobrium, is not so much the aims or values of agents but rather whether those agents are culpably unable—for want of will or discipline—to realize those aims. In addressing this second form that an agency deficit might assume, I complicate a bit the way in which we are typically inclined to think of agency. It is useful to think of agency as the capacity to direct oneself, with effect, toward the achievement of an end or state, either of oneself or of the world. The idea of autonomous agency referred to in chapter 2 would then involve the capacity to direct oneself toward a genuinely *preferred* or *endorsed* end or state. And it is natural enough to think of the actualization of agency as the exertion or exercise of one's capacity to produce an effect or to bring about a state of affairs. But often, if not always, the actualization of such first-order capacities is conditioned by capacities of the second order, capacities that enable or condition the exercise of capacities of the first order. I find it useful to think of second-order agency as the ability to acquire or avail oneself of the enabling or facilitating conditions—especially the epistemic conditions—of action in the first-order sense. The exercise of second-order agency consists in knowing how to put oneself in a position to exercise first-order agency.

In what follows, I focus on systematic or structural epistemic occlusions that compromise the exercise of first-order agency, occlusions for which the agents cannot be held responsible. Ideologically acquired beliefs furnish prime examples of such agency-compromising occlusions.[16] An example of John Locke's can be turned to my purposes here. I have in mind the situation of a person who is put into a cell and is led to believe, falsely, that all the doors are locked.[17] Such a person is objectively, from a third-person standpoint, able to leave the cell. But given the information made available to him, his ability to do so is compromised, and he cannot intelligibly avail himself of this opportunity. To the extent that the second-order capacity to acquire knowledge of the state of the doors was lacking, he would not be in a position to exercise his first-order capacity to walk out. One might expand this metaphorically by suggesting that he would be imprisoned by his *belief* that the door is locked rather than by an actual locked door. For a personal illustration of this idea, I often find that working in a local library—away from the hubbub and domestic distractions I would be likely to encounter in my home study—facilitates my ability to work in a concentrated fashion. My being aware of the alternative of the local library, and being able to avail myself of it, enhances my ability to focus uninterruptedly on the work at hand and consequently to be more productive than I otherwise would be. Compare this to the situation of children living in poverty who may well be fully *willing* to apply themselves to their studies but who are unaware of or are unable to avail themselves of requisite quiet spaces. Or consider high-achieving and ambitious, but low-income, high school students who fail to even *apply* to selective colleges and universities because they receive little, if any, counseling about how to do so or even that such an option is a real possibility for them.[18]

The lesson I draw from such considerations is that a genuine and fair assessment of agency must be informed by the agent's first-person perspective of what is possible, a perspective that informs expectations about outcomes of intentions to act—the likelihood of success. So the choices open to one will be a function of one's "picture of the world." First-order agency can be compromised in a nonculpable way—in a way that results from a limited hermeneutical horizon for which *the agent cannot be held responsible*—when a choice that could have been made or an action that could have been undertaken was not made or undertaken solely because the agent was systematically deprived of the otherwise socially available agency-enabling picture.

This suggests that we disaggregate two aspects of agency: its volitional component and its epistemic component. This would imply that a particular case of what may *appear* to be a lack of agency did not in fact result from a lack of volitional resources per se but rather from a lack of awareness of available courses of action, from epistemic-horizonal limitations. (There is, of course, a distinct class of cases in which agency is inculpably compromised, not because of a lack of awareness of options but rather when there is a veridical awareness of a lack of options. Although the remedies will differ, in both cases a fair assessment of agency will require hermeneutic access to the agent's web of beliefs.) This epistemic component figures centrally in the exercise of second-order agency in that the latter entails the ability to acquire the epistemic resources requisite to realizing first-order volitions.

If the conditions for second-order agency are blocked for some due to structural features of the societies in which they live, then it is unjust to demand, and unfair to expect, from them the same exercise of first-order agency as those more favorably positioned. How just is it to expect feats of first-order agency from segments of society bereft of the conditions that most of us can take for granted? It is such external obstacles to the exercise of first-order agency that are typically overlooked in neoconservative and neoimperialist accounts. Given that the sort of case I have in mind here involves a constriction of access to requisite epistemic resources when the agent is not culpable for that restriction, I take this sort of case—cases where agency is thwarted in a way for which the agent cannot be held culpable—to be an instance of an injustice of an epistemic sort. For here the agent is unfairly blamed for a compromise of agency that is caused by an epistemic occlusion that (a) is not acknowledged and (b) that results from structural factors over which the agent has no control.

It is in this sense that social and economic rights, and the material and epistemic conditions they would procure, can be understood to be conditions of first-order agency, say, of civil and political agency, and for this reason alone we incur the moral-political obligation to attend to such rights. The fact that second-order agency can be systematically undermined in such an arbitrary way means that a credible diagnosis of either of these agential pathologies, of values or of volition, will require a hermeneutic investigation aimed at construing the web of beliefs that agents actually have regarding the range of social options available to them as real and intelligible possibilities.

And this diagnostic deployment of hermeneutics is essential to underwriting critical social interventions that are guided by acknowledging the manifest injustice of expecting feats of first-order agency from segments of society bereft of the facilitating conditions that most of us can take for granted.

In his study's conclusion, McCarthy alludes to the tension in the global context between, on the one hand, the growing transnational solidarity around a "politics of human rights" and a deepening of a "human rights culture" and, on the other hand, a conflict between two dominant interpretations of human rights.[19] Developed societies tend to emphasize civil and political rights, whereas those regarded as developing societies tend to emphasize social and economic rights. This tension, he says, exerts a countervailing pressure that prevents a sufficient overlapping consensus on the extension of "human rights" to allow for even reasonable disagreement on the interpretation or application of the idea. That would be to say that proponents of the competing interpretations would, in some important sense, be talking past one another. One of the motivating factors in my having adduced the idea of second-order agency is that this concept provides a means of mediating these two horizons of interpretation. Attention to economic and social rights is a moral-political obligation because it is a condition of agency, of the ability to exercise civil and political rights.

A further advantage of my account of agency can be demonstrated if we use it to address one of the central issues in current discussions of the "adaptive preferences" of deprived persons. To avoid what I have criticized as the view that such people necessarily suffer from agency deficits, and to support the view that they are agents in the full sense, some scholars maintain that such people *are* acting in terms of their interests. For instance, recent trends in feminist scholarship that focus on deprivation emphasize a conception of agency that treats "agency as the capacity to make decisions and shape one's world in accordance with what one cares about, or to act in a way that reveals [one's] sense of what matters to [one]."[20] And such thinkers go on to claim that one can understand adaptive preferences to be genuine manifestations of agency in this sense. But this way of highlighting the agency of deprived women seems to lead to a dilemma. Serene Khader refers to this as the agency dilemma in feminist theory, to wit, should we see oppressed people as agents whose choices—even if they are life-diminishing or fail to be life-enhancing—are worthy of unquestioning respect or as passive victims who cannot make genuine choices?[21] My argument in favor of disaggregating the volitional and epistemic components of agency suggests that cases in which agency seems lacking need not be instances where volitional resources are lacking. So, in addition to providing me with a riposte to the "developmentalist's" charge of agency deficiency, disaggregating the volitional and epistemic aspects of agency allows me to avoid this so-called agency dilemma lurking in theories of deprivation. And that is because choices that are life-diminishing, or that fail to be life-enhancing, can be criticized as being "objectively bad" choices without presuming passivity, volitional deficits, or agential culpability on the part of such people.

An episode from the history of the practice of genital excision in the West is illustrative here. In the twentieth century, a number of Western women *chose* to undergo clitoridectomies, seeking relief from various "psychopathologies," psychopathologies that may well have been ideologically constituted.[22] Insofar as they were ideological in nature, i.e., could be understood to have a strategic provenance, this can be understood to be a case of cognitive deformation where there is the *distinct* issue of the epistemic injustice done to these women. That is, to the extent that this construal or construction of psychopathology is ideological, we can view this as a case of epistemic injustice rather than insist that such women were passive victims who lacked agency. Insofar as the mechanism of counterfactual dialogical critique outlined in chapter 2 issues in the exposure of the ideological nature of particular cultural interpretations, we can now view it as also addressing an epistemic condition of agency.

Furthermore, the claim that the volitional component of agency lacks defect in cases of "bad" choices is a fully defeasible claim. It follows as a corollary to my use of Locke's prisoner example that if the prisoner, desirous of freedom, *were* aware that the door was unlocked and with effort could be forced open, but nevertheless failed to exit, then this—all things being equal—*would* count as a culpable lack of agency. There can then, of course, be cases of genuine agential deficit, but my point is that we cannot make that discrimination in a meaningful way without the sort of investigation into the hermeneutic/epistemic situation of the agent that I am here advocating.

Accordingly, to determine whether or not the conditions obtain that would allow a charge of (culpable) agency deficiency to be meaningfully applied would require a hermeneutic investigation of the suspected agent's epistemic horizon or matrix of intelligibility. That is, being unable to act or to successfully pursue an end is not necessarily the result of a *volitional* deficit; it may well be occasioned by an inadequate epistemic/hermeneutic horizon for which the agent cannot be held culpable or responsible. I now want to claim that this necessary condition for the meaningful application of the expression "culpable agency deficiency" can be understood in terms of what I shall call the requirement of narrative representability. By this I mean that members of the target group of social concern should, in principle, be able to represent to themselves a narrative in which they figure as protagonists, a narrative that will take them in a continuous way without gaps from where they are, in all their concrete circumstances and identities, to circumstances that permit of life-enhancing behaviors. For a life-enhancing avenue for self-actualization to be concretely (that is, genuinely) accessible, it must be credible given the concrete material and psychological/epistemic circumstances within which the agent finds him- or herself. Given that it is the ability to acquire the enabling conditions of action, the exercise of second-order agency entails that the agent holds a view of the social world that allows for such narrative representability. It entails the epistemic status of knowing how to bridge the gap between one's current status and the status that one wills for oneself.

The significance of this "epistemic" component of agency can easily go unremarked as long as its satisfaction can be taken for granted. And for the socially privileged—those for whom its satisfaction is taken for granted, for whom the bridging of such gaps is effected so fluidly, fluently, and relatively effortlessly that the very existence of such gaps, and hence of the requisite epistemic tools for bridging them, goes virtually unnoticed—the requirement of second-order agency is itself invisible. At its limit, privilege *is* just the luxury of being unaware of, or of being blind to, the apparatus linking volition to effect. It is a condition of blissful hermeneutic oblivion and, as such, also of a distinctive modality through which epistemic injustice can be committed.[23]

The apparatus linking volition to effect—i.e., the enabling condition of agency in the first-order sense—has both a more or less purely epistemic dimension (consisting of both propositional and practical knowledge) and a concrete material dimension. By the latter, I refer to enabling infrastructures. An agent's cognitive relationship to them will manifest itself in that agent's social ontology or "picture of the world." Acknowledging this will encourage us to attend to both the social availability of resources and options and cognitive attitudes toward social availability simultaneously. To return to Locke's prisoner, we must ensure that the door is unbolted and that the prisoner is in a position to know it.

The significance of this apparatus and of the social ontology in which it is embedded and disclosed is strikingly apparent when we examine the touchstones typically deployed in neoconservative commentaries on agency. In such commentaries, the idea of "the unaided accomplishment of individual persons" serves as the idealization that informs assessments of agency.[24] The accomplishments of "unaided" individuals set the boundary conditions for assessments of agency. However, if "unaided accomplishment" refers to achievements won through individual effort alone and is meant to set aside the role of enabling conditions such as a certain degree of material prosperity, educational opportunity, an encouraging and supportive home and school environment, access to social networks, and so on, then few accomplishments, if any, can truly be said to have been unaided. To believe that they are so unaided would be an extreme case of blindness to the significance of such enabling conditions. This is a clearly unrealistic construal of the expression, and one that even the most tenacious among social conservatives would presumably relinquish upon reflection.

The most reasonable interpretation of the expression "unaided accomplishment" is that it refers to an accomplishment requiring no aid beyond what *most members of a given society can reasonably take for granted* given that society's material and intellectual resources, can take for granted in terms of material well-being, educational access, exposure and access to what is generally available in that society, and so on. Think of these as the "normal conditions" that establish the baseline beyond which accomplishment can meaningfully be viewed as aided in the requisite, and here pejorative, sense. Whether they are acknowledged to be so or not, these normal conditions are *enabling* conditions, enabling conditions that are not created by anyone's individual effort alone. In this context, the question I have been pursuing is, Why then charge individuals with agency deficiency when, through no fault of their own, these normal conditions do not obtain for them? Why insist that the least advantaged among us bear the additional burden of "proving" themselves under conditions that most of us do not have to face? None of this is to gainsay the psychological value, as a motivational strategy, of encouraging people to assume as much responsibility for their life conditions as they can. But it is to question the fundamental consistency, not to mention justice, of expecting, as a matter of social policy, feats from one segment of society that most members of that society are not required to perform. This would be tantamount to burdening some, and invidiously so, with the demand to display supererogatory volitional powers.

Moreover, this interpretation of "unaided accomplishment," in which its use implicitly presupposes that background normal conditions have been satisfied, implicitly treating them as "givens," leads to the following paradox. Social policies whose aim is to ameliorate material conditions and thereby to increase the scope of intelligible options for all—to assure that those conditions and options reach the threshold of "normal conditions"—are viewed as a form of aid in the pejorative sense, whereas achievements made on the basis of (preexisting and unacknowledged) normal conditions—the "standard" case—are not so viewed. This means that one would be said to have been aided in the relevant negative sense if, absent the normal enabling conditions, one is subsequently provided them, but that one would not be said to have been so aided if one in some sense "inherited" those conditions (calling to mind the proverbial case of scoring a triple by virtue of having been born on third base). Once we have acknowledged the role of normal conditions in human agency, as I have argued we must, how can a meaningful moral distinction be drawn between cases in which normal conditions are in force prior to volitional effort and cases in which those conditions are set in place after such effort, especially when we stipulate that the agent in question bears no responsibility for the conditions or the lack thereof? What justification can be given for this view of what does and does not count as unaided accomplishment and hence of the exercise of agency or its lack? So the burden is on those who would make *this* case for agency deficiency to determine where the line separating agential sufficiency and agential lack should be drawn, and to justify drawing it there.[25] For, as I have shown, there is ample reason to question the consistency and justice of drawing it in such a way that we are led to expect the supererogatory feats mentioned here only from some.

If what I have argued is sound—i.e., that the aid enabling the "unaided" accomplishments of the well-positioned is *hidden*, whereas for the poor it is simply lacking—then there is a gap between what existing social systems make available in principle and where the poor, even by their own best efforts, find themselves, a gap that cannot be bridged in the narratives that they can represent to themselves. Granting equal opportunity alone to individuals handicapped by the disadvantage of being nonculpably bereft of the normal conditions of agency does not constitute meeting them where they are or, as one commentator has recently put it, meeting "people at their point of need." Many will lack the wherewithal to make use of those opportunities because of those social, economic, or educational disadvantages. Lacking these resources and, therefore, also a reasonable basis for hope, they will lack what is crucial to productive effort, to agency in the full sense.[26]

I have argued that neither in the case of value-deficit claims nor that of agency-deficit claims can a person's behavior by itself be used to justify such a claim. In both cases, a hermeneutic investigation is needed. Put somewhat differently and in a manner reminiscent of Strawsonian presuppositions in the case of propositional truth claims, there is an "application condition" for claims of either agency or values deficit. Consistent with the requirement of narrative representability, the application condition is that "normal conditions" are in place such that the relevant actors can reasonably or plausibly be expected to be (hermeneutically) aware of certain "real possibilities," possibilities that are real *for them*, that can be realized in their action.

SITUATED AUTONOMOUS AGENCY

In chapter 2, I made the assumption that the affected women have agential capacities that can be invoked and deployed. There the conversationally guided discovery and exploration of options for their culturally indexed, that is, situated flourishing was put forward as a mechanism to enhance the compass of their agency. This exploration involved the consideration of alternative cultural interpretations, and this was, of course, integral to my claim that the interrogation of the status quo need not require the imposition of "external norms." The requirement of narrative representability that such women be met where they are—a requirement that this chapter highlights—was addressed in the previous chapter by a conversational model for encouraging them to entertain alternative cultural pathways for their flourishing. Indeed, agency is always in this way culturally saturated and mediated. It can plausibly be argued that cultures are sites for the acquisition and development of "agency skills" and that cultural transmission is a crucial mechanism of that acquisition.[27] Thus a given cultural matrix should be understood to be a scheme for determining what can intelligibly be done, and how.

This, however, suggests that hermeneutic oblivion is but one source of hermeneutical epistemic injustice. Another—and one that illustratively emphasizes how second-order agency is a distinctive *capacity*—is the refusal to acknowledge the *interpretive* agency of those at society's margins. The fact that our knowledge of the social world has an essentially interpretive nature has deep implications for our ability to exercise *social* agency. Failing to acknowledge this fact and its implications can render people vulnerable to a crippling form of epistemic injustice, to a violation that is distinctively hermeneutical in nature. For it means that the social world, its ontology and salient relations, is disclosed to social agents as configured in a specific and distinctive way. And the mode of its disclosure—the particular social phenomena, practices, and relations that can be meaningfully acknowledged in its terms—can determine the scope of our ability to intervene in that world, our social agency. This signals the importance of agency-enabling disclosures, of there being socially acknowledged interpretations—semantic organizations of the social field—that enable genuine agency in that they enable one intelligibly to "name" a problematic social experience and to respond accordingly. In chapter 2, I referred to the acknowledgment of such an interpretation as the recognition of its semantic authority. Public acknowledgment places at a putative agent's disposal semantic resources for active response by allowing for the publicly acknowledged disclosure of the "what" to which a response is required.

The significance of *this* cognitive component of agency—that is, the access to or capacity to *name* that which one's action is to address—underscores the importance of there being no arbitrary restrictions on participation in the conversational negotiation of interpretive frameworks for representing and articulating social experience. That the appropriate semantic resources are in place for interpreting social life then requires a specifically *hermeneutical* form of agency whose restriction is tantamount to yet another form of epistemic injustice, the injustice of arbitrarily restricting our ability to interpret reality in empowering ways. And this hermeneutical agency, activated in the struggle to win semantic authority for empowering social interpretations, is logically prior to the first-order social agency that depends on it for its focus. Such hermeneutical agency can serve to consolidate the semantic resources necessary to articulate the concepts requisite to meaningful response. The phenomena that we now describe as sexual harassment, "acquaintance rape," and police brutality can serve to illustrate this. The agency with which women and Blacks, respectively, are able to oppose such practices is directly proportional to the semantic authority that such descriptors have, that is, to the extent to which, for instance, sexual harassment, acquaintance rape, and police brutality are socially acknowledged as predicates that can be meaningfully applied to social experience. Keeping in mind the argument of chapter 2, we can now see that hermeneutic or semantic vulnerability can compromise agency in two distinct but related ways: it can limit our ability to name the wrongs that demand our response, and it can circumscribe our capacity to name the ways of being or the self-descriptions that we can "own." It threatens our ability to name both what we are against and what we are for, what we want to be. The democratization of social disclosure, the protection of spaces for the free exercise of this interpretive capacity in the negotiation of interpretive frameworks, is accordingly crucial for sustaining social, political, and cultural agency.[28]

4

TOWARD A HERMENEUTICS OF RACE

Biology, Race, Ethnicity, and Culture

My argument in chapter 1 to the effect that so-called natural kind terms should not be construed as bearing an isomorphic relationship to, to invoke Plato's expression, "nature's joints" is pertinent a fortiori to the status of the concept of race. Thus, in discussions of race, we should always be concerned to inquire after the conditions under which this modality of classification becomes a salient item of discourse, why it becomes privileged in highlighting or picking out the similarities and differences among us that matter. And to the extent that any discourse in which race figures reflects a structured social interpretation or construction, we need to interrogate the sorts of discourse in which the concept appears, to ask what interests they serve and what social strategies they enact. In short, and in a hermeneutical fashion, we need to ask, "To what questions is racial classification an answer?"

"Sameness vs. difference," like "kind vs. degree," are sliding signifiers; that is, their application must be understood to be relative to both altitude and *attitude*. Because the application of the concepts of both similarity and difference presuppose a three-place relationship—i.e., x is similar or dissimilar to y in virtue of some property or relation z—we must attend to the metric of similarity, z, which has risen to salience as a result of the interests or purposes at hand. The hermeneutic recontextualization of natural kinds in chapter 1 was an argument to the effect that such types of entity are most adequately understood to be the referents of descriptions that enable causal-explanatory practices. So, in these cases, z is a metric that is salient for causal-explanatory practice.

I have argued that, in science, natural kinds are "artifacts" or constructs that are instituted in the service of the epistemic goals of prediction and explanation. I argue here that—contrary to the inferences drawn by some philosophers from the results of recent population genetics research—the idea of race as ordinarily understood has little, if any, genuine scientific/biological salience. Accordingly, I am claiming that in the case of race the salience of the metric z cannot be its relevance to causal-explanatory practice within the natural sciences.[1] And, because ordinary language racial categories in themselves have little, if any, predictive or explanatory significance, their status, in comparison with the "genuine" natural kinds of science, is a fortiori artificial. Therefore, insofar as the idea of race continues to be a discursive topic, we must look elsewhere for the interests that underwrite the salience of its animating metric, perhaps, though not exclusively, to the interests in (social) control that are sustained and furthered by the continued deployment of such racial categories.

WHAT IS A RACE, ANYWAY?

We can characterize the ordinary or common sense conception of race as follows: (1) there are, generally speaking, three or perhaps as many as five nonarbitrarily partitioned major groupings of human beings; (2) the groups are discrete; (3) the groups are characterized by distinctive clusters of phenotypical traits; and, perhaps, (4) the major groups are stable natural kinds.

At issue are the presumed biological differences between socially labeled populations. Expressed more than a half century ago by the then president of the American Society of Human Genetics, Laurence Snyder, the consensus view among geneticists continues to be that "human populations differ one from another almost entirely in the varying *proportions* of the allelic genes of the various sets of hereditary factors, and not in the kinds of genes they contain."[2] There are numerous genetic similarities across all socially meaningful racial classifications and no genetic features that are entirely unique to any particular socially classified population.[3]

In spite of this consensus, there are distinguished philosophers of science who, although acknowledging the consensus, nevertheless insist that a scientifically respectable account of race can be provided. Central among such thinkers is the philosopher of biology Philip Kitcher. In a complexly woven and impressively nuanced essay, Kitcher is perhaps the first—and certainly the most influential—contemporary philosophical thinker to make an explicitly nonracist case for the *biological* salience of the idea of race.[4] Acknowledging that the phenotypic traits conventionally used to demarcate races neither have intrinsic significance nor have been shown to correlate with characteristics of intrinsic significance and, further, that intraracial diversity is far more pronounced than is interracial diversity, he nevertheless contests the claim that race has no biological significance.[5] He argues that the concept of race might indeed have biological significance, but that its significance is hostage to what are essentially cultural mechanisms of reproductive isolation. So, for Kitcher, race has biological significance, given a particular constellation of cultural intentions. That is, race has biological significance if we let it—if we want it to. He argues further that there may be good reasons for us to want it to have such significance, among others, reasons having to do with the desirability of preserving otherwise valued cultural traditions. His argument thus poses an uncomfortable dilemma: we might rid ourselves of the quite possibly ineliminably invidious effects of a system of racial classification, but such a liberation would come at a price that we might find too high to pay, namely, the possible disappearance of distinct ethnicities and diverse cultural traditions.

In this section, I briefly raise some questions about the model that Kitcher proposes as a reconstruction of the biological concept of race, and in the next section I question the terms in which he has posed this dilemma. Kitcher defines race genealogically. He adduces three conditions that are for him crucial components of a biologically based concept of race: (1) the presence of distinctive phenotypical differences as distinguishing features of pure races; (2) the heritability of these differences; and (3) mechanisms of reproductive isolation. The third component, mechanisms of reproductive isolation, is important in ensuring that residual mixed race populations remain small with respect to the population of the pure races.[6] Otherwise, the taxonomy instantiated by the various "founding populations" of the so-called pure races would cease to be relevant as a way of partitioning the species. In contexts in which there is a high frequency of interbreeding, this conception of racial partitioning would lose its point.

With regard to the first component, even if we were charitably to assume that Kitcher is referring to a distinctive range of variation of a phenotypical trait (and it should be kept in mind that, for some traits, much of the whole range of human variation can be observed within the African continent[7]), it is notoriously difficult to select the racially relevant phenotypical traits without begging questions. For example, superficial similarities in skin color, hair form, and nose shape, observable features that are popularly and traditionally used in identifying races, led scholars to place such groups as African pygmies and those of New Guinea in the same racial classification. These groups, however, differ dramatically in the hereditary components of their blood, factors that for a while were also considered to be dispositive markers for racial classification.[8] Geneticists regularly attest to the difficulty of finding a limited number of phenotypical traits that can be used in an absolute way to distinguish separate populations. Every phenotypical trait is continuously variable both within and across populations, and the range of variation of a given trait within a population overlaps with the range in others. Thus no phenotypical trait will serve unambiguously to classify an individual within a particular population. There is no phenotypical trait that can reliably serve as a label for a particular population.[9]

Moreover, what are taken to be racially salient traits do not vary concordantly. That is, such morphological features typically do not occur in clusters or bundles; they are not inherently linked or linked to each other at a genetic level. Rather, they vary independently of each other. This is because the characteristic frequencies of genotypes that are expressed in the phenotypes are the result of *independent* selection pressures. So a racial partition based, for example, on skin color would include many sub-Saharan Africans, Australian Aboriginal people, and the so-called Negritos of the Philippines. But the Negritos, for example, are otherwise genetically closer to the Asian people surrounding them.[10] So, depending on which distinctive phenotype one chooses, one gets different, noncongruent racial sortings.

The twin phenomena of discordant variation of phenotypical traits and of continuous variation of single traits serve to confound the project of partitioning our species into discrete clusters of traits that are isomorphic to the mutually exclusive categories that inform the commonsense understanding of racial groups. Evolutionary biologists refer to this continuous variation of traits as clinal. The range or spectrum of a trait, e.g., skin color, is said to form a cline if a gradient or change in the trait is correlated with a gradient in climate, geography, or ecology.[11] The physical traits that are deemed racial vary continuously in this way. As a consequence, as Naomi Zack points out, any partition that would distinguish the range of such a trait that is to be associated with one socially defined racial group from the range associated with another would have to be imposed arbitrarily and in a disorderly fashion.[12]

For example, not only does skin color vary continuously within, between, and among socially characterized racial groups, but there is considerable overlap among those groups with respect to this feature. A partition based on skin color that would be isomorphic to socially recognized racial categories cannot be drawn because it is not the case that every individual who is socially classified as Black, for example, would have darker skin than every individual classified as white (or that every individual socially classified as white would have lighter skin than every individual recognized as Black). Theoretically, one might get around this by drawing the partition separating racial groups in such a way as to avoid the embarrassing overlap, but this would be achieved at the price of either recategorizing some socially categorized Black individuals as white, for example, or some socially categorized white individuals as Black. In summary, a racial classification based on skin color would result in either an arbitrary, but orderly, partition (with the artificial, ad hoc boundary jiggling just mentioned) or one that fails to determine discrete groups.

Blood type is another phenotypical trait that has been commonly cited as a marker for racial classification. Unlike skin color, whose distribution within a reproductively isolated population can vary due to mating preferences, blood group distribution within such a population remains relatively stable.[13] There are approximately thirty-two blood group systems or classification schemes for demarcating blood type.[14] If we use differential frequencies of blood types from one blood group system, say, the familiar ABO system, to generate a population taxonomy, we get a different result than we would if we used differential frequencies of blood types from a different blood group system, say, the MN or Rh.[15] Different blood group systems yield noncongruent and sometimes cross-cutting population taxonomies. Therefore, blood type also fails to provide us with the requisite uniform variation of alleles that would univocally accord with socially recognized racial categories.[16]

No matter our choice of phenotypical trait, or of some combination thereof, the frequency distribution maps that are yielded will vary depending on what trait or combination of traits is selected, carving up the human species in different ways.[17] There seems to be an ineliminable arbitrariness in the traits selected for taxonomic relevance.[18] These considerations suggest that what should be taken to be phenotypically salient in dividing human populations into racial groups is underdetermined by science, and furthermore, to the extent that this is so, that *extra*-scientific intentions, *social* and *cultural* intentions, are brought to bear in such determinations.[19]

In a far-ranging refinement of Kitcher's argument, Michael Hardimon suggests another source of the salience that certain morphological features have for us, to wit, that certain visible features, and not others, are (naturally?) striking, salient, or "are obtrusively there."[20] But this suggests the idea of a "natural sensorium" in which certain properties stand out in an observer-invariant fashion as warranting designation as type-properties, whereas others recede into the background and do not. As I suggested at the beginning of this chapter, and in keeping with the hermeneutically informed perspective that guides my inquiry, it is difficult to conceive of such a sensorium that would come into focus either from "nowhere" or from all conceivable variants of human social and cultural horizons.[21] In any event, more would have to be said in order to address this hermeneutic demurral.

Even if we set aside the question of which phenotype(s) should be taken to identify racialized populations, the third component of Kitcher's account warrants scrutiny. Mechanisms of reproductive isolation are important in ensuring that the lines demarcating socially categorized or classified populations can constitute partial barriers to interaction, reproduction, and genetic migration.[22] However, this seems to leave us with a dilemma. Even with mechanisms of reproductive isolation in place, individuals cannot, of course, make a choice of mates based on a potential partner's genotype, but only on the observable phenotype. Individuals manifesting the preferred phenotype who are, say, heterozygous for the distinguishing alleles—and who are therefore not of the pure race—will, thus, like stealth bombers, be able to evade culturally based phenotype-sensitive isolating mechanisms. What would happen if only *one* such individual (displaying the preferred phenotype, but heterozygous at the relevant location) from a race other than the pure race, A, got through per hundred individuals of the pure race? Even though the mating of this individual and one of the pure race would produce offspring half of whom would be expected to be homozygous for the relevant trait, it is perhaps more realistic to consider what happens to the genome, the full set of genes, carried by the offspring. For all of the offspring, both those who are homozygous and those heterozygous for the relevant phenotypical trait, 50 percent of their genetic information will have come from a member of a race other than A. In later generations, a larger and larger fraction of the population will have some genetic information from the non-A race, i.e., will be of mixed race. Put another way, a smaller and smaller fraction of the population will be composed of individuals all of whose ancestors were of the pure race, thus violating one of the necessary conditions that Kitcher places on the concept of race and undermining a condition of the biological interest of this model.[23]

The pure race shrinks as the fraction of individuals with alien alleles increases (if my calculations are even roughly correct, the set of individuals of pure race will be swamped by the set of mixed race individuals fairly rapidly).[24] For instance—and although admittedly the rate of gene flow is undetermined—with respect to certain allelic frequencies and after fewer than sixty or so generations (and well within the time frame of the Common Era), the so-called Black Jews of Cochin, India show closer resemblance to their Hindu neighbors than they do to other Jewish groups who share their Palestinian ancestry.[25] (To the objection that this has to do with breeding populations, not races, it should be noted that for some genetic loci, the genetic difference between breeding populations from the same "race" can be greater than that between "races." For instance, the genetic difference at given loci between distinct endogamous communities *within* a given caste in Mumbai, India, was found to be as great as that between U.S. whites and Blacks.[26])

Of more direct relevance to the situation I am contemplating here is the fact that some evolutionary biologists set the threshold for the degree of exogamous mating necessary to establish population mixture—and thus render inapplicable the idea of distinct (pure) racial populations—low enough to make my concern quite plausible. Some suggest that, in a small population, as few as 1 percent of the matings per generation need to be exogamous to violate this condition that Kitcher places on the concept of race.[27] It seems that the only way to avoid this scenario is through the absolute isolation of the pure race from individuals who are heterozygous at key phenotypic loci, an isolation that would require additional measures, measures that are more artificial than those of culture alone.

The alternative, equally lacking in verisimilitude, would be to require the race-marking traits to be only those that manifest themselves recessively, that is, traits that appear only in the case of homozygous recessive alleles, and the races would be distinguished by traits controlled at different genetic loci (e.g., bald vs. blue-eyed). The point here is that individuals who are heterozygous at relevant loci simply would not manifest the target traits, and the cultural isolating mechanisms could work sufficiently well to keep the races relatively pure. So we have the following dilemma: to ensure the maintenance of pure races, *either* the isolating mechanisms must function with virtually *100 percent* efficiency, and not merely regulate interbreeding at low rates, *or*, equally implausibly, the distinctive traits that serve to distinguish the pure races must be traits that manifest themselves only recessively.

Putting this all together, it is difficult to see how this biological account of race connects in a meaningful way with what the so-called eliminativists with respect to race want to eliminate.[28] For the claim of the latter is that there is no biologically meaningful referent of the ordinary socially sanctioned racial categories, that there is no biological basis for the discourse they want to interrogate. Indeed, Kitcher acknowledges that the division of human groups drawn from considerations of population genetics may not accord with conventional racial divisions.[29] For these reasons, I am inclined to agree with Zack's suggestion that although Kitcher may have provided a successful account of inbreeding genealogical groups in general it is not an account of racial groups as they are ordinarily understood.[30]

The gross morphological features conventionally invoked to distinguish races do not correspond to biologically relevant markers of population difference and population membership, namely, the characteristic gene frequencies of different groups or the similarity in the sequence of base pairs in the DNA carried by different individuals in the same group, respectively. Given the implications of the discordant assortment of genes and the consequent arbitrariness of the way group distinctions get drawn, it is indeed difficult to argue that the ordinary language notion of race, to use Plato's apt expression, carves nature at its joints.

In this light, it is interesting to note that in a more recent essay Kitcher articulates a more "pragmatic" view of natural kinds that has a number of affinities with the account that I develop in chapter 1. In that essay, he maintains that nature is not self-announcing; it does not prescribe "the forms our language should take, [presenting itself as] nicely organized with fence-posts that our concepts must respect."[31] Rejecting the idea that there are natural fault lines that are discernible and traceable in an interest-free way, he highlights the role played by particular social purposes in drawing racial divisions.[32] This is, of course, a point with which I heartily agree, and I shall develop it in the second section of this chapter.

The hermeneutic position that I have developed does not countenance the interest-independence of kinds in general, be they "natural" or social. So eliminativist arguments rejecting such independence in the case of putatively biological kinds will not, for me, count as refutations of their reality any more than they would count against the reality of chemical elements. My interest is rather in the relationship between ordinary race-indexed discourse and biologically meaningful phenomena. I take a phenomenon to be biologically real or meaningful if and only if *it tracks the lines of demarcation that are taken to be salient for biological explanation and prediction*. My suggestion is that "race" is not a natural kind term, even in the minimalist hermeneutic/pragmatic sense of natural kind that I developed in chapter 1.[33]

When one surveys our species as a whole from the viewpoint of physical anthropology or population genetics, what is perhaps most striking is the continuity of variation, both phenotypically and genetically, within it. In other words, as I have suggested, human variation is for the most part clinal, varying linearly and gradually with geographic distance. Allele frequencies change smoothly across geographic regions with few sharp breaks; thus, so too do manifest phenotypical traits.[34] It is this "fact of continuity" that most insistently fuels suspicion of purportedly scientific attempts to partition our species into discrete clusters. No responsible account of population clusters or of the partitioning of the human population can dispense with an acknowledgment of the continuity displayed in the smooth gradient of allele frequency variation. Establishing partitions among continuously varying parameters, parameters that, in Kitcher's terms, fail to manifest themselves as "nicely organized with fence-posts that our concepts must respect," would require that *we* project or impose upon them metrics of similarity and difference, metrics that are presumably salient in context. Without such a metric, and the *justification* of such a metric in terms of its salience, any partitioning regime would be arbitrary.

Perhaps equally troubling is the possibility that a nested plurality of such metrics is on hand, yielding demographic units of differing sizes. Although written before we had access to the wealth of genetic information yielded by recently developed techniques for mapping the human genome, the tension—within the community of population biologists—between continuity and clustering, respectively, is nicely captured by the geneticist Cavalli-Sforza's opposition of "lumpers" to "splitters":

> The classification into races has proved to be a futile exercise for reasons that were already clear to Darwin. Human races are still extremely unstable entities in the hands of modern taxonomists, who define from 3 to 60 or more races. To some extent, this latitude depends on the personal preference of taxonomists, who may choose to be "lumpers" or "splitters." Although there is no doubt that there is only one human species, there are clearly *no objective reasons* for stopping at any particular level of taxonomic splitting. In fact, the analysis we carry out ... for the purposes of evolutionary study shows that the level at which we stop our classification is *completely arbitrary*.[35] (emphasis added)

There are thus two axes along which arbitrariness can impinge on a classification regime: a horizontal one, along which the continuum is parceled, and a vertical one, along which a particular parceled segment is further sliced and diced.

In addition to the question of the arbitrariness of the partition regime that parcels out subunits of our species, there is the question of whether the groups or clusters yielded by such a regime correspond to or match the groups that are ordinarily thought of as racial groups. Although my subsequent discussion will assume a trajectory that is different from his, Joshua Glasgow's summary of these two concerns as the arbitrariness objection and the mismatch objection to racial biological realism, respectively, is a useful organizing heuristic.[36] I pursue these questions in light of recent findings in the ever-expanding field of human genetics and genomic research (much of this data was unavailable at the time of Kitcher's first paper).

The most sustained challenge to the idea that ordinary racial classification has little if any biological significance is fueled by recent findings in the field of population genetics. New techniques in this field have enabled the identification of intraspecies population structures: biogenetically significant partitions based on genetic clustering.[37] Genetic clusters are groupings wherein the genetic distance between pairs of individuals within a group is less than that between groups. In other words, individuals within a cluster share with each other, on average, more alleles than they do with those in other clusters. So here, the metric of similarity, z, is shared polymorphism. Algorithms have been developed that—when operating on genetic information drawn from a worldwide sample of humans representing more than fifty different ethnic groups—produce partitioned clusters comprised of individuals who are assorted to achieve maximal genetic similarity among them.[38] The general idea is to find ways to place N objects (in this case, individuals) in groups to achieve maximal similarity within groups and maximal difference between groups. The number of such clusters to be generated is determined not by the program, but by the researcher. It turns out that when the number of clusters, K, into which the human population is to be subdivided is set to five, the resulting groupings of humanity closely match continental population groups—sub-Saharan Africa, Eurasia (Europe, North Africa, the Middle East, and Central and South Asia), East Asia, Oceania, and America.[39] Some scholars think this vindicates ordinary racial taxonomy and have seized on it to bolster a new case for the biological reality of race as ordinarily understood.[40]

But does this mean that such studies as these have managed to pull back the cloak to magically reveal nature's joints? Even if the K=5 result withstood attempts to reproduce it in clustering studies using different sets of genomic polymorphisms, humans, ethnic groups, and clustering algorithms—and it has been reproduced in most, but not all—there are nevertheless conceptual, empirical, and hermeneutic questions to be raised.[41]

If, for any K, d represents the maximum average genetic distance (from the center of a cluster) required for cluster membership and e represents the minimum genetic distance between the centers of two discrete clusters, then $e \geq 2d$. K will be inversely proportional to both d and e. This suggests that for any K there may be identifiable clusters that are intermediate between any of the K clusters. And this would mean that more clusters would have to be added to do justice to human genetic variation. Furthermore, any given cluster would then be more similar to adjacent clusters (i.e., the genetic distance e would be smaller).

Quite apart from this conceptual point, there may *in fact* be intervening populations that simply were *unsampled* in the relevant studies, in which case there may be unexamined "front end" assumptions about the choice of appropriate sampling frames of reference.[42] This would render the K = 5 result liable to the charge of being an artifact of the researcher's sampling scheme, a construct produced in part by the way in which separated populations were chosen for sampling from a more continuous distribution.[43] It has been pointed out that "if individuals were sampled continuously from region to region, it might be more difficult to infer genetic clusters that were inclusive of all or even most individuals in large geographical regions."[44] Accordingly, the population geneticist Michael Bamshad maintains that "the inclusion of such samples [drawn from geographically intermediate regions] demonstrates geographic continuity in the distribution of genetic variation and thus undermines traditional concepts of race."[45] Sampling bias notwithstanding, it remains the case that human genetic variation is characterized by clines, or spatial gradients of allele frequency, rather than by categorical variation between populations; the variation occurs as a function of genetic drift, selection and demographic history.[46] So even though in the original study K varied from two (yielding clusters comprised only of "Africans" and "indigenous Americans") to six (adding an *infracontinental* population from northwest Pakistan), in principle K can vary from 1 to n, where 1 is the redundant value of K that would encompass our entire species, and n is the value corresponding to partitions capturing the most finely grained demes or local breeding populations.

If K is an integer less than or equal to 3, then one might say, to use Cavalli–Sforza's terms, that this is the input of a "lumper"; if higher K values are chosen, it is the work of the "splitters." So we are led back to the issue of hermeneutic salience. And, as Kitcher points out in his later essay, the authors of the seminal 2002 study of human genetic partitioning do not claim that the K=5 clusters will play a significant role in the explanation of shared phenotypic features or of disease susceptibility.[47] (Indeed, the clustering algorithms typically operate only on neutral, noncoding polymorphisms and not on genes that are phenotypically expressed, although there may be nontrivial statistical correlations between neutral nucleotides and expressed genes.)

So, and especially in light of the fact of continuity, the case has yet to be made that the science *naturally* or inherently stops at K=5, or at any other partition value short of the number of worldwide demes for that matter, and there are important considerations to the contrary. Gadamer's hermeneutic account of the logic of question and answer is apposite here. Expanding on the work of R. G. Collingwood, Gadamer argues that in order to understand the meaning of a text or utterance, we need to have a sense of the question to which the text or utterance is an answer.[48] The question prefigures what sort of thing will be sought (and found). Although the natural sciences per se, for the most part, remained beyond his purview, Gadamer did highlight the role played by the question (or animating concern) in science, a concern that is often bracketed or unacknowledged in our ordinary understanding of science. He spoke of this bracketing as a "methodological abstraction" that characterizes inadequate conceptions of scientific practice; this abstraction entails taking the complete bracketing of ourselves, of our standpoint as inquirers, as an ideal. In this sense, the ideal is to provide descriptions that are describer-invariant. Gadamer's is thereby a critique of the ideal of *theoria*, of the ideal of a self-withholding or self-erasure that would enable a pure and unmediated seeing.

This methodological abstraction, Gadamer maintains, informs an orientation toward the world that takes out of play those very prejudices (quasi-transcendental presuppositions) that are constitutive of our experience. This abstraction conceals the hermeneutic fact, the fact that a particular result or account is meaningful or fully intelligible only with respect to the often unacknowledged question to which it is a reply. The acknowledgment of this hermeneutic fact requires a contextualizing of such results or accounts. As Gadamer puts it, "what is established by statistics seems to be a language of facts, but which questions these facts answer and which facts would begin to speak if other questions were asked are hermeneutical questions." For example, statistics correlating race with crime may well be the outcome of inquiries that failed to raise questions concerning the relationship of *social conditions* to criminal behavior. Gadamer concludes that even science, which in his view has institutionalized the fetishism of objectivity, must bow before the hermeneutic fact.[49]

Kitcher's remarks (in his later essay) on the partitioning result are illustrative of this hermeneutic fact. As he puts it, the grounding question that establishes the salience of the partition inquiry (and of the number of partitions sought) is, "How did our species reach its current distribution?"⁵⁰ So the clusters yielded by setting K=5 may facilitate our understanding of the history of human migration but may not be so useful in understanding disease susceptibility.

To relate this discussion to the question of the status of the race concept, we should keep in mind my earlier comments to the effect that judgments of similarity and difference are functions of altitude and attitude. There is an altitude from which we get two distinct populations globally (K=2), namely, Africans and Americans, and this result may indeed be useful for some purposes. And there are lower altitudes from which we get as many as seven or more such groups. As I have suggested, it is difficult to make a case for a *natural* or nonarbitrary altitude, an altitude from which nature's joints stand out in relief. For example, when K=6, a cluster emerges that consists of an isolated group, the Kalash, living in northwest Pakistan. Yet thinkers who maintain that genetic clusters are isomorphic to races deny that the Kalash are a race.[51] Why? What is so magical about the K=5 result? For both conceptual reasons and those arising from concerns about sampling bias (the adjudication of which is beyond the scope of this book), we should avoid any tendency to reify the clusters yielded in the K=5 result, that is, to think that there are any significant or important *in kind* differences among the so-identified clusters as if they contained different types of people. I certainly do not believe that this latter claim, about there being different types of individuals, would be endorsed by the philosophers who herald this result. But it seems that this is precisely what identifying such clusters with "races" does. How else could it be meaningful—i.e., nontautological in the sense that we do not simply stipulatively *define* the continent-based populations as races—to say that these population clusters are *also* races? After all, the extension class of "race" apparently does not include the Kalash. Why not? Are they not different enough? In this context, an observation of Glasgow's is telling: whether we get a "racial" rather than a "nonracial" set of clusters seems to be underdetermined by biological facts.[52] If labeling the clusters as races is to be informative (empirically meaningful), to what—in addition to what is meant by "genetic cluster"—does such a label commit us? What work—epistemologically, semantically, or metaphysically—does the predicate "race" do here? The genetic clusters are each characterized by distinctive *frequencies* of common traits, but there are no distinctive cluster traits (remember that each cluster will contain 93 to 95 percent of human genetic variation; the clusters are extremely heterogeneous), i.e., no distinctive traits possessed by clusters, no distinctive group traits.[53]

Thus far I have developed what in a loose way can be considered the arbitrariness objection. I now turn to what has been called the mismatch objection. Given that the ordinary conception of race implies the existence of nonarbitrarily partitioned discrete categories of human beings based on morphological differences, the mismatch between this conception and that of the population group has already been prefigured (that is, what constitutes a continental population group deviates too much from the ordinary concept of a race). So, my treatment of this issue will be relatively brief. The question at issue is: Are speakers who use "race" in its ordinary sense and those who use "continental population group" referring to the same thing? The partitioning established by studies of human population structure is based on neutral, noncoding components of the human genome, i.e., not the components that are responsible for phenotypical traits. Therefore, the clusters inferred from genetic data might correspond only crudely to ordinary racial categories, which are based on manifest physical traits. As I have pointed out, characteristics such as facial features and skin pigmentation, characteristics that are routinely used to group people by race, can be shared by groups that are genetically very different. Conversely, there can be vast morphological differences between populations that are genetically quite similar, such as those between the Ainu of northern Japan and other East Asian populations. In general, such physical traits are not good predictors of population group membership; indeed, they might imply a closer degree of relatedness (genetic or biological) than actually exists or vice versa.[54] So the determination of the extension class of "racial group" can often be at odds with that for "ancestral population group."

Despite the caveats adduced regarding it in chapter 1, Putnam's "twin earth" thought experiment is useful as a heuristic here. Just as our ordinary conception of water does not necessarily track the distinction between H_2O and some other molecular structure that has similar manifest properties, our ordinary conception of race does not track biologically significant distinctions between genetic ancestry clusters.[55]

The relationship between a racial description or classification, as a macroscopic manifest-level description, and a description at the genomic level is not—as Hardimon, for example, seems to imply—analogous to that between, say, physical observables such as pressure, temperature, or volume and microlevel phenomena such as molecules in motion.[56] Absent are the requisite coordinating definitions or rules of correspondence that would effect the bridging or coordinated tracking between the two levels, between the manifest "racialized" and latent genetic structures. The more appropriate analogy would be furnished by, say, the ordinary usage of "cedar," which is employed by nonbotanists to refer to various species of tree that are not even closely related.[57] In this latter case, ordinary language classification and scientific classification schemes barely overlap, and there are many other instances in which ordinary language subtends distinctions that divide scientific classes in ways that have little biological significance (e.g., frogs and toads, rabbits and hares, and onions and garlic).[58] Similar examples arise for racial classification in ordinary language practice. As I have indicated, the race-determining phenotypes for Blacks and Melanesians are quite similar. Both groups share a high frequency of dark skin pigmentation, curly black hair, full lips, round noses, etcetera; however, they constitute distinct population groups. Moreover, although it is difficult to deny that Hispanics are considered a racial group in the American racial vernacular, members of this class do not form a distinct biological population.[59] Clearly the ordinary language classifications of flora and fauna—think of the distinction between onions and garlic—serve a variety of human purposes, many of which are orthogonal to the interests of science. I suggest that racial classifications are of this sort.

Finally, a few brief observations regarding race and medicine, given the increasingly popular view that clinical genetics seems to support the association of biological findings with the social identities of research participants.[60] First, it turns out that setting $K=5$ is much less useful for explaining and predicting an individual's disease susceptibility and reaction to drugs than it is for understanding the history of human migration. Indeed, geneticists urge considerable caution when using population labels in biomedical settings.[61] It is true that knowledge of an individual's ancestry can be of use in predicting disease susceptibility, drug reactions, and so forth. But at issue is, What sort of marker is a good predictor of individual ancestry? For many of the reasons rehearsed previously, racial classification, as determined by the third-person observer's perspective, is only loosely correlated with geographic or genetic ancestry and is correlated to a degree that varies from loose, at best, to nonexistent, at worst.

However, in many cases, self-assessed racial identity may turn out to be correlated with the continental genetic cluster commonly associated with that identity (although, of course, ancestry inference from explicit genetic data of individuals is much more reliable). Nevertheless, even in such cases, the fact of membership in a genetically defined cluster does not guarantee that all individuals so classified will have a similar genetic composition.[62] It turns out that even though cluster membership can be reliably inferred from an individual's genetic makeup, such membership does not determine the proportion of an individual's ancestry that originated in different populations. Moreover, despite the possibility of accurate population assignment, individuals from different populations can be genetically more similar than individuals from the same population.[63] For example, it has been observed that two U.S. scientists of European origin shared fewer SNPs (single nucleotide polymorphisms) than either of them shared with one of their Korean counterparts.[64] Biomedically relevant phenotypes controlled by a dozen or fewer loci can thus be expected to show substantial overlap between populations.[65] That is, traits of biomedical interest cut across population boundaries. This can make inferences from an individual's population membership to their biomedically significant phenotypes unreliable. And this is especially the case for geographically proximate populations or admixed populations. In general, knowing a person's population of origin does not provide sufficient information to predict his or her genotype, because the majority of genomic variation occurs within, rather than between, populations.[66]

To understand how this can be the case—that is, how individuals from different populations can be more similar in a given respect than individuals from the same population—think of a genetically defined cluster as being characterized by an average over the aggregate genetic properties of a given population (one can think of it as determined by the frequencies of each allele in a population). So, although an individual can be reliably assigned to a cluster, such assignment does not per se indicate where in that cluster's variance (measure of dispersion of data about the mean or average) that individual would be located. An individual, i_A, within a given population or cluster, A, who is at one extreme of the variance for a given set of alleles in that population may be more similar to an individual, i_B, at an extreme in another, different, population, B, than i_A is to an individual from the other extreme of population A. If that set of alleles is responsible for a particular phenotypical trait, then an individual will be more similar to someone from another population with respect to that trait than to another member of the same population. Thus variation in such traits will be discordant not only, as I have pointed out, with "race" but also with population group classification.[67] For this reason, inference from an individual's population membership to his or her biomedically significant phenotype is unreliable.

The upshot of this is that such membership cannot, by itself, determine the actual genetic ancestry of an individual. To facilitate accurate predictions about disease susceptibility and outcomes, one would have to have a more fine-grained picture of the proportion of recent genetic ancestry an individual shares with members of one or more groups. So population group membership is of limited value for such predictions. Therefore, and a fortiori, race is at best too coarse a descriptor—too weak, and potentially misleading, a proxy for genetic ancestry—to be useful for clinical prediction. And this is especially so in the United States and Europe.[68] In a comprehensive review article providing an overview of the implications of the various attempts to partition our species, a group of researchers concludes that

> the small genomic differences between populations and the extensive allele sharing across continents explain why historical attempts to identify, once and for good [sic], major biological groups in humans have always failed. . . . [R]acial labels may not only obscure important differences between patients but also . . . have become positively useless now that cheap and reliable [sequencing] methods for genotyping are making it possible to pursue the development of truly personalized medicine.⁶⁹

In short, racial categorization is a poor and potentially confounding predictor of human biological diversity.

Neither of the two major, and overlapping, attempts to provide a scientific/biological basis for the partitioning of our species into significant groupings succeeds in demonstrating that *ordinary racial* classification has empirical significance. For Kitcher, races are understood by analogy to biological subspecies, i.e., as populations that are reproductively isolated from their conspecifics. For populationists such as Hardimon, the species is partitioned into ancestral breeding populations. Neither Kitcher's subspecies analogues nor the populationist's breeding populations correspond to the ordinary conception of distinct races.

It seems unavoidable, then, that racial classification is ineliminably a matter of *interpretation* and that such interpretations are parasitic on a set of purposes or interests. Insofar as race is understood as a social category, its utility as a proxy for the sort of "kind-type" that can be pressed into service for explanation and prediction is, to seriously understate the case, limited. So the ordinary concept of race is of limited utility as a scientific concept, and what is useful in the biologically significant populationist concept does not map onto the ordinary concept very tidily.

This is acknowledged even in the case of one of the more prominent and influential arguments for the claim that race is biologically real. In "The Meaning of 'Race': Folk Conceptions and the New Biology of Race," R. O. Andreasen concedes that the ordinary, commonsense conception of race refers not to a natural kind (the sort of particular that proves its mettle in scientific practice) but rather to a social kind (which may prove useful in accounting for "human social relations, racist beliefs and practices, and the like").[70] Unlike natural kinds (whether hermeneutically conceived or not), whose explanatory salience is understood to be independent of their social acknowledgment, the salience of *social* kinds is not retained across alternative possible social worlds. This is the case for ordinary racial distinctions, which often track particular social interests and agendas. One need only reflect on the different ways in which racial distinctions are deployed in the United States and, say, in Brazil, for instance.[71]

The aim of this section was to disaggregate race as ordinarily understood from the idea of an ancestral population group. The former has little if any biological significance, whereas the latter does, although in the case of the latter, different "altitudes" of differentiation will serve scientific projects embodying different "attitudes." Next I consider the concept of race as a category of social recognition.

ETHNICITY AND RACIAL IDENTITY

Given the foregoing, should "race" be retained as an element of our vocabularies? And, if so, why and how should it be so retained? As hermeneutics scholar Georgia Warnke has pointed out, how individuals are identified is a contextual matter, making such identification a matter of interpretation.[72] This suggests that we should examine the assumptions, interests, purposes, and agendas that are constitutive of a particular interpretive context when assessing the appropriateness of an identification.

An adequate treatment of this issue will require that we acknowledge what the social theorist Anthony Giddens has called a double hermeneutic.[73] There is not only the framework or context of salience from which ascriptions of racial identity are made, which frameworks and contexts determine the point of such classification and underwrite the classificatory categories as categories of social recognition. Think of interpretations based on these frameworks as interpretations that are made from a third-person perspective (which is itself a perspective, not a "view from nowhere"). There is also the matter of a classified individual's *self*-understanding, of the meaning to that individual of his or her actions, of the descriptions under which the individual understands his or her actions, possibilities, and so on. All of this is anchored in the first-person perspective. Both perspectives are sited within a corresponding context of interpretation, within a matrix of intelligibility. In most, if not all, cases, the actions and prospects of socially classified individuals become fully intelligible only when understood to be informed by the agent's acknowledgment of having been so classified, "objectified" as it were, from the third-person perspective.

With respect to the third-person perspective, it is crucial to acknowledge the ways in which racial typology is a historical and social product fashioned in the furtherance of particular social projects and agendas. As such, it is an interpretive product.[74] It is important, however, to recognize that it is not the case that all who are potentially affected by this product have contributed to its fashioning.⁷⁵ In other words, this interpretation lacks reciprocity; it is a product of asymmetrical hermeneutic participation. It is the outcome of what Miranda Fricker has aptly labeled hermeneutic injustice.⁷⁶ In this sense, racial typologies are therefore also large-scale instances of what I referred to in chapters 2 and 3 as an illegitimate denial of semantic authority to salient demographic strata, more often than not to the detriment of the members of those strata. Consequently, understanding racial classification as an interpretive phenomenon will reveal another way in which racial discourse is implicitly vulnerable to rational critique and therefore will display the internal connections between a hermeneutics of race and important aspects of Critical Race Theory. However, my discussion in chapters 2 and 3 adumbrates the way in which I would fill in this connection, and there is already a vast literature treating the phenomenon of racial identity from within the purview of Critical Race Theory, so I limit myself here to simply pointing it out.

As a category of social recognition, race is a social kind, and racial identity is a social construction. Again, the key hermeneutic idea is that of the context of salience. Insofar as race marks a description under which groups of people are treated in some distinctive way or other and a description under which those people react to such treatment—i.e., insofar as such people and groups can be said to be "racialized"—the concept has both predictive and explanatory salience. This is what I mean when I say that "race" designates a social kind. In this sense, it has been inscribed in the institutions and practices of society in such a way that those institutions and practices cannot be understood without recourse to the concept of race.⁷⁷ In this sense, the category may have both diagnostic and prescriptive value in that it can be invoked to explain human social relations, racist beliefs and practices, on the one hand, and, on the other, to focus social responses to those practices.

In my use of the expression "social kind," I do not intend so much to invoke a distinctive metaphysical status as to mark a distinction between sortings that figure in explanatory accounts that presuppose social recognition of those sortings and sortings that figure in causal explanatory accounts that do not presuppose such recognition. The former are social kinds, and the latter are natural kinds. From confirmed membership in racial group R, one can often make reliable predictions about how one is and has been treated, or how individuals who are taken to be members of group R are typically treated. But with the crucially important exception of matters pertaining to "environmental racism," one cannot make reliable predictions of biological or biomedical interest.[78]

Culminating in a position that is remarkably consonant with this book's hermeneutic frame of reference, Ian Hacking's conception of "dynamic nominalism" implies that "numerous kinds of human beings and human acts come into being hand in hand with our invention of the categories labeling them."[79] Drawing upon this, Anthony Appiah deploys a notion of identification that refers to the "process through which an individual intentionally shapes her projects—including her plans for her own life and her conception of the good—by reference to available labels, available identities."[80]

Building on these ideas and combining the first- and third-person perspectives, Robert Gooding-Williams develops a useful account of what is meant by the expression "a Black person." Such an individual is one who is socially classified as Black, acknowledges that she is so classified by identifying herself as Black, and "begins to make choices, to formulate plans, to express concerns, etc., in light of [her] identification of [herself] as black."[81] Such a person acquires an interpretive lens that brings her prospects, projects, and concerns into focus under a description of them as prospects, projects, and concerns of a person who is identified as Black. One is a Black person insofar as one's interpretive framework is shaped by one's acknowledgment of one's racial classification as Black.[82]

In this sense, "race is among the modes of identification that influence how we think and act."[83] In Charles Taylor's terms, racial identity can be understood as a lived self-interpretation, in this case as a matter of understanding oneself and one's prospects in terms of a reflexive identification with an ascribed identity. Among the Strawsonian or semantic presuppositions of assertions regarding racial identification, on Gooding-Williams's account, are the existence of social practices of ascribed classification and the consequent implications of that classification for one's life prospects. In short, it is difficult to see how racial identification could come into being in a nonracist society.

The central claim here is that it is a presupposition of this identity that the individual acknowledge her racial classification, not that she must endorse or embrace it. She may even loathe it. As long as the agent understands her actions under the description of responses to a particular social/racial classification, she understands herself and acts as a Black person. So, although it may be expressed in terms of a socially available menu of scripts for doing so, racial identification, perhaps unlike either cultural or social role identification, has a self-authorizing quality. Role identity carries with it an implicit normative component, such that one can be a failed parent or an inept postal clerk. One cannot, in the same way, be a failed Black person.[84] Such a status must, therefore, countenance a very wide range of behaviors: for example, when encountering another similarly classified individual, from going out of one's way to avoid overt acknowledgment of that individual to overtly standing in solidarity with those who have been so classified and treated accordingly (e.g., being a "race man").[85] Furthermore, racial identity, unlike cultural identity, seems to be an inherently responsive or reactive phenomenon (and Gooding-Williams is careful to distinguish Black Americans' racial self-understandings from their wider cultural identities). And, unlike cultural identity, racial identity does not entail subscription to a particular set of beliefs and practices.[86]

To fill in this picture, it is worth pointing out that this applies as well to white racial identity. If Black racial identity is characterized as a response to an invidious classification, then white racial identity would be characterized as a response to one's acknowledgment and expectation of one's *exemption* from such invidious classification. As is the case for being a Black person, there are a variety of ways of being a white person, but it might be useful to place these modalities into two broad categories: "negative" modalities, such as feelings of entitlement and superiority; and "positive" modalities, such as self-consciousness and responsibility. Among the negative modalities would be, at one extreme perhaps, the blissful hermeneutic oblivion of the privileged that I discussed in chapter 3, and at the other, the politics of white racial grievance now current in the United States and elsewhere, a politics waged in response to perceived threats to that entitlement.

Let us return to Kitcher's argument in "Race, Ethnicity, Biology, and Culture." The second major aspect of Kitcher's thinking on race is an elaboration of two arguments in favor of a continued social recognition of race as a *biologically* significant property of individuals: (1) an argument to the effect that such recognition is important to a society that values the preservation of cultural and ethnic diversity (and presumably this would be the case even in a nonracist society); and (2) an argument to the effect that it is essential if we are to fortify those individuals who are most likely to suffer racially indexed injustice and to seek redress on their behalf.[87] Kitcher will in effect maintain both that particular cultures need racially identified individuals and that racially identified individuals need those particular cultures. (In his later essay, "Does 'Race' Have a Future?," he focuses as well on racially indexed medical treatment protocols and health disparities, biomedical issues that were addressed in the previous section.)

I hope that it is apparent from the foregoing discussion that—as long as we do not take them to demarcate biologically meaningful distinctions— I believe that the use of racial categories is important for the diagnosis and treatment of social pathologies. My discussions of epistemic injustice, the withholding of facilitating conditions of agency, and so on in chapter 3 all point to the viability of the strategic use of racial categories. Accordingly, I devote the majority of my comments to Kitcher's first line of argument.

Here he develops a model for cultural transmission that is analogous to his account of biological descent, defining "ethnicity" in the following way:

E1 An ethnic division consists of a division of our species into non-overlapping subsets, where the subsets are the "pure" ethnicities. Individuals not belonging to any of the subsets are of mixed ethnicity.
E2 Pure ethnicities are closed under cultural transmission, i.e., the cultural "offspring" of "parents" all of whom are of ethnicity E are of ethnicity E.
E3 All cultural "ancestors" of any member of any pure ethnicity are of that ethnicity.[88]

A cultural "parent" need not be a biological parent; it could be anyone who is responsible for the dominant items of an individual's culture, including such an "offspring's" peers.

Assuming that the lines of cultural transmission produce discrete clusters, Kitcher avers that the preservation of cultural diversity will require mechanisms of partial cultural isolation, and that this in turn will require the continued recognition of the biological significance of race, of a racial substrate. He suggests that eliminativist attempts to replace the biological notion of race by the cultural notion of ethnicity will fail in this respect. His position on *race* is that ethnicity (cultural preference) performs the race-preserving work of reproductive isolation. His position on *ethnicity* seems to be that race and biological lineage are the lines through which ethnicity is handed down, so that the racial transmission of ethnicity performs the ethnicity preserving work of cultural isolation. Thus the systems of race and of ethnicity are mutually reinforcing.[89] This is the case, I believe, because ethnicity has for him two distinguishable features, one exercised horizontally and the other vertically: it acts horizontally in that it serves as a mechanism of reproductive isolation; it acts vertically in that it tends to be transmitted along lines of biological lineage. The horizontal, isolating feature ensures that the vertical biological lines of cultural transmission are also racialized lines.

Kitcher goes on to pose a challenging set of ethical and public policy questions as he turns his eye toward practices such as transracial adoption. He first poses a dilemma: in a society composed of ethnicities that are significantly unequal in terms of material endowment, the adoption of a child from the disadvantaged ethnicity by parents of the privileged ethnicity may be advantageous for the individual child but disadvantageous for the cultural tradition that she leaves, for she will no longer be available to it as a site of cultural transmission. He concludes that social policies directed toward individuals ultimately may lead to the "extinction" of "valuable" cultural traditions.[90]

Apart from the questionable Mendelian model of cultural transmission upon which this account relies,[91] this raises two sets of questions: (1) is it true that cultural preservation requires the social constraints that Kitcher has in mind, and (2) can such constraints be morally justified? Responding to the second set of questions would take me beyond the scope of this chapter;[92] however, I have already addressed several aspects of this issue—especially the connections among culture, autonomy, and agency—in chapter 2 and elsewhere.[93] Regarding the first set of questions, we should begin by noting that a pre-socialized child may have an ascribed racial classification, but she can no more "have" or "leave behind" a culture or ethnicity than a pre-linguistic child can have or leave behind *a* language. So, here, presumably, there can be "no issue of *violating* an ethnic identity she already has" and thus, given the material inequities at issue, "there would seem to be no reasons for opposing the adoption."[94] This is the argument that Kitcher seeks to undermine by asserting a prescriptive harmony between race and ethnicity.

At the current historical moment, it is true that children of parents from a particular ethnic group—children who would be positioned to be potential vectors of ethnic/cultural preservation—are likely, as a contingent matter of fact, to share the racial labels of their parents. Moreover, it is not implausible to argue that if the children, the majority of whom *happen* to share the racial labels of their parents, were out-adopted, the culture in question would suffer a deficit of sites of cultural transmission. However, this does not imply that being of race R (either in the sense of social classification or biological "nature") is proximally implicated here. Biological ancestry is only contingently related to the salient variable, namely, availability as a site of transmission. Therefore, it is not clear that the significance of biological ancestry to cultural preservation is sufficiently robust, as Kitcher suggests, to justify social policies of "offering to people of a particular racial group only limited opportunities for transferring to the dominant ethnicity." Here Kitcher offers as an example contemporary social policies aimed at protecting Native American cultural traditions by discouraging ethno-cultural emigration to the dominant ethnicity.[95] But this argument would apply *just as well* to a non–Native American child who was adopted by Native American parents and who would thereby become a potential site for cultural transmission (not a far-fetched scenario, given some of the traditional practices among Native Americans regarding the incorporation of "outsiders").[96] That is, one would have to make the same argument here discouraging her, the non–Native American child's, out-adoption. The arguments would, it would seem, have to be symmetrical. Any asymmetry would violate the stipulation that a presocialized child has no determinate ethnicity. The argument for encouraging a child to remain within the ambit of her parents' ethnicity has very little to do with race per se.

Nor is the connection between genealogy and culture sufficiently robust to underwrite the sentiment that "people should preserve 'their' culture."[97] In what sense does a culture belong to an individual simply by virtue of that individual's genealogy? If it did, then perhaps a presocialized child *would* have a culture. How could culture be "velcroed," as it were, onto an individual's phenotype as if it were carried along as a sort of "genetic endowment" or "genetic baggage"? Kitcher himself gives us reason to doubt the plausibility of this when he explicitly maintains that "the phenotypic characters used to pick out races neither have intrinsic significance nor are correlated with characteristics that are significant." His exhortation to bring race and ethnicity into harmony is therefore no more a call for retaining the biological offspring of parents whose culture is in question than it is an imperative to "recruit" outsiders to serve as sites of cultural transmission (except that, of course, practically speaking, it may be easier to retain than to recruit). So, *pace* Kitcher, it would seem that the argument for encouraging such children to remain within the ambit of their parents' ethnicity has very little to do with race per se, or in principle.[98]

Of course, there are indeed good reasons to protect particular cultures and to ensure a diversity of cultures.[99] However, the continuation of a network of cultural traditions does not always *require* a racial substrate or a racialized line of transmission, even when that network of traditions has arisen with and been historically maintained by distinctively racialized subjects. Over time, a given set of cultural practices can achieve relative autonomy and be codified as if it were a game that others can learn to play. Nevertheless, it is no doubt the case that extracting a cultural practice or product from its context of origin—a context forged in part as a response to the experiences of racialized subjects—can alter its meaning. And we cannot deny that, as Gooding-Williams puts it, African American cultural production has "been and continue[s] to be inflected by meanings and self-understandings that black persons have assigned to being black in a society that has been shaped by black slavery and antiblack racism."[100] Even so, as my proposal for a modified semantic holism in my discussion of language in chapter 1 suggests, one might think of regions of culture that can be isolated for certain purposes. Many of these regions will include facets or aspects of cultural practices that can be supported without the bearers of the supported traditions being members of the "race" historically associated with them, although it might well be a condition of that support that such nontraditional bearers will be conversant with the racially inflected meanings associated with those practices.[101] The blues tradition in African

American music is a case in point.[102] If a tradition inaugurated by a given group were uniquely dependent on members of that group for its preservation, I fear that the blues tradition might long ago have disappeared. And I recall a conversation in which Marian McPartland, a white British jazz pianist, while conversing with other jazz musicians referred to jazz, without irony, as "our music."[103] Reversing the vectors of transmission, one might think of the way in which the African American jazz clarinetist Don Byron has carried forward the Jewish musical tradition of klezmer, or of W. E. B. DuBois as he sits with a Shakespeare who fails to wince.

It is not clear that there is a need for the sort of cultural policing required to "keep the natives on the reservation." Mechanisms of cultural preservation do not *have* to be mediated by the concept of race or by a normative pressure that would enforce harmony between race and ethnicity. This is especially the case if we—in keeping with what I earlier referred to as a hermeneutics of suspicion—resist approaching cultural traditions and their dominant interpretations, or aspects of them, as having categorical value and instead think of them in terms of their value to individuals, either to those who are customarily associated with them or those who are not.

Kitcher expresses a related worry that, should we refuse to acknowledge race, the diverse cultural/ethnic heritages might not so much disappear altogether as become so thoroughly mixed that in the future we would be left with a society of ethnic hybrids and that this would be tantamount to a potentially stifling cultural homogeneity.[104] But, in some respects, that future is now. What else is it to be an American but *already* to be to a significant degree such a hybrid, although, to be sure, we probably each move in circles in which that hybridity is given a characteristic inflection, where different changes are rung on the theme?[105]

It is particularly the case in our "postmodern" and highly mediatized context that biological parents are not the only significant cultural parents. This is certainly in part what so bothers the religious right and what makes groups like the Amish stand out for us by their contrast with the norm. White teenagers still constitute the majority of the consumers of rap music, and not too long ago young white boys "wanted to be like Mike (Jordan)."

Although I am no fan of postmodernism, it seems that Kitcher tends to think that only if pure ethnicities are maintained in a state of splendid isolation could they make distinctive contributions. I am not unsympathetic to his concern, a concern he seems to share with DuBois, who—when he wrote "The Conservation of Races"—felt that Black people should resist assimilation in order to fully forge their distinctive message to humanity.[106] But this seems to restrict us to a purely aesthetic (in the Kantian sense) appreciation of multiculturalism or of "ethnic" differences. My view is that the plurality of cultural traditions make distinctive contributions because they both inform and address us. A tradition with which we are unfamiliar invites us to consider other possible ways of being, other possible ways to comport ourselves in the world, ways that may have been marginalized, forgotten, or even never acknowledged by us. In our encounter with such a tradition, our sense of human possibilities is expanded. If we take such invitations seriously, we might look at "our" tradition differently or enact, in varying degrees, a transformation of it.[107] In other words, some degree of ethnic hybridity just might be what results from allowing "pure" ethnicities to make distinctive contributions. And this process, having begun at least as far back as the seventeenth century in the United States, does not seem to have led to a stifling cultural homogeneity; indeed, it seems that what it is to be an American is constantly being negotiated and renegotiated.

Kitcher's second main argument for harmonizing race and ethnicity follows from his recognition that individuals who suffer mistreatment as racialized individuals stand to benefit from the strategic and cultural resources that are available within the ethnicity typically associated with the individual's "race." As I have indicated, I am quite sympathetic to this point, and I find this argument to be convincing. The cultural-expressive vocabulary that is characteristic of a distinct ethnicity is, at least in part, the product of its members' particular historical experience and of their ongoing social treatment. When that experience and treatment are corollaries of racial classification based on phenotypical properties, it stands to reason that such a vocabulary would embrace modes of response (and of resistance) to such racialized treatment. Certainly, then, for a racialized individual who is disadvantageously classified, access to the expressive resources of the ethnicity to which she is presumptively connected may be crucial to her ability to flourish. So, one can make a case for the coupling of racial ascription and at least a subset of ethnocultural practice in the case of racially stratified societies, the sort of society that provides the context for Gooding-Williams's account of what it is to be a Black person. For contained in that subset will be some of the strategies and scripts that would inform the actions undertaken by self-consciously racialized subjects. The cogency of this argument notwithstanding, it should be noted that, although it explicitly invokes race as a social kind, it in no way requires an appeal to a biological conception of race, and hence to what Kitcher refers to as the "concept of race" with its biological underpinnings.

I have been explicit in attempting to disaggregate and disentangle what Kitcher has impressively woven together, namely, biology, race, and culture. Kitcher has offered nonracist reasons of a *social* and *cultural* provenance for our continuing to acknowledge and maintain *biologically* defined racial distinctions. Abandoning discursive reference to race in this sense may well require us to give up prescriptive notions of identity that allow us to speak in terms of "violating" one's ethnic heritage or to speak of a cultural tradition as somehow belonging to someone simply because it was practiced by people who in some way or other physically resemble that individual. But I do not think that abandoning such discourse requires us to abandon the idea of the preservation and enhancement of cultural traditions. Given the social price exacted by such discourse and the dubious scientific value of it, should we not simply bid it "good riddance"?

5

CONCLUDING REFLECTIONS

Toward a New Reconciliation of Hermeneutics and Critical Theory, or Notes Toward a Hermeneutic Democracy

In his inaugural lecture at the University of Frankfurt, a lecture devoted to a broadly conceived critique of the "objectivist illusion," Habermas speaks of the connection between Enlightenment and processes of self-reflection.[1] Although undoubtedly related, he eventually came to distinguish between the concept of self-reflection necessary for emancipative reflection, on the one hand, and the Kant-styled transcendental self-reflection deployed in the project to determine the subjective conditions of possible knowledge *in general*, on the other.[2] Transcendental knowledge-generative frameworks are to be distinguished from factual and contingent knowledge-generative frameworks. Accordingly, emancipative self-reflection targets specific complexes of knowledge and power and can, therefore, expose the dogmatic character of particular worldviews and social practices. As Habermas puts it,

> self-reflection brings to consciousness those determinants of a self-formative process . . . which ideologically determine a contemporary practice and conception of the world. . . . [It] leads to insight due to the fact that what has previously been unconscious is made conscious in a manner rich in consequences.[3]

In this formulation, a central task of Critical Theory is to encourage reflexive awareness of the conditions of one's awareness. However, because Habermas understood hermeneutics per se to be restricted in its legitimate application to the understanding of utterances and the content of tradition, the potential to facilitate *critical* self-understanding was, for him, beyond its remit.[4]

This was very much my concern as I thematized throughout this study the methodological priority of the hermeneutic question (especially important in my interrogation both of the biological conception of race and of the practice of racial identification per se in chapter 4) as well as the quasi-transcendental world-disclosive function of socially and culturally indexed fundamental commitments. The idea was to bring to the fore an awareness of the conditions of our awareness that is distinctively hermeneutic. Throughout this work, my concern has been to demonstrate the scope of the critical/diagnostic significance of hermeneutics. By demonstrating the ways in which critical and reflexive perspectives can emerge from *within* socially and culturally embedded contexts, I view this as a contribution to the ongoing project of critical theory.

It is useful to take as a working definition of critical theory the following formulation: It is the project of bringing a "normative orientation towards the cognitive and experiential resources for . . . agents" who are inextricably socially and culturally situated and to diagnose "the extent to which social reality allows for the possible realization of normative goals."[5] My accounts of counterfactual dialogical critique, of social agency, and of the injustice of epistemic occlusion speak directly to the concerns of critical theory so understood. The modality of social critique proposed in chapter 2 is an account of the conditions of possibility for critical self-reflection on the part of culturally situated agents. It is one that allows for a reconstruction of the options available to such agents, a reconstruction that is enabled by a conversationally sustained imagination of legitimate cultural interpretations that are alternatives to the status quo. The requirement of narrative representability was introduced in chapter 3 as a diagnostic concept to determine the extent to which a given society could be understood by its members to permit the attainment of socially normed ideals of flourishing.

Here it is worth noting that both the critical apparatus of chapter 2 and the requirement of narrative representability in chapter 3 invoke the possibility of mediation as a facilitating condition of agency. Both take as a critical/diagnostic touchstone the possibility of constructing mediating stages—in chapter 2, between one's culture as currently understood and a more liberating conception, and in chapter 3, between one's current situation and one in which socially available modes of flourishing can be accessed. Being attentive to possible mediations between existing conditions and desired conditions was a hallmark of the immanent critique of the first generation of Critical Theorists, notably Max Horkheimer, Theodor Adorno, and Herbert Marcuse. And there are indeed "elective affinities" between the model of internal critique that I develop and its close cousin, immanent critique, but there are important differences.

Inspired by the Hegelian conception of "real possibility," a modal conception that emerges from the account of the dialectic of appearance and essence presented in Hegel's *Logic*, Adorno and Marcuse maintained that desired conditions could be understood to be latently present, as dispositional properties, in existing conditions, as the real possibilities of those existing conditions.[6] Thus understood, real possibility refers to the "not yet existent actuality of what exists." These theorists took such latent possibility to be the fulcrum for immanent critique, for a social critique that would not be burdened by an abstract separation of the "is" from the "ought."

A brief discussion of Adorno's deployment of the idea should suffice to illustrate the point. To circumvent subjective idealism and the "antinomies of bourgeois thought," Adorno follows Georg Lukács in asserting the "primacy of the object," of a social reality that could not be adequately captured by a conceptual framework that projects onto it a scheme of abstract types and their relations. Adorno used the term "nonidentical" to denote this nonconceptual content that constitutively resists conceptual capture and subsequent domestication. The nonidentical thus "underlies" manifest social experience and cannot be reduced to it. The astute dialectician, however, can discern, within existing social conditions and manifest experience, the potential for alternative social configurations, can discern the field of tension within which immediate appearance stands.[7] Or, as Marcuse put it, immediate appearance reveals persons and things in a perverted form, but we can also find in it concomitant possibilities of negating this perversion and realizing what could be instead.[8] These are the real possibilities afforded by existing totalities of circumstances.[9] Adorno suggests that we can discern these possibilities "when things in being are read as a text of their becoming." Adorno continues that

> the means employed in negative dialectics for the penetration of its hardened objects is *possibility*—the *possibility* of which their reality has cheated the objects and which is nonetheless *visible* in each one.[10] (emphasis added)

For existing conditions to be treated or read as a text in this way requires that they have "meaning-bearing" properties.[11]

Attentive deciphering of those meaning-bearing properties reveals "real possibility," the display of what could be in what is.

Now, despite their tendency to speak of the "visibility" of such real or concrete possibilities or their suggestion that such possibilities can be discerned in reality as forces and tendencies,[12] Marcuse's and Adorno's exploitation of the Hegelian concept of real possibility for the purposes of immanent critique cannot avoid the hermeneutic circle. In order for the meaning-bearing properties to be *activated* and subsequently discerned, there must be a hermeneutic projection on the field of immediate appearance, a meaning-activating projection enacted by situated and interested subjects.[13] Real possibility will then be what emerges from "readings" produced by such invested, practically engaged subjects and not what comes into view for the theoretical apprehension of a disinterested observer. In other contexts, Marcuse acknowledged the constitutive role of the subject with regard to such possibilities, and Max Horkheimer seemed to be quite clear-eyed about this as well: "a certain concern is also required if these tendencies are to be perceived and expressed."[14] When "hermeneutically chastened" in this way, this version of immanent critique is less vulnerable to the critique of objectivism expressed in Habermas's inaugural lecture and somewhat closer to the spirit of the internal critique I have pursued.

The conception of ideology and of ideology critique that is adumbrated in the development of my idea of counterfactual dialogical critique—especially given my emphasis on the plurivocity of cultural meaning and on cultural identity as a cluster concept—is an "immanent" conception in the sense that we need not import norms that are external to the cultural tradition sustaining a particular practice to put that practice into question. I have suggested that evidence of the strategic privileging of a particular cultural interpretation is prima facie evidence of its ideological status. In this sense, such a presumptively arbitrary restriction of what will be considered a candidate for recognition as a valid cultural interpretation or conception of sociocultural identity can be thought of as the hermeneutic analogue of what Habermas, in a discussion of the ideological function of culture, refers to as the distortions or "systemic restrictions placed on communication" whereby cultural traditions are "immunized against dissonant experiences."[15] Thus I have indicated the sense in which we can assess a cultural interpretation to be functioning ideologically without having to abstract from the self-understanding of the culture in question. An interpretation whose privileged or hegemonic status is achieved, for reasons that are typically invidiously strategic, at the cost of "shutting down" the conflict of interpretations to which cultural traditions are heir, of shutting down the interpretive "competition" that would otherwise play itself out both contemporaneously and historically, would in this sense count as ideological.[16]

One of the fundamental ways in which social power manifests itself is in the strategic promulgation and policing of the semantic resources for cultural interpretation and self-understanding.[17] This allows us to thematize the effects of power and to raise one of the central questions for critical theory: Whose situated cultural agency is served by existing socially sanctioned and authorized semantic resources and the cultural interpretations they promote? Systematic distributive asymmetries in such agency-enabling resources, particularly those that track socially discernible and acknowledged demographic fault lines such as race, class, and gender, will count as prima facie evidence of such an invidiously strategic formation.

More can be said about the concept of power as it figures in my account. One might argue, particularly if one is of a Foucauldian stripe, that all interpretive horizons arise as a result of strategic generation, and with a sufficiently broad understanding of "strategic," this may well be true. However, if all such horizons are strategically engendered in this sense, we nevertheless face the "Thales effect," namely, if everything is ultimately made of water, we still need some way of marking the distinction between the stuff that we drink and the stuff we drink it from. Therefore, the conception of power that is implicit in my discussion is one that contrastively distinguishes between strategic generation broadly conceived and the more narrow case of systematic, invidious generation and promulgation.[18]

With this, I hope to have clarified what Gadamer left unclear, namely, in what sense a hermeneutically underwritten distinction between legitimate and illegitimate prejudice can function as an effective proxy for ideology critique. The conception of ideology that is implicit in my account is hermeneutical in that it does not oppose a presumably theoretically underwritten and nonideological content to a culturally indexed set of beliefs, practices, or institutions whose content is being judged. Rather, the concern is with the *modality* with which a cultural self-understanding is put forward, not its content per se. Is it dogmatically asserted in a way that categorically preempts alternative interpretations so that it assumes the form of the sort of hardened object that so vexed Adorno, or not? This way of framing ideology critique avoids the presupposition of normative or epistemic privilege that has burdened traditional conceptions of ideology critique. And, as I have pointed out, this way of thinking about the project of cultural critique has the important practical advantage of mitigating the potentially compromising ambivalence that may accompany the moral agency of those who are wary of being perceived as condescendingly paternalistic in their interaction with differently situated actors.

Now, given the "embargo" on an a priori invocation of potentially question-begging external norms when formulating a critical response to situated practices, what will be the source of alternative understandings of cultural identity, and what will serve to motivate the requisite expansion of semantic resources? The short answer is the lived experience of individuals subject to those cultural interpretations. Although the tradition from which she takes up these matters is distinct from that of philosophical hermeneutics, Sally Haslanger's approach to the notions of ideology and ideology critique overlaps in a significant way with some of the concerns of this book.[19] I have in mind, in particular, her emphasis on the role played by culturally indexed background assumptions, or what she calls social meanings, in supplying the semantic fields on which intelligible speech and action draw (such semantic presuppositions were also referred to as social meanings in chapter 2 of this book, and in a previous book I referred to them as "prereflective meanings").[20] In this way, Haslanger is led to view propositional meaning and action description as derivative phenomena vis-à-vis the semantic background matrix that gives such assertions and descriptions sense. By locating ideology in this semantic space, as opposed to in the purely cognitive dimension of individually held belief, she is able to conceive of ideology critique in terms of a disruption of a semantic field or a reorganization of the way in which social space is configured.[21] This is fully compatible both with my insistence on the importance of assuring marginalized groups the semantic authority to name salient aspects of their experience (to name it as an instance of sexual harassment, police brutality, racial profiling, and so on) and with my highlighting the significance of being able to interrogate dominant cultural interpretations in order to permit less confining scripts for cultural identity (as I pointed out in the course of my discussion of female excision). Thus my discussion assumed the form, not of an abstract critique of problematic practices but rather took as its focus the semantic resources and cultural interpretations that legitimated those practices. Ideology critique as I have conceived it, therefore, would not demand that we measure a tradition or culture by the abstract requirements of "reason" but rather that we situate a given interpretation of it in relation to possible alternatives.

Haslanger helpfully goes on to point out that among the most effective resources for such critique will be "new experiences that highlight aspects of reality that were previously masked or obscured."[22] And harnessing such experiences in effective social movements is a modality for achieving public recognition of the inadequacy of dominant interpretations. It is worth noting here that by bringing to the foreground the linkages between cultural interpretations and the practices they make possible (or impossible), my argument can be understood to be an acknowledgment of what Habermas takes to be the urgency of submitting the world-disclosive power of cultural horizons to a critical forum.[23]

The implicit normative posture that has informed this work throughout is one in which social *legitimacy* and social self-understanding are coupled.[24] To wit, a fully legitimate self-understanding on the part of a society is one that is both (1) sufficiently reflexive to permit an acknowledgment of its own inadequacy in providing the semantic resources requisite to the situated autonomous agency of all of its members and (2) sufficiently hermeneutically charitable to acknowledge the various horizons of intelligibility from which its constituent stakeholders speak and act, horizons that provide the conditions that facilitate, or impede, agency. A social self-understanding that either arbitrarily excludes alternative configurations of social identity or arbitrarily occludes marginalized epistemic horizons is prima facie a flawed self-understanding. Just as there can be no final, privileged comprehensive meaning of a text, there can be no similarly privileged and final comprehensive sociocultural interpretation. As I have argued elsewhere, much in the same way that intercultural understanding constitutes an unfinished project, cultural self-understanding also does so.[25] Furthermore, much like a putatively comprehensive textual interpretation that fails to account for, and thereby incorporate, significant segments of a text, a selective and narrow cultural self-interpretation, one that fails to acknowledge marginalized horizons, must be adjudged inadequate.

In chapter 2, this inadequacy was highlighted in the form of a strategic fundamentalist gesture in which a particular and overly prescriptive framing of cultural identity brooked no competitors. This is the backdrop against which I discussed the practice of female excision. In chapter 3, it assumed the form of a failure to acknowledge the horizons from which marginalized agents speak and act, leading to the various misdiagnoses and epistemic injustices that follow from the fallacy of psychologizing the social. It is reflected in the "development" paradigm's failure to recognize the plurality of ontological, social, and normative backgrounds in which social agents are situated.[26] It is to such a failure that the requirement of narrative representability was addressed, a requirement that can serve as a catalyst to deepen the discussion of issues of global injustice and inequality by bringing into sharper relief the otherwise hidden epistemic structural components of inequality. In chapter 4, it assumes the form of a denial of semantic authority to the self-understanding of racially classified persons. In general, I have argued that attention to these hermeneutic inadequacies will be of benefit to the diagnosis and treatment of a variety of social pathologies: from cultural conventions that demand so-called adaptive preferences on the part of deprived women, to the practice of blaming the culture of the poor for their misery, and to failing to acknowledge the legitimate claims of those who struggle to have their perception of society acknowledged and to name salient aspects of their social experience (e.g., victims of sexual harassment, police brutality, racial profiling, and so on).

The claim, on the part of a dominant cultural interpretation, to represent the cultural self-understanding—and associated social configurations and practices—that *all*, after deliberate reflection on their own interests, would assent to is then the fulcrum about which my conception of ideology critique pivots. In this sense, I would then deem ideological any self-interpretation that is promulgated by a society that arbitrarily restricts the interpretive agency of its members and that thus undermines its semantic democratic character.[27] Semantic democracy, in which competing social interpretations can be granted public recognition, is a prerequisite of generalized social agency. The requisite reflexivity of a binding social interpretation, the first condition on social legitimacy alluded to previously, is facilitated by such a democratization of interpretive agency in which there are no arbitrary restrictions to participation in the interpretive practices that generate collectively binding and enabling social meanings. In this way, social legitimacy can be seen to require interpretive democracy. Thus my plea for hermeneutic democracy, for the democratization of social disclosure, and for the institutions that would enable and sustain it.[28]

The normative leverage that I exploit is provided by any claim, whether explicit or implicit, on the part of a sociocultural complex to have satisfied the conditions of reflexivity and hermeneutic charity. Such a claim, even if not explicitly made but only implicitly presupposed in the course of what is in fact a general misrecognition of the behavior and plight of others, furnishes me with the requisite toehold for a critical hermeneutics.

This normative lever assumes the form of an implicit claim to interpretive consensus in the discussion of cultural practices, in chapter 2, and the form of a demonstrably false assumption that "normal" conditions, both epistemic and material, are universally satisfied in the account of epistemic injustice, in chapter 3. In general, and throughout the range of topics taken up in this book, the normative pressure that burdens a given social self-understanding is understood to be generated from within, not imposed from without. The fulcrum is supplied by the internal claims implicitly raised. Although it is true that without such a fulcrum we would have to forfeit *this* critical avenue, it turns out that it is a rare society indeed that eschews all such internal validity claims.

This is because, as I noted in an earlier book, even the most insular of cultures implicitly raises the claim that its practices represent the best way for it to flourish.[29] Such a culture will operate with particular ideals of flourishing that, on that culture's own terms, it may be addressing ineffectually or in ways that are likely to fail. My analysis of what I have called second-order rationality is a minimalist conception of rationality that can be attributed to everyone as the inclination to question their practices—or modalities for realizing their ideals—when they can be brought to see how those practices and modalities are inadequate. The validity of this distinction between what members of a community believe or how they act and what, according to their own ideas, is reasonable for them to believe and how it is reasonable for them to act, authorizes a non-question-begging critical posture toward such cultural practices. This secures for us an internal critical purchase even in circumstances that may appear to be impervious to such approaches.

Furthermore, under current conditions of ubiquitous global covisibility, few societies, no matter how insular, can escape the gaze of others. As the cultural anthropologist Clifford Geertz once put it, "the deprovincialization of the world [means] we're going to be in each other's faces more."[30] Therefore, justification-demanding encounters that challenge parties to those encounters with the expectation to account for, to provide reasons for, their practices—to provide grounds that can be nonprovincially acknowledged *as* reasons—are likely to become increasingly unavoidable. And whether proffered sincerely or merely strategically and disingenuously, constitutive of such reasons is a vulnerability to critical scrutiny, from both without *and within*.

Appendix

TOWARD A HERMENEUTICS OF THE ETHICAL RESPONSE

Doing justice to the facticity of the other, to their genuine alterity, has been an abiding concern for the German phenomenologist Bernhard Waldenfels. Ever wary of a response to the other's facticity that threatens to assimilate the other to the self, he remains suspicious of the hermeneutic ideal of mutual or reciprocal understanding. Such an ideal, he maintains, is complicit with an Enlightenment universalism that ineluctably grants priority to a convergence and sameness that effaces the other's distinctiveness and difference. The hiatus between self and other that problematizes our understanding of the other also complicates the assessment of our moral obligation to the other. In his rejection of what he takes to be situationally indifferent moral rules that fail to acknowledge difference, Waldenfels, I argue, overlooks the conceptual resources of hermeneutics for delineating a "third way," an alternative both to the invocation of context blind and invariant moral rules and to a surrender to an ultimately normless relativism. This third way is captured by what I conceive of as a hermeneutically informed "fitting response" made in the context of an emergent and shared matrix of intelligibility.

In a number of influential essays and texts, Bernhard Waldenfels points out what he takes to be the deficiencies of traditional ethical theory insofar as it emphasizes the centrality of rules for ethical decision and the norms of universality and responsibility.[1] In "Toward a Responsive Ethics," Waldenfels indicates how what he calls a "responsive ethics" would remediate those shortcomings.[2] For him, a responsive ethics must start from the recognition of what he calls a "genuine *hiatus* between *you* and *me*, between the alien and the own" (emphasis added).[3] Given this gulf between self and other, he proposes an account of trust in order to recuperate the moment of sociality, the cement between self and other. In this appendix, I restrict myself for the most part to his critique of traditional ethical theory by examining the conception of responsive ethics that he proposes as an alternative to a traditional ethics of responsibility.

I agree with Waldenfels that when an other confronts us with an unforeseen demand, it is true that we cannot draw on our existing stock of responses already at hand. The response to the other's demand cannot simply follow *given* rules.[4] We must, as Waldenfels suggests, respond creatively. Our response cannot be *pre*-fabricated. As he says, in our response to the other, our "answers are not presented as offers on the counter[:] [t]he answers I give are to be invented."[5] Like musical interventions in jazz, such creative responses are improvisations; they are produced in the moment as a response to events in real time. However, I would insist that creative responses must also be "fitting responses," not merely arbitrary reactions. So to ask about the ethics of response or a responsive ethics is also to ask how we can meaningfully orient the production of relatively unpremeditated action undertaken in response to demands in real time.

I think that Schopenhauer's response to Kant's ethical theory is apposite here. Kant, of course, claimed that an action is moral if and only if it conforms to a principle or maxim that could be universalized, that morality demands that we perform those and only those actions that conform to the categorical imperative. Schopenhauer replied that this was tantamount to a kind of pedantry or rigorism, to the folly of being in the grip of a concept or maxim or rule and applying it doggedly no matter how different the situations of its application may be.[6] This would be a matter of not allowing one's discretion to recognize what is right, what is the "fitting response" in a particular case.

Both of the dominant traditions in modern ethical theory—the deontological orientation of Kant and the utilitarian/consequentialist tradition typically associated with Bentham and Mill—assume, despite their differences, that the role of the moral theorist is to seek "a fully explicit decision procedure for settling moral questions," to seek "explicit and univocal decision procedures."[7] What is morally right could then be fully specified by rules.

Insofar as this is so, neither tradition, in this sense, heeds Schopenhauer's complaint. Moreover, even if we decided that such a rule-based approach to ethics—whether a caricature of these traditions or not—was the best game in town, there is a conceptual issue that is insufficiently addressed, if not overlooked, by these traditions—namely, the problem of how general rules are to be applied to particular situations. Only if such rules were such that a full understanding of them would be sufficient for their correct application, only if they could be formulated in such a way that they required nothing in the way of contextual or indexical supplementation, could we apply them without having to exceed them in some way. But the rules associated with ethically mandated duties cannot be self-executing or self-interpreting. Their necessarily schematic character will always leave underdetermined just how and when we are to fulfill those mandates. And this would be the case as well for any proposed "metarule" for following such rules. There can be no rules for the application of rules. Looking for further rules governing the application of rules would inexorably lead us to circularity or to an infinite regress. Therefore, the correct application of such first-order ethical rules will require capacities of discernment that exceed our understanding of the content of the rules in question. This capacity is typically denoted by such terms as *phronesis* or judgment, referring to the faculty concerned with the appropriate application of general rules. The application of general moral rules in particular circumstances requires our ability to *judiciously* exceed what those schematic rules alone can tell us about our duties.[8] And, indeed, we can be said to have grasped the rules only when we can *perform* their application in concrete situations. Insofar as the verdict of such a judgment cannot preexist the performance itself, moral judgment is not a taxonomic but, to some degree at least, a creative faculty.

Although it is true that the schematic nature of rules necessitates the use of judgment in our application of them, we can nevertheless give reasons—reasons not drawn exclusively from the rule we are applying—for the choice we have made. Moral judgment can appeal to reasons, but it does not do so in virtue of any rule that makes something a reason. These reasons can perhaps be stylized as rules, but only after the fact. They would not be rules that preexisted the choice; rather, they would emerge in the situation of application. The moral rationality of a given action can be underwritten by its relationship to salient moral examples. Moral exemplars can in this way provide reasons.[9] Although it may be a matter of some controversy just how moral examples function as reasons, I believe that examples can be shown to function as reasons by virtue of the very same type of analogical reasoning from precedent that is used in common law legal reasoning.

Without getting too far into the weeds here, what these considerations suggest is that we must acknowledge that neither the rigid application of fully determinate rules, on the one hand, nor resigning ourselves to a sheer arbitrariness, on the other, exhaust the modalities through which we make moral decisions. I have adumbrated three possibilities: (1) algorithmically guided choice where reasons are conclusive, where there is a decision procedure with a unique result, and an agreed upon mechanism for definitively resolving disputes; (2) the condition of normless relativism or arbitrariness in which reasons are utterly irrelevant and where there are thus no agreed upon mechanisms for resolving disagreements; and (3) the hermeneutic domain of judgment, where reasons are relevant but not conclusive and where there is a more or less shared set of criteria to which one can appeal when giving reasons, although the appeal to no single interpretation of the criteria nor to any assignment of priorities to the criteria can be decisive. The idea of what I am calling the "fitting response" finds its place in this third space, the space between rule-dictated practice and the arbitrariness of "anything goes."

Because judgment is grounded in a creative insight that always, in a sense, "runs ahead" of rule-governed certainty and is thus never vouchsafed guarantees that promise success, the judgment that issues in the "fitting response" always carries with it the risk of losing one's way, of going astray. This is an unavoidable consequence of the freedom that it affords, but it is also more than an aimless meandering. For judgment takes its orientation from a contingently expandable matrix of intelligibility. Although there can be no algorithm for "the fitting response," that does not mean that the "fitting response" cannot be an "intelligible response."

I have gone on at some length about this because I think that Waldenfels has not given this "third space," the space of judgment, its due and that there is a price to be paid for this oversight. In his book, *The Question of the Other*, he claims that the "responsive difference," what he refers to as the genuine hiatus between the alien and the own, is effaced if the alienness in the other's demand is assimilated either to the "hermeneutic difference" or to the "regulative difference." By this I take him to mean that *if* we share with the other a system of rules for determining the meaning of expressions, or if there is a shared matrix of intelligibility, *then* the responsive difference is effaced. Put differently, he says that "responding *to the Other* differs radically from understanding *the Other* and coming to terms *with the Other.*" That is presumably because the demand of the other solicits a response that provokes new matrices of intelligibility or new rules.[10]

But how can this provocation succeed unless we can come to see those matrices and rules as intelligible (to us) extensions of our own? Waldenfels claims that the challenge of the other's demand puts our own possibilities into question.[11] But how can our possibilities be put into question (for us) unless *we* can come to find them questionable, unless some *intelligible* horizon of alternatives is presented? This seems to be a question of modality: all we can say is that the challenge could *possibly* put "our own possibilities into question," because we cannot know *that* it does until we have some intimation of its *relationship* to our possibilities. For instance, one might say that our possibilities can be put into question in that they do not seem adequate to address the demand of the other. Does not our coming to acknowledge this inadequacy require, no matter how inchoate, some sense of what *we take* the other to be demanding? In this sense, is it not the *intelligibility* of the other's solicitation that is at issue, and is not intelligibility the medium through which we are gauging the adequacy/inadequacy of our possibilities and our response? Our question then becomes, How do we adjust our matrices of intelligibility so that the demand of the other can be brought into focus, however provisional that focus may be? How are we to know what *direction* the alteration of our possibilities is to take? The negation occasioned by the demand of the other must, in this sense, be a *determinate* negation.

That determinate negation could, in turn, occasion the forging of a *medium* of exchange that is no more just "in our hands" than it is in the hands of the other. This would be an *emergent* horizon of intelligibility that would serve as the basis for a decidedly nonhomogeneous form of communion—a form that is structured on an ever-expanding shared vocabulary for discussing and representing, although *not* for standardizing, moral and cultural identity. Furthermore, this is explicitly *not* a universal metalanguage of the sort that would erase or assimilate cultural diversity. It does not, therefore, have the status of what Waldenfels calls the "third person position" that effaces difference and alterity.[12] This negotiated metalanguage—marking an emergent moment of communion as it enables the articulation of difference—is a *situated* metalanguage that is reflexively constituted by difference and alterity, a situated metalanguage co-constituted by self and other. I would thus contest the view that the other can be rendered intelligible only by reducing it to the same.

Why not think of alterity, then, as the provocation to extend our horizon in order to perform the feat of mutually situating "their" meanings in relation to ours? I should think that this would accommodate Waldenfels's concern to recognize genuine alterity's capacity to put *our possibilities* radically into question. And, as I have suggested, how else could our possibilities be put into question? What the expression "radical alterity" quite plausibly refers to is the fact that no understanding of the other is final, complete, not subject to further revision, and so on. There will always be more to say because the other's presence continually challenges any settled interpretive achievement. That is, "radical alterity" refers to the idea that understanding the "other" will always be an "unfinished project."

Waldenfels presents us with a false choice: the demand of the other exceeds meaning and intelligibility per se or it is fully intelligible in being an element of a *pre-given* set of options. Hence, if we quite rightly reject the notion that the *current* configuration of our matrices of intelligibility or of our practices of rule application will be adequate in meeting the challenge of the other's demand, then we are forced to accept the conclusion that the demand of the other exceeds meaning and intelligibility per se.

But how am I to know what direction my response is to take without at least some such provisional understanding, without some *sense* of the demand? If, as Waldenfels acknowledges, "that *with which* I respond owes its meaning to the challenge *to which* I respond,"[13] then must I not have at least a provisional understanding of the *meaning* of the challenge in order to even *orient* my response? If this is so, how can it be that "responding *to the Other* differs [so] radically from *understanding* the *Other* and coming to terms *with the Other*," especially when a proper conception of what it is to understand the other does not require what both Waldenfels and I would reject, namely, the assumption of the standpoint of the Third?

Furthermore, if we have no metric for gauging the demand of the other, what is the source of our confidence that the demand is a legitimate one *meriting* our response? Waldenfels speaks of the "ambivalence of alienness," oscillating between incitation and menace. These are situations where he acknowledges that we are forced to evaluate.[14] In his commentary on the story of Abraham and Isaac, Kierkegaard points out that when Abraham received the call from God to sacrifice Isaac, he had no metric or set of rules that would have allowed him to authenticate this call. He had no means to assure himself that it was indeed the call of God, as opposed to the solicitation of the Devil. Indeed, from the public standpoint of the ethical stance, it could only have been interpreted as either a diabolical command or as a psychotic event. Here Waldenfels's discussion of trust finds its place, the place in which faith enters in Kierkegaard's account.

Waldenfels's analysis of trust is developed to address a particular problem. If, as he assumes, the hiatus between ego and alter is genuine, then we must face the "problem" of how the sociality of community can be generated.[15] But, as I have suggested, we should be wary of accepting that premise. Much as Heidegger averred that the problem of knowledge, in particular the problem of the "external world," arose for philosophy only because it took as its starting point the *artificial separation* of human reality and world, making it problematic whether or not what is "outside" of consciousness could be faithfully represented "inside," I am left to wonder whether the problem of sociality arises for Waldenfels, at least in part, because of the *assumption* of a similarly artificial gulf.

It follows from the foregoing that one can contest Waldenfels's use of "assimilation" to refer to the necessarily distortive refashioning of the heterogeneous material of alterity to fit a previously established matrix or mold, to refer to the sort of polishing away of rough and characteristically distinctive edges of which Derrida accused philosophy in his "White Mythology." As the basis for an alternative to this idea of assimilation as erasure, the conception of understanding that I propose does conceptually involve an act of assimilation, but the act of assimilation involved is a dialectical one in that it is highly unlikely that the matrix invoked at the beginning of the process will prove adequate to its end. What Waldenfels seems to overlook is, as I have argued, that *we may have to change* in order to "situat[e] the other's meaning in relation to the whole of our own meanings or situat[e] ourselves in relation to it."[16] That is, he is captive to the falsely dichotomous picture of "theirs *or* ours," in which "ours" is by implication taken to rigidly resist transformation. The limits of our horizons are elastic. There is thus no line establishable a priori that demarcates what is internal to a self-description from what is necessarily external to it, and this attests to the possibility of a contingently expandable sense of who "we" are. The alterity of others that I find to be salient is an alienness that we can transform into intelligibility to an arbitrarily great degree, even if not exhaustively.

An "ethics of otherness" is not the only alternative to the normalization and the bureaucratization of the court and the clinic.[17] The bureaucratic colonization of the lifeworld and the merely procedural legitimacy of laws can be contested by protecting a space for the risk of the unpremeditated outcomes of genuinely dialogical communicative participation and contestation.[18]

NOTES

INTRODUCTION

1. For recent anthologies aimed at broadening the purview of hermeneutics, see Georgia Warnke, ed., *Inheriting Gadamer: New Directions in Philosophical Hermeneutics* (Edinburgh: Edinburgh University Press, 2016); and Ming Xie, ed., *The Agon of Interpretations: Towards a Critical Intercultural Hermeneutics* (Toronto: University of Toronto Press, 2014).
2. Hans-Georg Gadamer, *Truth and Method*, 2nd rev. ed., trans. Joel Weinshamer and Donald G. Marshall (New York: Continuum, 2002), 475–76.
3. Gadamer, *Truth and Method*, 173–97.
4. Gadamer, *Truth and Method*, 306–7, 374–75, 397, 576; Lorenzo C. Simpson, *The Unfinished Project: Toward a Postmetaphysical Humanism* (London: Routledge, 2001), 80–87.
5. Gadamer, *Truth and Method*, 300–307.
6. Cf. Charles Taylor, *Philosophy and the Human Sciences* (Cambridge: Cambridge University Press, 1985), 9; and Charles Taylor, "Theories of Meaning," in *Human Agency and Language*, vol. 1 (Cambridge: Cambridge University Press, 1985).
7. Hans-Georg Gadamer, *Philosophical Hermeneutics* (Berkeley: University of California Press, 1976), 63.
8. Gadamer, *Truth and Method*, 429, 435–36.
9. Gadamer, *Truth and Method*, 444.
10. Gadamer, *Philosophical Hermeneutics*, 13.

11. Gadamer, *Philosophical Hermeneutics*, 11.
12. Lorenzo C. Simpson, *Technology, Time and the Conversations of Modernity* (London: Routledge, 1995); and Simpson, *The Unfinished Project*.
13. See, for instance, Jürgen Habermas, *On the Logic of the Social Sciences* (Cambridge, MA: MIT Press, 1988), 143–70; and Hans-Georg Gadamer, "On the Scope and Function of Hermeneutical Reflection," in *Philosophical Hermeneutics*, trans. David E. Linge (Berkeley: University of California Press, 1976). I offer a brief account of this exchange in Simpson, *Technology, Time and the Conversations of Modernity*, 92–94.
14. Habermas, *On the Logic of the Social Sciences*, 166–70.
15. Gadamer, "On the Scope and Function of Hermeneutical Reflection," 31.
16. Paul Ricoeur, *Freud and Philosophy: An Essay on Interpretation* (New Haven, CT: Yale University Press, 1965), 32–36.

1. TWIN EARTH AND ITS HORIZONS: ON HERMENEUTICS, REFERENCE, AND SCIENTIFIC THEORY CHOICE

1. This fabulation was loosely inspired by Richard Rorty, "Texts and Lumps," in *Philosophical Papers*, Vol. 1, *Objectivity, Relativism, and Truth* (Cambridge: Cambridge University Press, 1991), 78–92. Although obviously a caricature, I think it captures some of the salient differences in philosophical styles.
2. Cristina Lafont, *The Linguistic Turn in Hermeneutic Philosophy*, trans. José Medina (Cambridge, MA: MIT Press, 1999).
3. Martin Heidegger, *On the Way to Language*, trans. Peter D. Hertz (San Francisco: Harper Collins, 1971), 60–68; and Martin Heidegger, "The Letter on Humanism," in *Martin Heidegger: Basic Writings*, ed. David F. Krell (New York: Harper and Row, 1977), 193.
4. Hans-Georg Gadamer, *Truth and Method*, 2nd rev. ed., trans. Joel Weinshamer and Donald G. Marshall (New York: Continuum, 2002), 443.
5. Cf. especially, Lafont, *The Linguistic Turn*; and Cristina Lafont, *Heidegger, Language and World-Disclosure*, trans. Graham Harman (Cambridge: Cambridge University Press, 2000).
6. Lafont, *The Linguistic Turn*, 228–29.

7. Jürgen Habermas, *The Philosophical Discourse of Modernity: Twelve Lectures*, trans. Frederick Lawrence (Cambridge, MA: MIT Press, 1987), 319; partially cited in Lafont, *The Linguistic Turn*, 222.
8. Lafont, *The Linguistic Turn*, 222.
9. This agreement need not be explicit. It is not that the certainty that a topic is shared is typically *itself* thematized as a topic in the conversation, although there can certainly be cues that it is not shared, cues that can in turn instigate an investigation to determine whether it is or not. When faced with a surprising or deep disagreement, interlocutors can ask each other if they are referring to an x with the properties 1 . . . n to assure themselves that they are indeed talking about the same thing. The more elaborate the description that yields consensus, the more confident are the interlocutors that they are talking about the same thing. The more falsifiable is the claim that they are addressing the same topic, the more they can be assured of it if they retain consensus.
10. Lafont, *The Linguistic Turn*, 112n35.
11. Cristina Lafont, "Hermeneutics," in *The Blackwell Companion to Heidegger*, ed. H. Dreyfus and M. Wrathall (Cambridge, MA: Blackwell, 2005), 281.
12. Norwood Russell Hanson, *Patterns of Discovery: An Inquiry Into the Conceptual Foundations of Science* (Cambridge: Cambridge University Press, 1958), 4–30.
13. Israel Scheffler, *Science and Subjectivity* (Indianapolis: Bobbs-Merrill, 1967); Israel Scheffler, "Vision and Revolution: A Postscript on Kuhn," *Philosophy of Science* 39 (1972): 366–74; Dudley Shapere, "The Structure of Scientific Revolutions," *The Philosophical Review* 73 (1964): 383–94; Dudley Shapere, "Meaning and Scientific Change," *Mind and Cosmos: Essays in Contemporary Science and Philosophy*, ed. R. Colodny (Pittsburgh: University of Pittsburgh Press, 1966), 41–85; and Dudley Shapere, "The Paradigm Concept," *Science* 172 (1971): 706–9. The account presented here is informed by the discussion in Gerald Doppelt, "Kuhn's Epistemological Relativism," in *Relativism: Cognitive and Moral*, ed. M. Krausz and J. Meiland (Notre Dame: University of Notre Dame Press, 1982), 113–46. See also W. H. Newton-Smith, *The Rationality of Science* (London: Routledge, 1999), 158–73.
14. Doppelt, "Kuhn's Epistemological Relativism," 117–18.

15. See Avrum Stroll, *Twentieth-Century Analytic Philosophy* (New York: Columbia University Press, 2000), 220–30.
16. Stephen Schwartz, ed., *Naming, Necessity, and Natural Kinds* (Ithaca, NY: Cornell University Press, 1977), 20–34.
17. Hilary Putnam, "Meaning and Reference," in *Naming, Necessity, and Natural Kinds*, ed. Stephen Schwarz (Ithaca, NY: Cornell University Press, 1977), 119–32.
18. Stroll, *Twentieth-Century Analytic Philosophy*, 244.
19. For example, *pace* Putnam and Kripke, John Justice argues that even the bits of language that would seem to most uncontroversially effect their reference directly, bits such as proper names and indexicals, have a referent-determining Fregean sense. John Justice, "The Semantics of Rigid Designation," *Ratio* 16 (2003): 33–48. Taking as his point of departure the embarrassment that direct reference theories face when confronted with the phenomenon of fictive objects, Avrum Stroll, *pace* Marcus and Geach, rejects the idea that fictive objects cannot be objects of reference and simply denies that proper names are necessarily rigid designators, thus challenging the notion that there is a relevant difference between names and descriptions with respect to referential power. Avrum Stroll, "Proper Names, Names and Fictive Objects," *Journal of Philosophy* 95 (1998): 522–33.
20. Ruth Barcan Marcus, "Modalities and Intensional Languages," *Synthese* 13 (1961): 309; reprinted in Ruth Barcan Marcus, *Modalities: Philosophical Essays* (Oxford: Oxford University Press, 1993), 3–38.
21. Marcus, "Modalities and Intensional Languages," 309–10.
22. Martin Heidegger, *Being and Time*, trans. John Macquarrie and Edward Robinson (New York: Harper and Row, 1962), 199, H 156–57.
23. Heidegger, *Being and Time*, 203–4, H 161.
24. John Dupré, "Natural Kinds," chap. 46 in *A Companion to the Philosophy of Science*, ed. W. H. Newton-Smith (Oxford: Blackwell, 2000), 315.
25. Dupré, "Natural Kinds," 311; and Scott Soames, *Philosophical Analysis in the Twentieth Century* (Princeton, NJ: Princeton University Press, 2003), 2:440.
26. Dupré, "Natural Kinds," 315–16.
27. On the problematic status of essentialism in the concept of species membership, see also Joseph LaPorte, *Natural Kinds and Conceptual Change* (Cambridge: Cambridge University Press, 2004), 52–62.

28. Richard Rorty, *Philosophy and the Mirror of Nature* (Princeton, NJ: Princeton University Press, 1979), 276.
29. Cf. Keith Donnellan, "Proper Names and Identifying Descriptions," *Synthese* 21 (1970): 335–58; and Saul Kripke, "Naming and Necessity," in *Semantics of Natural Language*, ed. Donald Davidson and Gilbert Harman (Dordrecht: D. Reidel, 1972), 253–355; cited in Rorty, *Philosophy and the Mirror of Nature*, 288n24.
30. Rorty, *Philosophy and the Mirror of Nature*, 294–95. Rorty suggests that even here reference, as opposed to merely "talking about," is anchored in intentional attitudes. Cf. Rorty, *Philosophy and the Mirror of Nature*, 289–95.
31. See Hilary Putnam, *Meaning and the Moral Sciences* (London: Routledge, 1976), 125–26.
32. In an earlier work, I give an account of what I call the scientific "prejudice" and of the nature of the field of referents it projects. Lorenzo C. Simpson, *Technology, Time, and the Conversations of Modernity* (London: Routledge, 1995), 33–39.
33. See Putnam, *Meaning and the Moral Sciences*, 123.
34. Rorty, *Philosophy and the Mirror of Nature*, 299; cf. also with Joseph Margolis, *The Persistence of Reality: Texts Without Referents* (Oxford: Basil Blackwell, 1989), 235–71.
35. Cf. Linda Martín Alcoff, *Real Knowing: New Versions of the Coherence Theory* (Ithaca, NY: Cornell University Press, 1996), 169, 176, 198, 222.
36. See Hilary Putnam, *Mind, Language, and Reality* (New York: Cambridge University Press, 1975), 124–25.
37. Gadamer, *Truth and Method*, 378, 388.
38. On sameness of reference, there are no guarantees, but as I point out in Note 9, there are constraints. And there may well be cases in which the assessment of descriptive/referential harmony may require more than attending to what people say, but also to what they do. Even if our interlocutors do not deploy a vocabulary for picking out a particular referent that is readily translatable into ours, they may well have practices that overlap saliently with those that we associate with the referent. That is, they may treat a class of objects in ways that are *analogous* to the ways we treat a class of things that are of referential interest. So harmonizing interpretations can involve both what we say and what

we do. For further discussion of this idea in the context of meaningful cross-cultural conversation, see Lorenzo C. Simpson, *The Unfinished Project: Toward a Postmetaphysical Humanism* (London: Routledge, 2001), 78–98.

39. Simpson, *The Unfinished Project*, 78–98.
40. For a discussion of this example, see LaPorte, *Natural Kinds and Conceptual Change*, 126–30.
41. Hans-Georg Gadamer, *Philosophical Hermeneutics*, trans. David E. Linge (Berkeley: University of California Press, 1976), 63.
42. Simpson, *The Unfinished Project*, 91–92.
43. John Searle, "Proper Names," *Mind* 76 (1958): 166–73; and John Searle, *Speech Acts* (Cambridge: Cambridge University Press, 1969), 55. See also P. F. Strawson, *Individuals: An Essay in Descriptive Metaphysics* (London: Methuen, 1959), 180–83, 190–94.
44. Moreover, it can be argued that such a cluster-of-descriptions view fares no worse than does the causal theory of reference when it comes to blocking drastic shifts of reference across theory change. LaPorte, *Natural Kinds and Conceptual Change*, 116–18.

Arriving at a position similar to the one I propose but from a different route, Gilbert Harman and Ned Block also suggest that the holist can avoid the aporetic quagmires of incommensurability and nonintertranslatability "by replacing the dichotomy between agreement and disagreement with a gradient of similarity of meaning." Ned Block, "Holism: Mental and Semantic," in *Routledge Encyclopedia of Philosophy*, ed. E. Craig (London: Routledge, 1998). I would go further here by suggesting that if speakers from distinct theoretical contexts were mutually and systematically assured of the similarity of meaning, then it would be unintelligible, except from a third-person standpoint, to suggest that there is disagreement where agreement is presumed. The metric for assessing adequate similarity would be determined by the purposive contexts in which the interlocutors are engaged. This would have the linguistic implication that, as Nelson Goodman has suggested, synonymy designates a similarity relation, one of sufficient similarity with respect to a given purpose or set of concerns. Nelson Goodman, *The Structure of Appearance* (Cambridge, MA: Harvard University Press), 1951.

45. Writing from an explicitly hermeneutical standpoint, Dimitri Ginev argues for the continuity across historical/conceptual change of a shared historical constitution of the theoretical scientific world. Dimitri Ginev, *A Passage to the Hermeneutic Philosophy of Science* (Amsterdam: Rodopi, 1997), 62–66. This continuity is assured by virtue of the fact that subsequent theories can be understood to be interpretations of previous ones. In a related spirit, Fine and Earman also adduce evidence to the effect that Einstein, in his special theory of relativity, understood "mass" in the same way that it is understood in Newtonian mechanics. Arthur Fine and J. Earman, "Against Indeterminacy," *Journal of Philosophy* 74, no. 9 (1977): 535–38.
46. Unlike some writers who, appropriately enough, are impressed by the notion of the theory ladenness of experience, I do not believe that acknowledging that there is no "language-independent framework of *experiences* that scientific theories are about" is necessarily to abet the vitiation of the relative distinction between theoretical discourse and experience. See, for example, Steven Vogel, *Against Nature: The Concept of Nature in Critical Theory* (Albany: State University of New York Press, 1996), 128. I have claimed that the fact that there is no linguistically innocent experience does not mean that there cannot be paradigm invariant experience. Or put in a slightly different way, the theories that constitute data are *not* ineluctably the theories that are at issue in rendering an account of the data.
47. Lafont, "Hermeneutics," 282.
48. Reflecting more broadly on the hermeneutical concept of tradition, tradition represents a normative phenomenon in that it determines what can be meaningfully predicated of worldly things. It determines the conditions of intelligibility to which we are subject, what can be said, for instance, without making category mistakes. Analogous to the verificationist criterion of meaning, the structure of tradition does not determine what *is* true or false but what sorts of claims are candidates for having truth value of various sorts. So the truth that shows in a happening of tradition is like the appearance of a logical space, not of a claim about what position in that logical space is being occupied.

 I contend that, ultimately, the concept of tradition, as a determinate context whose limits and determinateness can be specified prior to a hermeneutic encounter, does not do the delimiting work that we might expect of it if it is to make the hermeneut's insistence that interlocutors "must share the same tradition" meaningful when providing an account of what emerges or results from such an encounter. See Gadamer, *Truth and Method*, 293, 295. Given the priority of Gadamer's logic of question and answer, the tradition in which an act of understanding takes place is *always constructed* as opposed to found (in such a way that it can be identified before the encounter and reidentified after the encounter). The tradition that, according to Gadamer, I must share with my interlocutor is always going to be, at least in part, the product of the questions that *I* can see her responses as answers to. Therefore, no matter how exotic or recondite her "actual" tradition may be, I always *write her into* my tradition, or better perhaps, she is always being written into my tradition—or better yet, we are written into each other's tradition—in virtue of my unavoidable projection of the questions that I understand her to answer. Ultimately, I maintain that for hermeneutics, in this sense, "tradition" refers to any connection that humans can make (the tradition of humanity), and perhaps for reasons similar to Davidson's argument that a plurality of conceptual schemes is unintelligible, there cannot be a plurality of traditions for hermeneutics. At the very least, these considerations justify a blurring of the distinction between discourse within a tradition and discourse across traditions. Although arriving at this conclusion via a different route than the one I take here, Gadamer would seem to concur with my claim that tradition is singular: "everything contained in historical consciousness is in fact embraced by a single historical horizon." Gadamer, *Truth and Method*, 304.

49. See also my arguments against this inside/outside metaphor in Simpson, *Technology, Time, and the Conversations of Modernity*, 95–132. In addition, see my argument against there being a difference in kind between intracontextual and intercontextual discourse in Simpson, *The Unfinished Project*, 81–83, 104–5, 109–10.

50. See Bas van Fraassen, *The Scientific Image* (Oxford: Clarendon Press, 1980), 41–44, 64.

51. Ronald N. Giere, "Theories," in *A Companion to the Philosophy of Science*, ed. W. H. Newton-Smith (Oxford: Blackwell, 2000), 521.

52. It is essential to Lafont that our understanding of entities acknowledge "that they may be different from what and how we understand them as being." Lafont, "Hermeneutics," 282. But does she mean different from what and how we *currently* understand them to be, or from what we *in principle* can understand them to be? If the former, then this emendation can easily be accommodated within hermeneutics; if the latter, then it is true that a decisive break with hermeneutics would be required. But is what is implied in this view plausible? Again, she believes that fallibilism requires direct reference. This is but a repetition of the claim that to acknowledge the theory ladenness of data is ineluctably to commit oneself to relativism. But this simply does not follow as long as the theories being tested are logically independent of the theory that informs the data.

We can distinguish between what can be referred to as more or less observational vocabularies, on the one hand, and as more or less theoretical vocabularies, on the other, although no sharp distinction can be drawn between the two. We may determine what dimensions of experience or logical spaces will be of interest in an investigation of nature, but we do not thereby determine just what *position* in that logical space nature will turn out to occupy. For example, we might determine that electrical current as measured by an ammeter is a relevant logical space, but we do not thereby determine just what ammeter reading will obtain—we can only make intelligent guesses or predictions about it.

Second, it is not clear to me that many postempiricist philosophers of science do justice to the relative stability of nature at this second or phenomenal level. Unless one adopts a problematic holistic conception of scientific meaning whereby the entire observational language used by a theoretical paradigm to characterize its data has its meaning ineluctably and exhaustively "infected" or determined by the paradigm's own unique meanings, it does not follow that, as Steven Vogel, among others, has written, "if scientists see the world differently after a paradigm shift then the very conditions of objectivation themselves would seem to have changed." Instead, one would have to acknowledge that observation statements can have a relative stability across paradigm changes. Vogel, *Against Nature*, 128.

Our conceptions of the empirical world are no doubt informed by prevailing theories about it, but such conceptions are *relatively* more stable than are those theories; the scope of agreement about facts of observation is far wider than is the scope of agreement about the theoretical apprehension of those facts. To deny this is to deny the obvious fact that there can be disagreement at the theoretical/explanatory level about how to account for facts that the disputants acknowledge. The Hanson-inspired distinction among levels of "seeing as" is also relevant here: *Both* Tycho Brahe and Kepler see the scene before them *as* one in which the distance between the Sun and the Earth's horizon is increasing; however, one sees it *as* the Sun rising and the other sees it *as* the horizon falling away. And although Joseph Priestly and Antoine-Laurent Lavoisier conceptualized the stuff involved in combustion differently, one construing it as "phlogiston" and the other as "oxygen," they could nevertheless agree on relevant experiments.

2. CRITICAL FUSIONS: TOWARD A GENUINE "HERMENEUTICS OF SUSPICION"

1. See Lorenzo C. Simpson, *The Unfinished Project: Toward a Postmetaphysical Humanism* (London: Routledge, 2001).
2. Simpson, *The Unfinished Project*, 78–80, 89.
3. Bernhard Waldenfels, "Der Andere und Der Dritte im interkulturelller Sicht," in *Ethik und Politik aus interkultureller Sicht*, ed. R. A. Mall and N. Schneider (Amsterdam: Rodopi, 1996), 71–83; and Bernhard Waldenfels, *The Question of the Other* (Hong Kong: Chinese University Press, 2007).
4. Richard Rorty, "What Can You Expect from Anti-Foundationalist Philosophers?: A Reply to Lynn Baker," *Virginia Law Review* 78, no. 3 (Apr., 1992): 719–27.
5. Hans-Georg Gadamer, "The Hermeneutics of Suspicion," *Man and World* 17 (1984): 313–23.
6. Hans-Georg Gadamer, "The Scope and Function of Hermeneutical Reflection," in *Philosophical Hermeneutics*, trans. David E. Linge (Berkeley: University of California Press, 1976), 31.
7. In keeping with this, in Simpson, *The Unfinished Project*, I elaborated an argument for what I call "humanity as an unfinished project," an argument that suggests that humanity is to be understood in a

postmetaphysical fashion, is to be understood as *forged* rather than *found*. This position was developed in part to propose an alternative, in discussions of community and difference, to liberal appeals to an overlapping consensus; to the communitarian failure to do justice to difference; and to postmodern tendencies to valorize fragmentation.

8. Simpson, *Unfinished Project*, 83.
9. On the obstacles posed to intercultural translation by asymmetrical power relations, see Talal Asad, "The Concept of Cultural Translation in British Social Anthropology," in *Writing Culture: The Poetics and Politics of Ethnography*, ed. James Clifford and George E. Marcus (Berkeley: University of California Press, 1986).
10. See Simpson, *Unfinished Project*, 87.
11. Hans-Georg Gadamer, *Truth and Method*, 2nd rev. ed. (New York: Continuum, 2002), 293–94.
12. I also address this issue in chapter 1 in my discussion of topic identification.
13. There are two constraints on the metalinguistic predicates that are invoked in a situated metalanguage. On the one hand, we have to avoid vacuity; the predicates must have sharp enough boundaries to be meaningfully applied. On the other hand, we need capaciousness; the predicates must be flexible and expansive enough to subsume competing conceptions. So the *Sache* or topic that we dialogically adduce in the analogical process I discuss here must be fashioned at a sufficiently "low altitude" to have adequately concrete criteria of application to *exclude* some candidates from inclusion. Yet such a topic must have purchase at a sufficiently high altitude or level of generality to embrace or fuse conceptions on both sides of an intercultural dialogue. There has been a great deal of discussion among cultural anthropologists, art historians, and philosophers of art regarding the transcultural status of aesthetic judgment that usefully illuminates these issues. Participants in that discussion have demonstrated, for instance, that judgments of aesthetic merit have *meaning* on both sides of cultural divides. The social anthropologist Howard Morphy has argued, for example, that, when "aesthetic" is taken to name the dimension within which *formal* properties are apprehended independently of function, the "aesthetic" meets the criteria that I have adduced for a viable cross-cultural predicate. In this way, he offers an illuminating account of the cross-cultural

purchase of the concept of the aesthetic. Howard Morphy et al., "Aesthetics Is a Cross Cultural Category," in *Key Debates in Anthropology*, ed. Tim Ingold (London: Routledge, 1996), 258. To illustrate this point, many experts claim that, despite differences in what counts as aesthetically satisfying, many African societies, for example, seem to acknowledge a meaningful, if not absolute, distinction between aesthetic value and functional sufficiency. See Robert Ferris Thompson, "Esthetics in Traditional Africa," *Art News* 66 (1968): 44–45, 63–66; and the summary discussion in Frank Willett, *African Art* (New York: Thames and Hudson, 1971), 208–22. As H. Gene Blocker implies, even if members of the culture in question do not have anything in their vocabulary corresponding to our word "art," they may well have practices that overlap saliently with those that we associate with art. H. Gene Blocker, *The Aesthetics of Primitive Art* (Lanham, MD: University Press of America, 1994), 147–48. That is, they may treat a class of objects in their world in ways that are *analogous* to the ways we treat art objects.

14. Indeed, the cultural theorist Stuart Hall has suggested that because one's identity is a matter of the articulation of one's self-conception in the context of the changing, and perhaps conflicting, resources for intelligibility ("ideologies") that one encounters, identity is a malleable property. Stuart Hall, *Essential Essays, vol. 2: Identity and Diaspora*, ed. David Morley (Durham, NC: Duke University Press, 2019), 69.

15. See Simpson, *Unfinished Project*, 139–40.

16. See, for example, Thomas McCarthy, *Race, Empire, and the Idea of Human Development* (Cambridge: Cambridge University Press, 2009), 243.

17. Bhikhu Parekh, *Rethinking Multiculturalism: Cultural Diversity and Political Theory* (Cambridge, MA: Harvard University Press, 2000), 148. This is a position to which Gadamer is sympathetic, for he reminds us that "the closed horizon that is supposed to enclose a culture is an abstraction." Gadamer, *Truth and Method*, 304.

18. United Nations Research Institute for Social Development, *Gender, Justice, Development and Rights* (New York: UNRISD Workshop, June 3, 2000); cited in Monique Deveaux, "A Deliberative Approach to Conflicts of Culture," *Political Theory* 31 (December 2003): 780–807.

19. See Simpson, *The Unfinished Project*, 105, 109–10, 112.

20. See, for example, Deveaux, "A Deliberative Approach to Conflicts of Culture."
21. Akeel Bilgrami, "What Is a Muslim? Fundamental Commitment and Cultural Identity," *Critical Inquiry* 18 (1992): 821–42.
22. Bilgrami, "What Is a Muslim?," 823. When we think of the controversy surrounding the so-called Rushdie affair, we should note that, given the highly charged and contested nature of intracultural struggles to articulate and systematize expressions of cultural identity, the Muslim reaction to Salman Rushdie's *The Satanic Verses*, and to the *fatwah* that followed its publication calling for his death, was hardly uniform. See Sadik J. Al-Azm, "The Importance of Being Earnest About Salmon Rushdie," *Die Welt des Islams* 31, no. 1 (1991): 1–49, esp. 34.
23. Bilgrami, "What Is a Muslim?,"823; and Akeel Bilgrami, "Rushdie. Islam, and Postcolonial Defensiveness," *Yale Journal of Criticism* 4 (Fall 1990): 301–11.
24. Yael Tamir, "Liberal Nationalism," *Philosophy and Public Policy* (Winter/Spring 1993): 4.
25. I have discussed the within group struggle to expand the moral imaginary in terms of persuading members of dominant social groups to acknowledge the semantic authority of claims put forth by others. On the concept of semantic authority, see Simpson, *The Unfinished Project*, 110–11; and Lorenzo C. Simpson, "Humanism and Cosmopolitanism After '68," *New Formations* 65 (Fall 2008): 57–58, 64–65. By this I mean to highlight the importance of ensuring that a claim made by a particular social group has a claim on all, that it be recognized as a general claim. This would compel interlocutors both to make perspicuous the hermeneutic and social contexts implicated in such a claim *and* to make a genuine and open-minded effort to assess the extent to which such a claim is generally compelling, that is, the extent to which it has purchase beyond the specific sociocultural context of its generation. Such a general claim would be one that *addresses* everyone, one that ultimately invites reply. It is a claim that is to be taken seriously by *all* as a *candidate* for a perspicuous description of the world, one that renders salient features that should command respectful attention. Such an acknowledgment involves treating the other's claim as making a claim on all, not by demanding acknowledgment or accession by force but by getting

each to recognize that it is addressed to them as a possible way for all to view the world that they share. And it might be discovered that mutual efforts to understand the heretofore marginalized or newly emergent descriptions may initiate social learning processes whereby what was previously seen as (merely) private becomes a matter of right, bearing with it concomitant demands for public recognition and regulation.

To treat a claim as general in this way is to treat it as a speech act that imposes a mutual burden: the "addressee" assumes the obligation of taking the claim seriously enough to enter, along with the sender, a dialogically constituted space of reasons and reasoning in considering its general applicability; the "sender" assumes an obligation to justify the claim or a particular application of a term or to persuade the addressee, again in a mutually forged justificatory language, of the usefulness of so applying the term. To treat a claim as general in this way is to take it up in such a way that we are willing genuinely to risk having our view of things challenged, without of course there being any *guarantee* that we will be so persuaded. General claims remain defeasible, criticizable claims. But to fail to seek to understand, and to take such claims seriously *as claims*, is to fail to give the other her due. To take examples from our society, to treat, say, sexual harassment and police brutality as merely descriptions of social interaction from the points of view of women and Blacks, respectively, with no presumption that these descriptions will have *general semantic authority*, is to enact a restriction that would allow these issues to be understood as simply idiosyncratic matters of "their perception," where *their* perception has unfortunately become *our* collective problem, a problem to be handled perhaps strategically rather than to be understood as a matter of what their perception *reveals* about our *common* social reality.

26. On the latter, see Simpson, *The Unfinished Project*, 83, 91–92.
27. Deveaux, "A Deliberative Approach to Conflicts of Culture," 788.
28. On the occasion of a seminar that the cultural anthropologist Renato Rosaldo offered at the Humanities Institute at SUNY Stony Brook on September 9, 1999, I understood him to offer the following methodological advice in response to a question I put to him concerning strategic representation: One should in the first instance take what is said at face value but be prepared to question it when, for instance,

conversations with others seem to contradict it or when the respondent's own behavior seems to belie what s/he has said. Then go on to hazard interpretive projections of the form, "what would be the case if what the 'informant' has said is true? or false?" Then, making the process recursive, return to engage the interlocutor in a confirmatory or disconfirmatory dialogue informed by what one has learned.

29. See Lorenzo C. Simpson, "On Habermas and Particularity: Is There Room for Race and Gender on the Glassy Plains of Ideal Discourse?," *Praxis International* 6 (1986): 338.

30. Jürgen Habermas, *Legitimation Crisis*, trans. Thomas McCarthy (Boston: Beacon, 1975), 114.

31. Habermas, *Legitimation Crisis*, 114.

32. The health implications of female genital cutting have been well-documented. See, for example, UN Office of the High Commissioner for Human Rights, *Human Rights Fact Sheet 23: Harmful Traditional Practices Affecting the Health of Women and Children* (Geneva: United Nations, August 1995); cited in Sally Sheldon and Stephen Wilkinson, "Female Genital Mutilation and Cosmetic Surgery: Regulating Non-Therapeutic Body Modification," *Bioethics* 12 (1998): 263–85.

33. Here I am not concerned to address the putative inconsistency or hypocrisy of Western objections to such practices while apparently tolerating potentially dangerous forms of cosmetic surgery aimed at increasing sexual desirability. See Sheldon and Wilkinson, "Female Genital Mutilation and Cosmetic Surgery." I am concerned to elaborate mechanisms for critical response to such practices that are untethered to "Western" views.

34. The idealization implied in the notion of "safe" spaces is deployed as an assumption in my argument for the metaethical claim that non-question-begging, critical cross-cultural conversations can be meaningfully held. It does not address the equally important political question of how such spaces are to be created, maintained, and respected as sources of proposals that are treated as candidates for semantic authority, that is, as candidates for general social recognition and acknowledgment.

35. On this spectrum of procedures, see Anna Elisabetta Galeotti, "Relativism, Universalism, and Applied Ethics: The Case of Female Circumcision," *Constellations* 14 (March 2007): 91–111.

36. Amy Allen provides a gloss on the concept of autonomy that is useful for the concerns of this chapter, namely, that autonomy is the capacity of "critical reflection: the capacity to reflect critically upon the state of one's self . . . on the norms, practices, and institutions that structure [one's life] . . . and, on this basis to chart paths for future transformation." Amy Allen, *The Politics of Our Selves: Power, Autonomy, and Gender in Contemporary Critical Theory* (New York: Columbia University Press, 2008), 2.

37. A plausible gloss on the idea of autonomous choice would be to say that a preference is chosen autonomously when it can be reflexively endorsed and when such endorsement entails the assumption, on the part of the agent, of the responsibility to defend or justify that preference to a relevant community of peers if challenged. A further plausible condition, if not an explicit "Strawsonian" prerequisite, of a meaningful autonomy claim is an awareness of alternative intelligible options. For further discussion of the first point, of the "communicative" conception of autonomy, see Kenneth Baynes, "The Self and Individual Autonomy in the Frankfurt School," in *The Routledge Companion to the Frankfurt School*, ed. Peter Gordon, Axel Honneth, and Espen Hammer (London: Routledge, 2018), 424–38; and Paul Benson, "Taking Ownership: Authority and Voice in Autonomous Agency," in *Autonomy and the Challenges to Liberalism*, ed. John Christman and Joel Anderson (Cambridge: Cambridge University Press, 2005), 101–26.

38. For a consideration of this issue, see Marina Oshana, *Personal Autonomy in Society* (Hampshire, UK: Ashgate, 1988), 123–42. The spheres of culture that are "autonomy eligible" may vary, both historically and geographically. On this, see Jürgen Habermas, *Theory of Communicative Action*, Vol. 1, *Reason and the Rationalization of Society* (Boston, MA: Beacon, 1985), 340; and Jürgen Habermas, *Moral Consciousness and Communicative Action*, trans. Christian Lenhardt and Shierry Weber Nicholsen (Cambridge, MA: MIT Press, 1990), 199. See also Baynes, "The Self and Individual Autonomy in the Frankfurt School." My concern, of course, is to situate my conversational model within contexts in which autonomy claims are made and exchanged.

39. My account of autonomy blends aspects of both what in the literature are referred to as *internalist* and *externalist* accounts of the

phenomenon. Although I concentrate here on internalist aspects of autonomy, namely, on second-order endorsement of first-order choices and preferences, there are externalist aspects of my account as well. See Oshana, *Personal Autonomy in Society*, 21–23, 87. Even in cases in which the requisite second-order endorsement is forthcoming, I ask whether or not the conditions governing what is available to particular social agents as a first-order preference are invidious or arbitrary. A further point is that even if we acknowledge that endorsement per se is insufficient as a criterial property of autonomy and require that autonomous agents also assume the burden of discursively defending their choices, such agents are obliged only to assume responsibility for responding to challenges that are appropriate and intelligible to them given their own evaluative standpoint or matrix of intelligibility (cf. Benson, "Taking Ownership," 113). So this emendation would remain compatible with the hermeneutic account that I wish to develop here. To act autonomously is to act on reasons, and what will count as a reason for an agent is determined by the web of significance in which she finds herself.

40. See Miranda Fricker, *Epistemic Injustice: Power and the Ethics of Knowing* (Oxford: Oxford University Press, 2007), 152–53.
41. See note 25 above.
42. In this way, my position addresses one of the concerns expressed in "recognitional" accounts of autonomy, namely, the semantic vulnerability that can compromise autonomous agency. See, for example, Joel Anderson and Axel Honneth, "Autonomy, Vulnerability, Recognition, and Justice," in *Autonomy and the Challenges to Liberalism*, ed. John Christman and Joel Anderson, 127–49.
43. Maendeleo Ya Wanawake, "FGM—Advocacy Strategy for the Eradication of Female Genital Mutilation in Kenya," 2000, http://www.maendeleo-ya-wanake.org/. See also Jane Njeri Chege, Ian Askew, and Jennifer Liku, "An Assessment of the Alternative Rites Approach for Encouraging Abandonment of Female Genital Mutilation in Kenya," in *Frontiers in Reproductive Health* (Washington, DC: United States Agency for International Development, 2001). The implementation of institutionalized alternatives to excision, access to those alternatives, and the *awareness* of the existence of and potential access to them on the part of female agents collectively address an important dimension

of agency that I discuss in the next chapter. They are illustrative of what I call conditions of second-order agency. I argue that we should distinguish between agential capacities of the first order, to wit, the capacity to produce an effect or to bring about a state of affairs (in the case under consideration, perhaps to lead a life that combines social flourishing and bodily integrity), and agential capacities of the second order, to wit, the awareness of and the ability to acquire or to avail oneself of the enabling or facilitating conditions of agency in the first-order sense. The latter, second-order capacities are then those that condition the exercise of capacities of the first order. Satisfaction of the conditions of second-order agency can be understood as an enabling condition of self-transformation in that it contributes to the motivational support requisite to the actualization of emancipatory self-transformation. See Allen, *The Politics of Our Selves*, 12.

44. Celia W. Dugger, "A Movement to End Female Genital Mutilation Spreads in Senegal," *New York Times*, October 16, 2011.

3. AGENCY, THE "POLITICS OF MEMORY," AND REPARATIVE JUSTICE: HERMENEUTICS AND THE POLITICS OF DEVELOPMENT

1. Thomas McCarthy, *Race, Empire, and the Idea of Human Development* (Cambridge: Cambridge University Press, 2009).
2. See the discussion in chapter 4.
3. McCarthy, *Race, Empire, and the Idea of Human Development*, 103–7.
4. Barack Obama, "Remarks by the President in the Eulogy for the Honorable Reverend Clementa Pickney," White House Office of the Press Secretary, June 26, 2015, https://obamawhitehouse.archives.gov/the-press-office/2015/06/26/remarks-president-eulogy-honorable-reverend-clementa-pinckney.
5. McCarthy, *Race, Empire, and the Idea of Human Development*, 10. As evidence of the continuing currency of the "culture of poverty" thesis in our policy discourse, I note that Republican congressman and former vice presidential candidate Paul Ryan deployed it as late as spring 2014 in a town hall meeting. And an even more recent recrudescence of this idea can be found in David Brooks, "The Nature of Poverty," *New York Times*, May 1, 2015.

6. McCarthy, *Race, Empire, and the Idea of Human Development*, 11.
7. See Serene J. Khader, *Adaptive Preferences and Women's Empowerment* (Oxford: Oxford University Press, 2011), 56.
8. See my discussion of semantic authority in chapter 2; see also Miranda Fricker, *Epistemic Injustice: Power and the Ethics of Knowing* (Oxford: Oxford University Press, 2007), 145–6.
9. Glenn Loury, "The Moral Quandary of the Black Community," *The Public Interest* 79 (Spring 1985): 19.
10. Brooks, "The Nature of Poverty," A31.
11. See Lorenzo C. Simpson, *The Unfinished Project: Toward a Postmetaphysical Humanism* (London: Routledge, 2001), 80–87.
12. See Charles Taylor, "Interpretation and the Science of Man," *Review of Metaphysics* 25, no. 1 (1971): 17–38; also cited in Paul Rabinow and William Sullivan, eds., *Interpretive Social Science* (Berkeley: University of California Press, 1979), 68.
13. Thomas McCarthy, "Rationality and Relativism: Habermas's 'Overcoming of Hermeneutics'," in *Habermas: Critical Debates*, ed. J. B. Thompson and David Held (Cambridge, MA: MIT Press, 1982), 70.
14. See Lorenzo C. Simpson, *Technology, Time, and the Conversations of Modernity* (London: Routledge, 1995), 106–7, 201, 202n21.
15. See McCarthy, *Race, Empire, and the Idea of Human Development*, 161.
16. Here I have in mind, as paradigm cases, strategically generated false beliefs whose falsehood the agent is not in a position to detect.
17. See John Locke, *An Essay Concerning Human Understanding*, book 2, chap. 21, par. 10.
18. See Andrew Delbanco, "Our Universities: The Outrageous Reality," *New York Review of Books* 62, no. 12 (July 9, 2015): 38–39.
19. McCarthy, *Race, Empire, and the Idea of Human Development*, 235.
20. Khader, *Adaptive Preferences*, 31, 113. Khader's is, in part, an argument for the agential capacities of oppressed or marginalized groups. Mine is an argument against the assumption of a lack of agency without the requisite hermeneutic diagnosis.
21. Khader, *Adaptive Preferences*.
22. See Diana Tietjens, "Feminism and Women's Autonomy: The Challenge of Female Genital Cutting," *Metaphilosophy* 31, no. 5 (October 2000): 475.
23. This oblivion is a symptom of the epistemic gap between the first-person perspective of the agent and the third-person perspective of the

judging observer, and it can assume at least two forms: oblivion to the perhaps inculpably compromised hermeneutic horizon of the agent or to the unjustly distributed material resources that occasion the unacknowledged true beliefs such an agent may have about that unjust distribution, i.e., the agent's realization that "the game is rigged."

24. Glenn C. Loury, "Beyond Civil Rights," *New Republic* (October 7, 1985): 25.

25. It is perhaps worth pointing out that my argument here is, in part, an argument to "denaturalize" what I have called the normal conditions and that such a strategy has similar benefits here to those we reap when it is deployed in cognitive and intellectual contexts that seem quite remote from the one considered here. Two examples come readily to mind: the physics of motion, or dynamics, and human sexuality. The history of dynamics can be construed as a story punctuated by various conceptions of what constitutes natural or normal motion. For Aristotle, natural or "unaided" terrestrial or sublunary motion was linear motion that came to an end (a rock falling to the earth or a pushed wagon eventually coming to a stop). Galileo challenged this idea of natural motion, suggesting that both were special cases of motion, in both cases of motion begun and ended by the impress of external forces. The idea that an object set in motion would continue, following an unending path across the earth's surface, unless external forces were acting on it—Galileo's idea of inertia—represented an advance that expanded the scope of dynamic explanations. Similarly, Newton's challenge to Galileo's new idea of natural, inertial motion ultimately led to a dynamic theory of even broader explanatory scope. And the same can be said of Einstein's relationship to Newtonian mechanics. With regard to human sexuality, one need only reflect on what has been gained by rethinking the "natural" status of heterosexuality.

26. See also Thomas Nagel, "The Policy of Preference," in *Mortal Questions* (Cambridge: Cambridge University Press, 1979), 92–93.

27. The conditions for the acquisition of autonomy skills are discussed in Diana Tietjens Meyers, "Decentralizing Autonomy: Five Faces of Selfhood," in *Autonomy and the Challenges to Liberalism*, ed. John Christman and Joel Anderson (Cambridge: Cambridge University Press, 2005), 36–40. I believe that these conditions apply as well, ceteris paribus, to agency.

28. In the case of responding to experiences of oppression, I am referring to necessary, but of course not sufficient, conditions of agency. A woman may well recognize, say, that she is being sexually harassed but may nevertheless find herself unable to actively counter it because of her other beliefs concerning socially available options.

4. TOWARD A HERMENEUTICS OF RACE: BIOLOGY, RACE, ETHNICITY, AND CULTURE

1. Here I want to distinguish the concept of race that circulates within and informs everyday social life from the population genetics concept of geographic ancestry group. On the connection between the concept of race and the population geneticist's concept of a geographical ancestry group, Sean L. Simpson in private conversation has spoken of "race" as being a weak proxy for ancestral history. See Michael D. Hardimon, *Rethinking Race: A Case for Deflationary Realism* (Cambridge, MA: Harvard University Press, 2017), 156–59.
2. Cited in Morris W. Foster and Richard R. Sharp, "Race, Ethnicity, and Genomics: Social Classifications as Proxies of Biological Heterogeneity," *Genome Research* 12 (2002): 844–50.
3. Foster and Sharp, "Race, Ethnicity, and Genomics," 845.
4. Philip Kitcher, "Race, Ethnicity, Biology, Culture," in *In Mendel's Mirror: Philosophical Reflections on Biology* (Oxford: Oxford University Press, 2003), 230–57. My remarks here are based on a commentary on Kitcher's original unpublished paper that I delivered at a conference on race held at Rutgers University in 1994. My discussion here is revised to reflect the later, published version of Kitcher's remarks, which version is, to some extent, responsive to my original commentary. See Kitcher, "Race, Ethnicity, Biology, Culture," 253n1.
5. Kitcher, "Race, Ethnicity, Biology, Culture," 232.
6. Kitcher, "Race, Ethnicity, Biology, Culture," 236, 233.
7. See Rick A. Kittles and Kenneth M. Weiss, "Race, Ancestry, and Genes: Implications for Defining Disease Risk," *Annual Review of Genomics and Human Genetics* 4 (2003): 44.
8. Audrey Smedley, *Race in North America: Origin and Evolution of a Worldview* (Boulder, CO: Westview Press, 1999), 293n12.

9. Of course, our inability to say which racial classification applies to an individual does not imply that the very idea of such classification is bankrupt, that is, the idea that there are distinct populations characterized by distinctive clusters of manifest traits. The discussion that follows addresses this latter idea.
10. Christopher Wills, "The Skin We're In," *Discover Magazine*, November 1, 1994, 80. Cf. also Luigi Luca Cavalli-Sforza, *History and Geography of Human Genes* (Princeton, NJ: Princeton University Press, 1994).
11. See L. C. Dunn, *Heredity and Evolution in Human Populations* (Cambridge, MA: Harvard University Press, 1965), 100–101.
12. Naomi Zack, *Philosophy of Science and Race* (New York: Routledge, 2002), 43–46.
13. Zack, *Philosophy of Science and Race*, 50.
14. Each such system is correlated with particular kinds of antigen (molecules found on the surface of red blood cells). The familiar ABO system is one such blood group system.
15. Dunn, *Heredity and Evolution in Human Populations*, 101.
16. Zack, *Philosophy of Science and Race*, 51.
17. Alexander Alland Jr., *Human Diversity* (Garden City, NY: Anchor Books, 1973), 54.
18. As Naomi Zack puts it, the salient phenotypical traits "vary independently within social racial groups and neither singly nor together do the variations fall into discrete groups that can be correlated with social racial categories." Zack, *Philosophy of Science and Race*, 56. That said, Zack seems to mischaracterize the nature of Kitcher's project. The reconstruction of the concept of race that Kitcher undertakes aims to make the case for a "possible biological foundation for a division of our species into races." Kitcher, "Race, Ethnicity, Biology, Culture," 239. It is not intended to be a demonstration that there is such a foundation. In other words, Zack seems to take the conditions that Kitcher puts forward as categorical claims rather than as hypothetical or proleptic proposals. Cf. Naomi Zack, "Ethnicity, Race, and the Importance of Gender," in *Race or Ethnicity? On Black and Latino Identity*, ed. Jorge J. E. Gracia (Ithaca, NY: Cornell University Press, 2007), 111–15.
19. Although it is beyond the scope of this investigation, the foregoing discussion of the inadequacy of phenotypic description for racial

classification also places into question Michael Hardimon's recently proposed account of what he calls the minimalist concept of race. Hardimon, *Rethinking Race*, 27–64. It seems that Hardimon's concept of *race* is more adequately captured by the concept of *cline*. His argument to the effect that "minimalist races" are biologically real implies that such a concept has what philosophers of science would call empirical import (the condition of having predictive and explanatory implications). It is difficult to discern just what empirical import "minimalist race" has in addition to that of a cline, or what empirical significance is added by giving clinal variations racial designations. Indeed, Hardimon's response to the objection that visible phenotypical differences among groups is not biologically relevant is, in effect, to adduce an argument supporting the biological salience of clines (Hardimon, *Rethinking Race*, 79–84). Thus it is difficult to avoid the conclusion that such a concept is expressive of little more than a potentially misleading redundancy. For another appraisal of Hardimon's position, see Zack, "Ethnicity, Race, and the Importance of Gender," 107–110.

20. Hardimon, *Rethinking Race*, 7; Michael O. Hardimon, "The Ordinary Concept of Race," *Journal of Philosophy* 100 (September 2003): 454–55.

21. See also Zack, "Ethnicity, Race, and the Importance of Gender," 108–9; and Linda Martin Alcoff, *Visible Identities: Race, Gender and the Self* (Oxford: Oxford University Press, 2006), 126–27. Alcoff cites Foucault to the effect that the perceptual intelligibility of a salient visible difference requires an appropriate interpretive framework. In a later essay, Kitcher, too, appears to be somewhat sympathetic to the point I raise here. See Philip Kitcher, "Does 'Race' Have a Future?," *Philosophy & Public Affairs* 35, no. 4 (Fall 2007): 299–300.

22. Foster and Sharp, "Race, Ethnicity, and Genomics," 846.

23. Kitcher, "Race, Ethnicity, Biology, Culture," 235.

24. Although he is addressing a different situation—namely, one where the isolating barriers have been taken out of play—and not the one I am contemplating here, it is worth noting that Kitcher acknowledges that in the case of a population consisting of two pure races, both of whose endogamous and exogamous mating rates are equal, it could take as few as ten generations or less for either of the two to disappear (Kitcher, "Race, Ethnicity, Biology, Culture," 238).

25. Dunn, *Heredity and Evolution in Human Populations*, 114. For a more recent account of this population, see Yedael Y. Waldman et al., "The Genetic History of Cochin Jews of India," *Human Genetics* 135, no. 10 (October 2016): 1127–43.
26. Dunn, *Heredity and Evolution in Human Populations*, 119.
27. See John H. Relethford, "Models, Predictions, and the Fossil Record of Modern Human Origins," *Evolutionary Anthropology* 8 (1999): 8; and Milford H. Wolpoff, John Hawks, and Racel Caspari, "Multiregional, Not Multiple Origins," *American Journal of Physical Anthropology* 112 (2000): 129–36.
28. Kitcher, "Race, Ethnicity, Biology, Culture," 232.
29. Kitcher, "Race, Ethnicity, Biology, Culture," 241, 244, 247; cf. Smedley, *Race in North America*, 287. Furthermore, as I have suggested, if there is a significant reduction in global reproductive isolation, it is an implication of Kitcher's account that even though we may have racialized ancestries, we may get to the point at which biological races may no longer exist. Furthermore, the sociohistorically sensitive nature of the application conditions for Kitcher's conception of biological race means that, for instance, even if—based on statistically low rates of intermarriage—a partition could be drawn between Africans and Caucasians in the contemporary United States, the empirical basis for such a partition distinguishing Asians and Caucasians, or Asians and Africans even, has not been provided. See Kitcher, "Race, Ethnicity, Biology, Culture," 239–42; and Joshua Glasgow, "On the New Biology of Race," *Journal of Philosophy* 100 (September 2003):469–70. It also bears mentioning that Kitcher's account, in which reproductive isolation plays a defining role, would counterintuitively allow what we would regard as distinct social classes, such as that of the English aristocracy, to count as different races. This would certainly seem to be at odds with the ways in which "race" is ordinarily understood. Kitcher, "Race, Ethnicity, Biology, Culture," 244; Glasgow, "On the New Biology of Race," 470–71.
30. Zack, "Ethnicity, Race, and the Importance of Gender," 115.
31. Kitcher, "Does 'Race' Have a Future?," 299–300. In the course of his account, he very helpfully reminds us that there is just one world, nevertheless, in the sense that it is comprised of "the so-far undifferentiated totality of what is independent of us."

32. Kitcher, "Does 'Race' Have a Future?," 302.
33. I note here that, unlike Kitcher in his later essay, I do not claim that race is not a natural kind because there are no natural kinds. Kitcher, "Does 'Race' Have a Future?," 298–303. Rather, my view is that there is a pragmatic sense in which there are natural kinds, but race is not among them.
34. See Dunn, *Heredity and Evolution in Human Populations*, 100; Alland, *Human Diversity*, 52–56; Hardimon, *Rethinking Race*, 24–25; and Michael Bamshad, Stephen Wooding, Benjamin A. Salisbury, and J. Claiborne Stephens, "Deconstructing the Relationship Between Genetics and Race," *Nature Reviews Genetics* 5 (August 2004): 601.
35. Cavalli-Sforza et al., *History and Geography of Human Genes*, 19. The most recent authoritative statement on this issue is perhaps Cavalli-Sforza's to the effect that because there is no evidence of a discontinuous distribution of genetic markers across our species there is no biological basis for human racial classification. See Guido Barbujani, Arianna Magagni, Eric Minch, and Luigi Luca Cavalli-Sforza, "An Apportionment of Human DNA Diversity," *PNAS* 94 (1997): 4516–19.
36. Joshua Glasgow, *A Theory of Race* (New York: Routledge, 2009), 94–108.
37. The results of the seminal study can be found in N. Rosenberg, J. Pritchard, J. L. Weber, H. M. Cann, K. K. Kidd, L. A. Zhivotovsky, et al., "Genetic Structure of Human Populations," *Science* 298, no. 5602 (2002): 2381–85.
38. For a brief but helpful overview of clustering algorithms, see Quayshawn Spencer, "Philosophy of Race Meets Population Genetics," *Studies in History and Philosophy of Biological and Biomedical Sciences* 52 (2015): 47–49. I have also benefited from discussions about these matters with the biostatistician Sean L. Simpson.
39. Marcus W. Feldman, "The Biology of Ancestry: DNA, Genomic Variation, and Race," in *Doing Race: 21 Essays for the 21st Century*, ed. Hazel R. Marcus and Paula M. L. Moya (London: W. W. Norton, 2010), 147; and Quayshawn Spencer, "A Radical Solution to the Race Problem," *Philosophy of Science* 81, no. 5 (2014): 1025–38.
40. Cf. Hardimon, *Rethinking Race*, 84–97; Spencer, "A Radical Solution to the Race Problem"; and Spencer, "Philosophy of Race Meets Population Genetics," 47–49.

41. As of this writing, it has been replicated in 69 percent of subsequent studies. See Spencer, "Philosophy of Race Meets Population Genetics,"48n14. However, there have been methodological objections to the study's design. See, for example, Kenneth M. Weiss and Jeffrey C. Long, "Non-Darwinian Estimation: My Ancestors, My Genes' Ancestors," *Genome Research* 19 (2009): 703–10.
42. Kittles and Weiss, "Race, Ancestry, and Genes," 44.
43. Kittles and Weiss, "Race, Ancestry, and Genes," 56; David Serre and Svante Paabo, "Evidence for Gradients of Human Genetic Diversity Within and Among Continents," *Genome Research* 14, no. 9 (September 2004): 1679–85. Rosenberg replies to this objection, but it is not clear that he addresses the sampling problem per se. Rosenberg et al., "Clines, Clusters, and the Effect of Study Design on the Inference of Human Population Structure," *PLOS Genetics* 1, no. 6 (December 2005): 660–71. See also Glasgow's discussion of the Rosenberg reply. Glasgow, *A Theory of Race*, 106.
44. The authors go on to point out that, at the time of their writing and two years after the K=5 result, "the sampling of individuals from many parts of the world (such as sub-Saharan Africa, India, North and South America) has been extremely limited even though genetic diversity in some of those regions . . . seems to be higher than in many parts of the world and there is substantial genetic structure among African populations." Bamshad et al., "Deconstructing the Relationship Between Genetics and Race," 601.
45. Michael J. Bamshad, Stephen Wooding, W. Scott Watkins, Christopher T. Ostler, Mark A. Batzer, and Lynn B. Jorde, "Human Population Genetic Structure and Inference of Group Membership," *American Journal of Human Genetics* 72, no. 3 (2003): 587. Such population sampling effects have also been demonstrated by D. J. Witherspoon, S. Wooding, A. R. Rogers, E. E. Marchani, W. S. Watkins, M. A. Batzer, and L. B. Jorde, "Genetic Similarities Within and Between Human Populations," *Genetics* 176, no. 1 (2007): 356–57.
46. Serre and Paabo, "Evidence for Gradients of Human Genetic Diversity," 1679; Kittles and Weiss, "Race, Ancestry, and Genes," 37.
47. Kitcher, "Does 'Race' Have a Future?," 305.
48. Hans-Georg Gadamer, *Truth and Method*, 2nd rev. ed., trans. Joel Weinsheimer and Donald G. Marshall (New York: Continuum, 2002), 369–79.

49. Hans-Georg Gadamer, *Philosophical Hermeneutics*, trans. David E. Linge (Berkeley: University of California Press, 1976), 11, 13.
50. Kitcher, "Does 'Race' Have a Future?," 306.
51. For example, see Hardimon, *Rethinking Race*, 88.
52. Glasgow, *A Theory of Race*, 106. Another index of the arbitrariness with which the number of salient distinct genetic clusters is determined is the following:

 > "Consistent with the evidence that the root of the human mtDNA phylogenetic tree is in Africa, initial studies of genomic diversity indicated that Africans have the highest levels of diversity among any living population as well as extensive population substructure; a study of genome-wide microsatellite DNA variation in more than 3,000 Africans identified *14* ancestral population clusters that correlate broadly with geography, culture and language. Genome-wide single nucleotide polymorphism (SNP) genotyping studies largely supported these observations. The findings of these and other studies indicate that African populations have maintained a large and subdivided structure throughout their evolutionary history and that *the deepest splits between human populations lie in sub-Saharan Africa*" (italics added). Rasmus Nielsen, Joshua M. Akey, Mattias Jakobsson, Jonathan K. Pritchard, Sarah Tishkoff, and Eske Willerslev, "Tracing the Peopling of the World Through Genomics," *Nature* 541 (2017): 304.

 As a corollary of this, one of this study's authors reports that "we compared European and Asian populations to each other, and they were more similar than any two African populations we looked at." Sarah Tishkoff, cited in Jessica Wapner, "Out of Africa," *Newsweek* July 27–August 3, 2018, 25. So should K be set to equal 5 or 18 or even more?
53. If this argument in favor of genetic continuity is valid, then why is it that various genetics-based enterprises such as Ancestry.com can now so accurately determine one's continental ancestry? Such companies have genetic data from a number of populations on file. With a given individual's genotype, it is possible to determine the population cluster from which it has the least genetic distance and to thereby link that individual to his/her ancestral population. As Serre and Paabo point out, the fact of continuity does not rule out the possibility that "individuals can be assigned to culturally predefined populations on the basis of their genotypes." Serre and Paabo, "Evidence for Gradients

of Human Genetic Diversity," 1683. This is because in such an assignment one is allowing for a *range* of genotypes (among individuals) to be correlated with a single *culturally predefined* continental population. However, individuals whose genotypes fall within various subranges within any given range could have been reliably assigned to more narrowly defined, subcontinental population groups. The assignment of an individual to a culturally predefined and predelineated population group is not a determination of where that individual is located in the multidimensional clinal space of that population. As Glasgow usefully summarizes this line of argument, "perfect assignment of individuals to populations is not tantamount to a demonstration that we do not as a whole make up a continuous population." Glasgow, *A Theory of Race*, 107. And, as Feldman points out, the reverse is not the case, in that knowing a person's geographic origin will not enable us to infer his or her genotype, because "the majority of genomic variation occurs within, rather than between, populations." Feldman, "The Biology of Ancestry," 151.

54. Bamshad et al., "Deconstructing the Relationship Between Genetics and Race," 601.
55. Putnam's device is particularly useful in helping to illuminate how we might disaggregate the ordinary concept of race and the biological concept of population group. This directly contradicts Hardimon's claim for their correspondence. Hardimon, *Rethinking Race*, 9.
56. Hardimon, *Rethinking Race*.
57. John Dupré, *The Disorder of Things: Metaphysical Foundations of the Disunity of Science* (Cambridge, MA: Harvard University Press, 1993), 31; John Dupré, "Natural Kinds," in *A Companion to the Philosophy of Science*, ed. W. H. Newton-Smith (Oxford: Blackwell, 2000), 316.
58. Dupré, *The Disorder of Things*, 27–34; Dupré, "Natural Kinds," 316.
59. Quayshawn Spencer, "Philosophy of Race Meets Population Genetics," 50, 52.
60. If such classifications were taken to be the appropriate labels, there is always the question of *which* such social classifications should be used. As Foster and Sharp point out, "choosing how to socially identify donors as members of social populations is not a trivial or self-evident matter. An individual donor, for instance, may be known simultaneously as a

resident of a particular Indian village in Arizona, a member of the Hopi tribe, a descendant of a Laguna family (through a paternal ancestor who is not explicitly noted in matrilineal Hopi society), a Native American, and as someone of Spanish ancestry (owing to 18th-century intermarriages between Lagunas and Spaniards) in addition to being a member of the general U.S. population. Each of these identities, or several in combination, would . . . [result] in somewhat different scientific findings about genetic variation in relation to specific social categories . . . , depending on which label or labels are placed on an individually anonymous DNA sample.

"This potential for scientific inaccuracy in defining social categories and in recording them for specific donors could reduce the value of their association with specific genetic findings." Foster and Sharp, "Race, Ethnicity and Genomics," 847.

61. Witherspoon et al., "Genetic Similarities Within and Between Human Populations," 351. A case in point here is the controversy surrounding the drug BiDil, a so-called race-based medicine that has been approved for use by African American men with congestive heart failure. In addition to questions about the design of the efficacy study (the research leading to its approval tested the drug only in African American populations, leaving unexamined its efficacy in other populations), such factors as chronic social stress and diet were not examined as possible confounding variables. So the drug's efficacy is in no way dispositive of the issue of the importance of genetic factors. For a helpful overview, see H. Brody and L. Hunt, "BiDil: Assessing a Race-Based Pharmaceutical," *Annals of Family Medicine* 4, no. 6 (November 2006): 556–60; and Sheldom Krinsky, "The Art of Medicine: the Short Life of a Race Drug," *The Lancet* 379 (January 14, 2012): 114–15. I am grateful to David Ratner for alerting me to this literature. See also note 78 below.

62. Bamshad et al., "Deconstructing the Relationship Between Genetics and Race," 606.

63. Witherspoon, et al., "Genetic Similarities Within and Between Human Populations," 351–59.

64. Sung-Min Ahn, Tae-Hyung Kim, Sunghoon Lee, et al., "The First Korean Genome Sequence and Analysis: Full Genome Sequencing for a Socio-Ethnic Group," *Genome Research* 19, no. 9 (September 2009):

1622–29; cited in Guido Barbujani, Silva Ghirotto, and Francesca Tassi, "Nine Things to Remember About Human Genome Diversity," *Tissue Antigens* 82, no. 3 (2013): 159.

65. Witherspoon et al., "Genetic Similarities Within and Between Human Populations," 357.
66. Somewhere between 89 and 94 percent of the genetic variation in our species resides within a given population, so only 6 percent to 11 percent of the variation occurs between populations with different continental ancestries. Feldman, "The Biology of Ancestry," 151, 143–44.
67. Witherspoon et al., "Genetic Similarities Within and Between Human Populations," 358; see also Foster and Sharp, "Race, Ethnicity and Genomics," 844, 845.
68. Bamshad et al., "Deconstructing the Relationship Between Genetics and Race," 606, 607.
69. Barbujani, Ghirotto and Tassi, "Nine Things to Remember," 155.
70. R. O. Andreasen, "The Meaning of 'Race': Folk Conceptions and the New Biology of Race," *Journal of Philosophy* 102, no. 2 (February 2005): 105. On this point, see also Sally Haslanger, *Resisting Reality: Social Construction and Social Critique* (Oxford: Oxford University Press, 2012), 306–9.
71. See, for example, Stanley R. Bailey, *Legacies of Race in Brazil: Identities, Attitudes, and Politics in Brazil* (Stanford, CA: Stanford University Press), esp. chaps. 3, 8, 9.
72. Georgia Warnke, "Race, Gender and Antiessentialist Politics," *Signs: Journal of Women in Culture and Society* 31, no.1 (2005): 105.
73. See Anthony Giddens, *New Rules of Sociological Method: A Positive Critique of Interpretive Sociologies*, 2nd ed. (Stanford, CA: Stanford University Press, 1993), 9. However, I do not here deploy this idea in the way that Giddens had in mind. I refer to two levels of interpretation whereby one level, the first-person level, is causally related as a response to the other level, the third-person perspective. Perhaps "dual perspective hermeneutic" is more apposite than is "double hermeneutic" to capture what I intend here.
74. For an extended discussion of racial identification as a species of interpretation, see Georgia Warnke, *After Identity: Rethinking Race, Sex and Gender* (Cambridge: Cambridge University Press, 2007).

75. I have phrased this point in this way to highlight the contrast between this situation and one that would meet the requirements of normative legitimacy as laid out, for example, by Habermas in his account of moral/practical deliberation.
76. Miranda Fricker, *Epistemic Injustice: Power and the Ethics of Knowing* (Oxford: Oxford University Press, 2007), 147–75.
77. See Andrew J. Pierce, "Reconstructing Race: A Discourse-Theoretical Approach to a Normative Politics of Identity," *Philosophical Forum* 43, no.1 (Spring 2012): 29.
78. For present purposes, I include under the rubric of environmental racism all racist and race-indexed practices and experiences that, cumulatively, have actual physiological effects. On the latter, with regard to infant and maternal mortality and morbidity (phenomena that persist across socioeconomic class lines for African Americans), see Linda Villarosa, "Why America's Black Mothers and Babies Are in a Life-or-Death Crisis," *New York Times Magazine* April 11, 2018; also see the fairly extensive literature on Arline Geronimus's so-called weathering hypothesis, e.g., Arline Geronimus, Margaret Hicken, Danya Keene, and John Bound, " 'Weathering' and Age Patterns of Allostatic Load Scores Among Blacks and Whites in the United States," *American Journal of Public Health* 96 (May 2006): 826–33. I am grateful to Robert Gooding-Williams for bringing this literature to my attention. The current (as of spring of 2020) COVID-19 pandemic offers the most recent, and startling, illustration of how racial disparities in health outcomes can be traced to race-indexed practices and experiences.

One might also include here possible epigenetic effects of racial practices. Although such practices cannot alter the underlying DNA itself, they can possibly lead to an alteration in the way that genes work, in gene expression, and such change can be heritable. However, the notion of transgenerational transmission of epigenetic markers is very far from settled. Nevertheless, even if we assumed that epigenetic alteration in gene expression can be inherited, for this to be a plausible source of incipient racialization it would seem that the exogenous environmental triggers would have to act selectively in such a way that they would be highly correlated with just those populations that were already understood to fall under a particular racial category.

On the contrary, it would seem that the environmental precursors to epigenetic modification would correlate, perhaps, with socioeconomic status but only, at best, very weakly with ascribed racial classification. For example, environmental stressors might disproportionately affect poor people in general, but not necessarily people of African heritage in particular. I am grateful to Sean L. Simpson for bringing this phenomenon to my attention and to David Ratner for further discussion.

79. Ian Hacking, "Making Up People," in *Forms of Desire: Sexual Orientation and the Social Constructionist Controversy*, ed. Edward Stein (New York: Routledge, 1992), 87.
80. Kwame Anthony Appiah and Amy Gutmann, *Color Conscious: The Political Morality of Race* (Princeton, NJ: Princeton University Press, 1996), 78.
81. Robert Gooding-Williams, "Race, Multiculturalism, and Democracy," *Constellations* 5, no. 1 (1998): 23.
82. In this sense, Gooding-Williams's conception of what it is to be a Black person is relevant to my discussion of agency in chapter 3.
83. Chike Jeffers, "The Cultural Theory of Race: Yet Another Look at Du Bois's 'The Conservation of Races'," *Ethics* 123, no. 3 (2013): 403–26.
84. Relevant to this is Gooding-Williams's discussion of the incoherence of understanding this mode of identification in terms of its authenticity or lack thereof. See Gooding-Williams, "Race, Multiculturalism, and Democracy," 24–25.
85. The first part of this example is drawn from my own experience as an incoming freshman on an overly white Yale College campus. One of my very scarce Black classmates almost walked into a tree in his attempt to avoid acknowledging me on Yale's "Old Campus."
86. See Appiah and Gutmann, *Color Conscious*, 88–89.
87. Kitcher, "Race, Ethnicity, Biology, and Culture," 110–14. He discusses these issues at length in this essay but also adverts to them in the later essay, Kitcher, "Does 'Race' Have a Future?," 309, 311.
88. Kitcher, "Race, Ethnicity, Biology, and Culture," 107.
89. Kitcher, "Race, Ethnicity, Biology, and Culture," 108–9.
90. Kitcher, "Race, Ethnicity, Biology, and Culture," 111.
91. Regarding the quasi-Mendelian model, there are a number of disanalogies between cultural transmission and genetic transmission, salient

among them being the fact that there are creative discontinuities in the transmission of ethnicity (even from one's biological parents) because of ineluctable acts of reinterpretation and reinvention as ethnicity is passed down from generation to generation. See James Clifford, *The Predicament of Culture: Twentieth-Century Ethnography, Literature, and Art* (Cambridge, MA: Harvard University Press, 1988), 341. Kitcher acknowledges that his analysis depends on this model, and he notes its defeasibility. See Kitcher, "Biology, Race, Ethnicity, and Culture," 110.

92. It is hardly clear that this need necessarily remain a situation structured by the either/or of individual salvation or cultural preservation. It would rather be one that demands social and economic reform to enable both individual flourishing and cultural viability. If adults of the disadvantaged ethnicity had the wherewithal to provide children access to the riches of "their" culture and to ensure the material well-being of children, then this dilemma would not have to detain us. And even if the tradeoff that he outlines were ineliminable, we should ask who is the "we" whose lives might be enriched at the possible expense of a given individual—those who are sufficiently privileged to have access to the resources of cultural diversity, those who, by hypothesis, are likely to belong to the advantaged ethnic group? This question highlights the socially heterogeneous nature of the "we." Furthermore, there is an interesting, if not paradoxical, tension between the presumptive appreciation of cultural diversity and the requirements (i.e., the reciprocal nonappreciation of the culture of others) for maintaining it. The "we" that appreciates such diversity must be distinct from the "we" whose culture is to be preserved. One's position on this issue is likely to be strongly colored (if I may use that term) by one's position in our society's social, economic, and racial matrix.

93. In chapter 2, I address the relationships and potential tensions between cultural imperatives and individual autonomy and agency. This set of issues is also highlighted in the well-known volume devoted to Charles Taylor's essay in Amy Gutmann, ed., *Multiculturalism: Examining the Politics of Recognition* (Princeton, NJ: Princeton University Press, 1994). In Jürgen Habermas's contribution to that volume, he maintains that an individualistically construed theory of rights, correctly understood, requires the recognition of collective identities. For among the

protections afforded individuals must be the recognition and protection of the intersubjective contexts from which their identities are forged and that sustain their capacities for agency. However, because the cultivation and protection of individual autonomy is the fulcrum of Habermas's argument for the recognition of group rights, the idea of individual autonomy at the same time sets the formal limits on the right to cultural recognition. This puts Habermas in a position to endorse the public recognition of social and cultural difference but also to worry about the oppressive potential of what can be called "identity politics," that is, the tendency to embrace overly prescriptive, and therefore restrictive, accounts of ethnic/cultural membership and to assume that such membership is obligatory and definitive of one's identity. Jürgen Habermas, "Struggles for Recognition in the Democratic Constitutional State," in *Multiculturalism: Examining the Politics of Recognition*, ed. Amy Gutmann (Princeton, NJ: Princeton University Press, 1994); see also Lorenzo C. Simpson, "Multiculturalism," in *The Cambridge Habermas Lexicon*, ed. Amy Allen and Eduardo Mendieta (Cambridge: Cambridge University Press, 2019). In addition to this quasi-Herderian argument for cultural preservation as an agential resource, one can make aesthetic and pedagogical arguments. Perhaps having in mind some amalgam of the two, W. E. B. Du Bois spoke of the distinctive "gifts" that distinct "races" provide to the world. See W. E. B. DuBois, "The Conservation of Races," in *W. E. B. Du Bois: A Reader*, ed. David Levering Lewis (New York: Henry Holt, 1995). Kitcher's might be a neo-Du Boisian project, but he does not provide an explicit argument here, relying instead on an unexamined analogy with our interest in the preservation of biological species. In Lorenzo C. Simpson, *The Unfinished Project: Toward a Postmetaphysical Humanism* (London: Routledge, 2001), I discuss the pedagogical potential for edification and enhanced self-knowledge that can emerge from meaningful cross-cultural encounters.
94. Kitcher, "Biology, Race, Ethnicity, and Culture," 111.
95. Kitcher, "Biology, Race, Ethnicity, and Culture," 111.
96. Intertribal adoption and intermarriage were customary during the pre-Columbian era. There were rituals of adoption to mark the integration of new members, and they were considered full members of

the adopting tribe. This included "exchanges" of children as a means of fostering intertribal peace, in which the adopted children were socialized into the customs and language of the adopting tribe. Moreover, extending into the nineteenth century in Canada there were intermarriages with French fur hunters of European descent, where the resulting children were considered full members of the relevant tribe, and in the United States, especially during their migrations from east to west, Native Americans adopted abandoned or orphaned white children they encountered, children who became full members of their respective tribes of adoption. See Roxanne Dunbar-Ortiz, *An Indigenous People's History of the United States* (Boston: Beacon, 2014); J. T. Garrett and Michael Garrett, *The Cherokee Full Circle: A Practical Guide to Ceremonies and Traditions* (Rochester, VT: Bear and Company, 2002); and Russel Thornton, "Tribal Membership Requirements and the Demography of 'Old' and 'New' Native Americans," *Population Research and Policy Review* 16 (1997): 33–42. Of course, with current economic and social incentives for being able to document Native American heritage, tribal membership rules have become more strict, but this is a situation of relatively recent origin. I am grateful to my assistant, Giada Mangiameli, for her research into this matter.

97. Kitcher, "Race, Ethnicity, Biology, and Culture," 111.
98. Kitcher, "Race, Ethnicity, Biology, and Culture," 90.
99. Cf. Gutmann, *Multiculturalism: Examining the Politics of Recognition.*
100. Gooding-Williams, "Race, Multiculturalism, and Democracy," 32.
101. Indeed, the more the performance by such "outsiders" is informed by such an appreciation, the more "authentic" it will be and the less likely it is to be perceived as an illegitimate form of cultural appropriation. This has become an issue in the wake of the institutionalization of jazz education in American universities and conservatories. I provide a general account of the nature and possibility of such "cross-cultural" understanding in chap. 4 of Simpson, *The Unfinished Project*.
102. African American cultural production is no doubt inflected by the meanings its agents assign to being Black in this society. Nevertheless, there are aesthetic imperatives that inform its various domains of artistic expression that allow us to view certain works or products from the standpoint of their having a relatively self-contained unity and, in that

sense, as having an autonomous value in themselves, a value that can be recognized independently of the context of their generation. Of course, many of those imperatives themselves may have their origins and distinctive salience within racialized contexts, and whatever their origin, they must be appreciated in order to experience the expressive unity of works fashioned in response to them. For instance, it may not be irrelevant to the forms that Charles Mingus's compositions and performances on the bass assumed that he was not allowed to pursue study of the cello at a local conservatory because he was Black. Yet those compositions and performances can be appreciated on their own in musical terms.

103. Again, I do not want to give short shrift to the crucially important and vexed issue of cultural appropriation. I cannot settle it here, but to mitigate matters I shall restrict the unproblematic use of "our" to those non-Black musicians who acknowledge the African American foundation of the musical practice. On the matter of "outsiders" carrying on cultural traditions, I am reminded of a recent account of a woman of European descent who had become the link for the continuation of a medically important healing tradition practiced by native peoples of Central America. The last living practitioner, an old man of Mayan descent, had passed it on to her.

104. Kitcher, "Race, Ethnicity, Biology, and Culture," 112–13.

105. For discussions of the hybrid nature of American culture, see Ralph Ellison, *Going to the Territory* (New York: Vintage, 1987); and Albert Murray, *The Omni-Americans* (New York: Vintage, 1983).

106. DuBois, "The Conservation of Races," 23–26.

107. I develop this point in Simpson, *The Unfinished Project*.

5. CONCLUDING REFLECTIONS: TOWARD A NEW RECONCILIATION OF HERMENEUTICS AND CRITICAL THEORY, OR NOTES TOWARD A HERMENEUTIC DEMOCRACY

1. Jürgen Habermas, *Knowledge and Human Interests*, trans. Jeremy J. Shapiro (Boston: Beacon, 1968), 301–17. Habermas here follows Edmund Husserl in understanding the "objectivist illusion" to refer to an objectivism that *naively* correlates theoretical propositions with

metaphysically independent matters of fact taken to be established independently of the inquirer's context.
2. See Jürgen Habermas, "A Postscript to *Knowledge and Human Interests*," *Philosophy of the Social Sciences* 3 (1975): 182.
3. Jürgen Habermas, *Theory and Practice*, trans. John Viertel (Boston: Beacon, 1973), 22–23.
4. Hermeneutics assumed a somewhat broader role in Habermas's social theory in *The Theory of Communicative Action* insofar as that account is structured by the complementary frameworks of system and hermeneutic lifeworld. Jürgen Habermas, *Theory of Communicative Action*, vol. 2, *Lifeworld and System: A Critique of Functionalist Reason*, trans. Thomas McCarthy (Boston: Beacon, 1985).
5. Hans-Herbert Kogler and L'ubomir Dunaj, "Beyond Ethnocentrism: Towards a Global Social Theory," in *Social Theory and Asian Dialogues*, ed. Ananta K. Giri (Singapore: Palgrave Macmillan, 2018), 71, https://doi.org/10.1007/978-981-10-7095-2_5.
6. G. W. F. Hegel, *Hegel's Science of Logic*, trans. A. V. Miller (London: George Allen and Unwin, 1969), 396–97, 479–80, 550–53.
7. Theodor Adorno, "Sociology and Empirical Research," in *The Positivist Dispute in German Sociology*, ed. and trans. Glyn Adey and David Frisby (London: Heineman, 1969), 69.
8. Herbert Marcuse, *Negations: Essays in Critical Theory*, trans. Jeremy J. Shapiro (Boston: Beacon, 1968), 67.
9. Marcuse, *Negations*; and Hegel, *Hegel's Science of Logic*, 547.
10. Theodor Adorno, *Negative Dialectics*, trans. E. B. Ashton (New York: Continuum, 1973), 52.
11. On the idea of object's having meaning-bearing properties in Adorno's conception of them, see Brian O'Connor, *Adorno's Negative Dialectic: Philosophy and the Possibility of Critical Rationality* (Cambridge, MA: MIT Press, 2004), 56.
12. Marcuse, *Negations*, 75.
13. I elaborate this point with explicit reference to Marcuse in Lorenzo C. Simpson, "Marcuse, Time and Technique: Concerning the Rational Foundations of Critical Theory," *Philosophical Forum* 4 (1986): 245–70.
14. See Herbert Marcuse, *One Dimensional Man: Studies in the Ideology of Advanced Industrial Society* (Boston: Beacon, 1964), 150; and Max

Horkheimer, *Critical Theory: Selected Essays*, trans. Matthew J. O'Connell et al. (New York: Continuum, 2002), 213.

15. Habermas, *The Theory of Communicative Action*, vol. 2, *Lifeworld and System*, 187, 189. Here, of course, Habermas is giving an analysis of the ways in which the sphere of culture, as a whole, can function ideologically by serving to legitimate social inequality. My concern is with how a privileged *interpretation* within such a sphere can function ideologically.

16. In the course of my argument, I have occasionally used "ideology" in more conventional ways, but with the expectation that the context makes clear how it is being used.

17. One can clearly see such a policing of cultural self-understanding and corresponding strategic framing of identity at work within the ambit of major religious traditions, within Christian fundamentalism, for example, or in the case of some of the political strategies enacted in highly prescriptive accounts of Muslim identity. On the politics of representation within Islamic societies, see Dale F. Eickelman and James Piscatori, *Muslim Politics* (Princeton, NJ: Princeton University Press, 1996).

18. This can be instructively compared, I think, with the position that Amy Allen—a thinker whose influences are drawn both from Foucault and from the tradition of critical theory—articulates with respect to the relation between emancipation and power. In her recent work, she proposes a conception of emancipation in which emancipation does not mean freedom from power relations altogether but rather means more specifically freedom from states of domination, where "domination" refers to a state in which relations of power have become ossified or hardened in such a way that the free flow of power relations has congealed, rendering some individuals less capable of exercising power than others. See Amy Allen, The End of Progress: Decolonizing the Normative Foundations of Critical Theory (New York: Columbia University Press, 2016). Therefore, and in a way that closely parallels the distinction I wish to draw here between invidious generation and strategic generation *überhaupt*, she advocates drawing a distinction between, on the one hand, domination as it refers to structural asymmetries of power and, on the other hand, power tout court. See Amy Allen, The Politics of Our Selves: Power, Autonomy, and Gender in Contemporary Critical Theory (New York: Columbia University Press, 2008), 54.

19. See Sally Haslanger, "Racism, Ideology, and Social Movements," *Res Philosophica* 94, no. 1 (January 2017): 1–22.
20. Haslanger, "Racism, Ideology, and Social Movements," 7–10, 12–14. My conception of "prereflective meaning" is discussed in Lorenzo C. Simpson, *Technology, Time, and the Conversations of Modernity* (London: Routledge, 1995). And this idea might be usefully compared to what Charles Taylor refers to as "intersubjective meaning." See Charles Taylor, "Interpretation and the Sciences of Man," *Review of Metaphysics* 25, no. 1 (1971): 3–51.
21. Haslanger, "Racism, Ideology, and Social Movements," 10.
22. Haslanger, "Racism, Ideology, and Social Movements," 10, 11.
23. Cf. Jürgen Habermas, *The Philosophical Discourse of Modernity: Twelve Lectures*, trans. Frederick Lawrence (Cambridge, MA: MIT Press, 1987), 154, 205, 319–20.
24. I am fully aware that no adequate account of legitimacy can avoid fundamental questions regarding the distribution of *material* resources. My aim here is to address necessary, though not sufficient, conditions of legitimacy.
25. On the epistemology of intercultural understanding, see Lorenzo C. Simpson, *The Unfinished Project: Toward a Postmetaphysical Humanism* (London: Routledge, 2001).
26. Published after the formulation of the argument in this book—and, indeed, citing some of my earlier work along these lines—Hans-Herbert Kogler and L'ubomir Dunaj attempt to reconstruct, for a variety of cultural contexts, the conditions that provide for critical openings. See Kogler and Dunaj, "Beyond Ethnocentrism."
27. This point can be usefully compared to Seyla Benhabib's conception of "democratic interpretive iteration," in which she has in mind the conditions on the legitimate application of transnational norms within particular sociocultural contexts. See Seyla Benhabib, *Dignity in Adversity: Human Rights in Troubled Times* (Cambridge: Polity Press, 2011), 125–31.
28. For some time now, Habermas has been explicit in acknowledging the necessary role played by lifeworldly, *sittliche* contexts in enabling the agential capacities of individuals. See, for example, Jürgen Habermas, "Struggles for Recognition in the Democratic Constitutional State," in *Multiculturalism: Examining the Politics of Recognition*, ed. Amy

Gutmann (Princeton, NJ: Princeton University Press, 1994), 113. And he has demonstrated increased appreciation for the centrality of hermeneutic processes both "vertically," in determining the shape assumed by transnational norms when applied in the context of particular political cultures, and "horizontally," where such processes are engaged in responding to threats to consensus-based understandings of collective identity within societies challenged by cultural difference. See Jürgen Habermas, *An Awareness of What Is Missing: Faith and Reason in a Post-Secular Age* (Cambridge: Polity Press, 2010). For a brief general discussion of this, see Lorenzo C. Simpson, "Multiculturalism," in *Cambridge Habermas Lexicon*, ed. Amy Allen and Eduardo Mendieta (Cambridge: Cambridge University Press, 2019). Insofar as Habermas's focus in the work under discussion is on "multicultural" societies in transition and the consequences of such processes for the vertical interpretation of supranational norms and the horizontal project of achieving social consensus, my focus is somewhat broader. I have been concerned with the plurality of ways in which even a relatively homogeneous or "monocultural" society could understand itself, with the possible plurality of its self-interpretations, owing, at least in part, to the variety of distinct social positions occupied by its members.

29. See Simpson, *The Unfinished Project*, 72, 94–95.
30. David Berreby, "The Unabsolute Truths of Clifford Geertz," *New York Times Magazine*, April 9, 1995, 44.

APPENDIX: TOWARD A HERMENEUTICS OF THE ETHICAL RESPONSE

1. See, for instance, Bernhard Waldenfels, *The Question of the Other* (Hong Kong: Chinese University Press, 2007); and Bernhard Waldenfels, "Der Andere und der Dritte in interkultureller Sicht," in *Ethik und Politik aus interkultureller Sicht*, ed. R. A. Mall and N. Schneider (Amsterdam: Rodopi, 1996).
2. Bernhard Waldenfels, "Toward a Responsive Ethics," paper presented at Stony Brook University, New York, November 12, 2010. This appendix is drawn from the commentary I presented on that occasion.
3. Waldenfels, "Toward a Responsive Ethics," 13.

4. Bernhard Waldenfels, *The Question of the Other*, 24.
5. Waldenfels, "Toward a Responsive Ethics," 10.
6. Arthur Schopenhauer, *The World as Will and Representation*, trans. E. F. J. Payne (New York: Dover, 1966), 1:59–60.
7. See Charles Larmore, *Patterns of Moral Complexity* (Cambridge: Cambridge University Press, 1987), ix, 10.
8. Larmore, *Patterns of Moral Complexity*, 7, 9.
9. Larmore, *Patterns of Moral Complexity*, 14, 8.
10. Waldenfels, *The Question of the Other*, 33, 24.
11. Waldenfels, *The Question of the Other*, 25.
12. Bernhard Waldenfels, "Der Andere und der Dritte in interkultureller Sicht."
13. Waldenfels, *The Question of the Other*, 24.
14. Waldenfels, "Toward a Responsive Ethics," 13.
15. Waldenfels, "Toward a Responsive Ethics," 13.
16. Cf. Hans-Georg Gadamer, *Truth and Method*, 2nd rev. ed., trans. Joel Weinsheimer and Donald G. Marshall (New York: Continuum, 2002); cited in Robert Bernasconi, " 'You Don't Know What I'm Talking About': Alterity and the Hermeneutical Ideal," in *The Specter of Relativism: Truth, Dialogue, and Phronesis in Philosophical Hermeneutics*, ed. Lawrence K. Schmidt (Evanston, IL: Northwestern University Press, 1995), 186.
17. Waldenfels, "Toward a Responsive Ethics," 20.
18. Cf. Lorenzo C. Simpson, *The Unfinished Project: Toward a Postmetaphysical Humanism* (London: Routledge, 2001), 86.

BIBLIOGRAPHY

Adorno, Theodor. *Negative Dialectics*, trans. E. B. Ashton. New York: Continuum, 1973.

———. "Sociology and Empirical Research." In *The Positivist Dispute in German Sociology*, ed. and trans. Glyn Adey and David Frisby, 68–86. London: Heineman, 1976.

Ahn, Sung-Min, Tae-Hyung Kim, Sunghoon Lee, et al. "The First Korean Genome Sequence and Analysis: Full Genome Sequencing for a Socio-Ethnic Group." *Genome Research* 19, no. 9 (September 2009): 1622–29. 10.1101/gr.092197.109.

Al-Azm, Sadik J. "The Importance of Being Earnest About Salmon Rushdie." *Die Welt des Islams* 31, no. 1 (1991): 1–49.

Alcoff, Linda Martín. *Real Knowing: New Versions of the Coherence Theory*. Ithaca, NY: Cornell University Press, 1996.

———. *Visible Identities: Race, Gender and the Self*. Oxford: Oxford University Press, 2006.

Alland, Alexander, Jr. *Human Diversity*. Garden City, NY: Anchor, 1973.

Allen, Amy. The Politics of Our Selves: Power, Autonomy, and Gender in Contemporary Critical Theory. New York: Columbia University Press, 2008.

———. *The End of Progress: Decolonizing the Normative Foundations of Critical Theory*. New York: Columbia University Press, 2016.

Anderson, Joel, and Axel Honneth. "Autonomy, Vulnerability, Recognition and Justice." In *Autonomy and the Challenges to Liberalism: New Essays*, ed. John Christman and Joel Anderson, 127–49. Cambridge: Cambridge University Press, 2005.

Andreasen, R. O. "The Meaning of 'Race': Folk Conceptions and the New Biology of Race." *Journal of Philosophy* 102, no. 2 (February 2005): 94–106.

Appiah, Kwame Anthony, and Amy Gutman. *Color Conscious: The Political Mortality of Race*. Princeton, NJ: Princeton University Press, 1996.

Asad, Talal. "The Concept of Cultural Translation in British Social Anthropology." In *Writing Culture: The Poetics and Politics of Ethnography*, ed. James Clifford and George E. Marcus, 141–64. Berkeley: University of California Press, 1986.

Bailey, Stanley R. *Legacies of Race in Brazil: Identities, Attitudes, and Politics in Brazil*. Stanford, CA: Stanford University Press, 2009.

Bamshad, Michael J., Stephen Wooding, W. Scott Watkins, Christopher T. Ostler, Mark A. Batzer, and Lynn B. Jorde. "Human Population Genetic Structure and Inference of Group Membership." *American Journal of Human Genetics* 72, no. 3 (March 2003): 578–89. https://doi.org/10.1086/368061.

Bamshad, Michael, Stephen Wooding, Benjamin A. Salisbury, and J. Claiborne Stephens. "Deconstructing the Relationship Between Genetics and Race." *Nature Reviews Genetics* 5 (August 2004): 598–609. https://doi.org/10.1038/nrg1401.

Barbujani, Guido, Silva Ghirotto, and Francesca Tassi. "Nine Things to Remember About Human Genome Diversity." *Tissue Antigens* 82, no. 3 (2013): 155–64. doi:10.1111/tan.12165.

Barbujani, Guido, Arianna Magagni, Eric Minch, and L. Luca Cavalli-Sforza. "An Apportionment of Human DNA Diversity." *PNAS* 94 (1997): 4516–19.

Barcan Marcus, Ruth. "Modalities and Intensional Languages." *Synthese* 13 (1961): 303–22; reprinted in *Modalities*. Oxford: Oxford University Press, 1993.

Baynes, Kenneth. "The Self and Individual Autonomy in the Frankfurt School." In *Routledge Companion to the Frankfurt School*, ed. Peter Gordon, Axel Honneth, and Espen Hammer, 424–38. London: Routledge, 2018.

Benhabib, Seyla. *Dignity in Adversity: Human Rights in Troubled Times*. Cambridge: Polity Press, 2011.

Benson, Paul. "Taking Ownership: Authority and Voice in Autonomous Agency." In *Autonomy and the Challenges to Liberalism*, ed. John Christman and Joel Anderson, 101–26. Cambridge: Cambridge University Press, 2005. https://doi.org/10.1017/CBO9780511610325.007.

Bernasconi, Robert. " 'You Don't Know What I'm Talking About': Alterity and the Hermeneutical Ideal." In *The Specter of Relativism: Truth, Dialogue, and Phronesis in Philosophical Hermeneutics*, ed. Lawrence K. Schmidt, 178–94. Evanston, IL: Northwestern University Press, 1995.

Berreby, David. "The Unabsolute Truths of Clifford Geertz." *New York Times Magazine*, April 9, 1995, 44. https://www.nytimes.com/1995/04/09/magazine/unabsolute-truths-clifford-geertz.html.

Bilgrami, Akeel. "Rushdie. Islam, and Postcolonial Defensiveness." *Yale Journal of Criticism* 4 (Fall 1990): 301–311.

———. "What Is a Muslim? Fundamental Commitment and Cultural Identity." *Critical Inquiry* 18 (1992): 821–42.

Block, Ned. "Holism: Mental and Semantic." In *Routledge Encyclopedia of Philosophy*, ed. E. Craig, 488–93. London: Routledge, 1998. http://www.rep.routledge.com/article/WO15SECT5.

Blocker, H. Gene, *The Aesthetics of Primitive Art*. Lanham, MD: University Press of America, 1994.

Brody, Howard, and Linda Hunt. "BiDil: Assessing a Race-Based Pharmaceutical." *Annals of Family Medicine* 4, no. 6 (November 2006): 556–60.

Brooks, David. "The Nature of Poverty." *New York Times*, May 1, 2015. https://www.nytimes.com/2015/05/01/opinion/david-brooks-the-nature-of-poverty.html.

Cavalli-Sforza. Luigi Luca, et al., *History and Geography of Human Genes*. Princeton, NJ: Princeton University Press, 1994.

Chege, Jane Njeri, Ian Askew, and Jennifer Liku. "An Assessment of the Alternative Rites Approach for Encouraging Abandonment of Female Genital Mutilation in Kenya." In *Frontiers in Reproductive Health*. Washington, DC: United States Agency for International Development, 2001.

Clifford, James. *The Predicament of Culture: Twentieth-Century Ethnography, Literature and Art*. Cambridge, MA: Harvard University Press, 1988.

Davidson, Donald, and Gilbert Harman, eds. *Semantics of Natural Language*. Dordrecht: D. Reidel, 1972.

Delbanco, Andrew. "Our Universities: The Outrageous Reality." *New York Review of Books* 62, no. 12. July 9, 2015, 38–39. https://www.nybooks.com/articles/2015/07/09/our-universities-outrageous-reality/.

Deveaux, Monique. "A Deliberative Approach to Conflicts of Culture." *Political Theory* 31 (December 2003): 780–807.

Doppelt, Gerald. "Kuhn's Epistemological Relativism." In *Relativism: Cognitive and Moral*, ed. M. Krausz and J. Meiland, 113–46. Notre Dame: University of Notre Dame Press, 1982.

DuBois, W. E. B. *A Reader*, ed. David Levering Lewis. New York: Henry Holt, 1995.

Dugger, Celia W. "A Movement to End Female Genital Mutilation Spreads in Senegal." *New York Times*, October 16, 2011.

Dunbar-Ortiz, Roxanne. *An Indigenous People's History of the United States*. Boston: Beacon, 2014.

Dunn, L. C. *Heredity and Evolution in Human Populations*. Cambridge, MA: Harvard University Press, 1965.

Dupré, John. *The Disorder of Things: Metaphysical Foundations of the Disunity of Science*. Cambridge, MA: Harvard University Press, 1993.

———. "Natural Kinds." In *A Companion to the Philosophy of Science*, ed. W. H. Newton-Smith, chap. 46. Oxford: Blackwell, 2000.

Eickelman, Dale F., and James Piscatori. *Muslim Politics*. Princeton, NJ: Princeton University Press, 1996.

Ellison, Ralph. *Going to the Territory*. New York: Vintage, 1987.

Feldman, Marcus W. "The Biology of Ancestry: DNA, Genomic Variation and Race." In *Doing Race: 21 Essays for the 21st Century*, ed. Hazel R. Marcus and Paula M. L. Moya, 136–59. London: Norton, 2010.

Fine, Arthur, and J. Earman. "Against Indeterminacy." *Journal of Philosophy* 74, no. 9 (1977): 535–38.

Foster, Morris W., and Richard R. Sharp. "Race, Ethnicity, and Genomics: Social Classifications as Proxies of Biological Heterogeneity." *Genome Research* 12 (2002): 844–50. doi:10.1101/gr.99202.

Fricker, Miranda. *Epistemic Injustice: Power and the Ethics of Knowing*. Oxford: Oxford University Press, 2007.

Gadamer, Hans-Georg. *Philosophical Hermeneutics*, trans. David E. Linge. Berkeley: University of California Press, 1976.

———. "The Hermeneutics of Suspicion." *Man and World* 17 (1984): 313–23.

———. *Truth and Method*, 2nd rev. ed., trans. Joel Weinsheimer and Donald G. Marshall. New York: Continuum, 2002.

Galeotti, Anna Elisabetta. "Relativism, Universalism, and Applied Ethics: The Case of Female Circumcision." *Constellations* 14 (March 2007): 91–111.

Garrett J. T., and Michael T. Garrett. *The Cherokee Full Circle: A Practical Guide to Ceremonies and Traditions*. Rochester, VT: Bear, 2002.

Geronimus, Arline, Margaret Hicken, Danya Keene, and John Bound. "'Weathering' and Age Patterns of Allostatic Load Scores Among Blacks and Whites in the United States." *American Journal of Public Health* 96 (May 2006): 826–33.

Giddens, Anthony. *New Rules of Sociological Method: A Positive Critique of Interpretive Sociologies*, 2nd ed. Stanford, CA: Stanford University Press, 1993.

Giere, Ronald N. "Theories." In *A Companion to the Philosophy of Science*, ed. W. H. Newton-Smith, 515–24. Oxford: Blackwell, 2000.

Ginev, Dimitri. *A Passage to the Hermeneutic Philosophy of Science*. Amsterdam: Rodopi, 1997.

Glasgow, Joshua. "On the New Biology of Race." *Journal of Philosophy* 100 (September 2003): 456–74.

———. *A Theory of Race*. New York: Routledge, 2009.

Gooding-Williams, Robert. "Race, Multiculturalism, and Democracy." *Constellations* 5, no. 1 (1998): 18–41.

Goodman, Nelson. *The Structure of Appearance*. Cambridge, MA: Harvard University Press, 1951.

Habermas, Jürgen. *Knowledge and Human Interests*, trans. Jeremy J. Shapiro. Boston: Beacon, 1968.

———. "A Postscript to *Knowledge and Human Interests*." *Philosophy of the Social Sciences* 3 (1973): 157–89.

———. *Theory and Practice*, trans. John Viertel. Boston: Beacon, 1973.

———. *Legitimation Crisis*, trans. Thomas McCarthy. Boston: Beacon, 1975.

———. *Theory of Communicative Action*. Vol. 1, *Reason and the Rationalization of Society*, trans. Thomas McCarthy. Boston: Beacon, 1985.

———. *The Theory of Communicative Action*. Vol. 2, *Lifeworld and System: A Critique of Functionalist Reason*, trans. Thomas McCarthy. Boston: Beacon, 1987.

———. *The Philosophical Discourse of Modernity: Twelve Lectures*, trans. Frederick Lawrence. Cambridge, MA: MIT Press, 1987.

———. *On the Logic of the Social Sciences*, trans. Shierry Weber Nicholsen and Jerry A. Stark. Cambridge, MA: MIT Press, 1988.

———. *Moral Consciousness and Communicative Action*, trans. Christian Lenhardt and Shierry Weber Nicholsen. Cambridge, MA: MIT Press, 1990.

——. "Struggles for Recognition in the Democratic Constitutional State." In *Multiculturalism: Examining the Politics of Recognition*, ed. Amy Gutmann, 107–48. Princeton, NJ: Princeton University Press, 1994.

——. *An Awareness of What Is Missing: Faith and Reason in a Post-Secular Age*. Cambridge: Polity Press, 2010.

Hacking, Ian. "Making Up People." In *Forms of Desire: Sexual Orientation and the Social Constructionist Controversy*, ed. Edward Stein, 69–87. New York: Routledge, 1992.

Hall, Stuart. *Essential Essays, vol. 2: Identity and Diaspora*. Ed. David Morley. Durham, NC: Duke University Press, 2019.

Hanson, Norwood Russell. *Patterns of Discovery: An Inquiry Into the Conceptual Foundations of Science*. Cambridge: Cambridge University Press, 1958.

Hardimon, Michael O. "The Ordinary Concept of Race." *Journal of Philosophy* 100 (September 2003): 437–55.

——. *Rethinking Race: A Case for Deflationary Realism*. Cambridge, MA: Harvard University Press, 2017.

Haslanger, Sally. *Resisting Reality: Social Construction and Social Critique*. Oxford: Oxford University Press, 2012.

——. "Racism, Ideology, and Social Movements." *Res Philosophica* 94, no. 1 (January 2017): 1–22.

Hegel, G. W. F. *Hegel's Science of Logic*, trans. A. V. Miller. London: George Allen and Unwin, 1969.

Heidegger, Martin. *Being and Time*, trans. John Macquarrie and Edward Robinson. New York: Harper and Row, 1962.

——. *On the Way to Language*, trans. Peter D. Hertz. San Francisco: Harper Collins, 1971.

——. *Basic Writings*, ed. David F. Krell. New York: Harper and Row, 1977.

Horkheimer, Max. *Critical Theory: Selected Essays*, trans. Matthew J. O'Connell et al. New York: Continuum, 2002.

Ingold, Tim, ed. *Key Debates in Anthropology*. London: Routledge, 1996.

Jeffers, Chike. "The Cultural Theory of Race: Yet Another Look at Du Bois's 'The Conservation of Races.'" *Ethics*, 123, no. 3 (2013): 403–26.

Justice, John. "The Semantics of Rigid Designation." *Ratio* 16 (2003): 33–48.

Khader, Serene J. *Adaptive Preferences and Women's Empowerment*. Oxford: Oxford University Press, 2011.

Kitcher, Philip. *In Mendel's Mirror: Philosophical Reflections on Biology*. Oxford: Oxford University Press, 2003.

———. "Does 'Race' Have a Future?" *Philosophy and Public Affairs* 35, no. 4 (Fall 2007): 293–317.

Kittles, Rick A., and Kenneth M. Weiss. "Race, Ancestry, and Genes: Implications for Defining Disease Risk." *Annual Review of Genomics and Human Genetics* 4 (2003): 33–67.

Kogler, Hans-Herbert, and L'ubomir Dunaj. "Beyond Ethnocentrism: Towards a Global Social Theory." In *Social Theory and Asian Dialogues*, ed. Ananta K. Giri, 69–106. Singapore: Palgrave Macmillan, 2018. https://doi.org/10.1007/978-981-10-7095-2_5.

Krinsky, Sheldon. "The Short Life of a Race Drug." *The Lancet* 379 (January 14, 2012): 114–15. https://doi.org/10.1016/S0140-6736(12)60052-X.

Lafont, Cristina. *The Linguistic Turn in Hermeneutic Philosophy*, trans. José Medina. Cambridge, MA: MIT Press, 1999.

———. *Heidegger, Language and World-Disclosure*, trans. Graham Harman. Cambridge: Cambridge University Press, 2000.

———. "Hermeneutics." In *Blackwell Companion to Heidegger*, ed. H. Dreyfus and M. Wrathall, 265–84. Cambridge, MA: Blackwell, 2005.

LaPorte, Joseph. *Natural Kinds and Conceptual Change*. Cambridge: Cambridge University Press, 2004.

Larmore, Charles. *Patterns of Moral Complexity*. Cambridge: Cambridge University Press, 1987.

Locke, John. *An Essay Concerning Human Understanding*. London: Thomas Basset, 1690.

Loury, Glenn C. "The Moral Quandary of the Black Community." *Public Interest* 79 (Spring 1985).

———. "Beyond Civil Rights." *New Republic* (October 7, 1985): 22–25.

Marcuse, Herbert. *One Dimensional Man: Studies in the Ideology of Advanced Industrial Society*. Boston: Beacon, 1964.

———. *Negations: Essays in Critical Theory*, trans. Jeremy J. Shapiro. Boston: Beacon, 1968.

Margolis, Joseph. *The Persistence of Reality: Texts Without Referents*. Oxford: Basil Blackwell, 1989.

McCarthy, Thomas. "Rationality and Relativism: Habermas's 'Overcoming of Hermeneutics.'" In *Habermas: Critical Debates*, ed. J. B. Thompson and David Held, 57–78. Cambridge, MA: MIT Press, 1982.

———. *Race, Empire, and the Idea of Human Development*. Cambridge: Cambridge University Press, 2009.

Meyers, Diana Tietjens. "Feminism and Women's Autonomy: The Challenge of Female Genital Cutting." *Metaphilosophy* 31, no. 5 (October 2000): 469–91.

———. "Decentralizing Autonomy: Five Faces of Selfhood." In *Autonomy and the Challenges to Liberalism*, ed. John Christman and Joel Anderson, 27–55. Cambridge: Cambridge University Press, 2005.

Murray, Albert. *The Omni-Americans*. New York: Vintage, 1983.

Nagel, Thomas. *Mortal Questions*. Cambridge: Cambridge University Press, 1979.

Newton-Smith, W. H. *The Rationality of Science*. London: Routledge, 1999.

Nielsen, Rasmus, Joshua M. Akey, Mattias Jakobsson, Jonathan K. Pritchard, Sarah Tishkoff, and Eske Willerslev. "Tracing the Peopling of the World Through Genomics." *Nature* 541 (2017): 302–10.

O'Connor, Brian. *Adorno's Negative Dialectic: Philosophy and the Possibility of Critical Rationality*. Cambridge, MA: MIT Press, 2004.

Obama, Barack. "Remarks by the President in the Eulogy for the Honorable Reverend Clementa Pickney. White House Office of the Press Secretary." June 26, 2015. https://obamawhitehouse.archives.gov/the-press-office/2015/06/26/remarks-president-eulogy-honorable-reverend-clementa-pinckney.

Oshana, Marina. *Personal Autonomy in Society*. Hampshire, UK: Ashgate, 1988.

Parekh, Bhikhu. *Rethinking Multiculturalism: Cultural Diversity and Political Theory*. Cambridge, MA: Harvard University Press, 2000.

Pierce, Andrew J. "Reconstructing Race: A Discourse-Theoretical Approach to a Normative Politics of Identity." *Philosophical Forum* 43, no.1 (Spring 2012): 27–49.

Putnam, Hilary. *Mind, Language and Reality*. New York: Cambridge University Press, 1975.

Rabinow, Paul, and William Sullivan, eds. *Interpretive Social Science*. Berkeley: University of California Press, 1979.

Relethford, John H. "Models, Predictions, and the Fossil Record of Modern Human Origins." *Evolutionary Anthropology* 8 (1999): 7–10. https://doi.org/10.1002/(SICI)1520-6505(1999)8:1<7::AID-EVAN4>3.0.CO;2-O.

Ricoeur, Paul. *Freud and Philosophy: An Essay on Interpretation*, trans. Denis Savage. New Haven, CT: Yale University Press, 1965.

Rorty, Richard. *Philosophy and the Mirror of Nature*. Princeton, NJ: Princeton University Press, 1979.

———. *Philosophical Papers*, vol. 1: *Objectivity, Relativism and Truth*. Cambridge: Cambridge University Press: 1991.

———. "What Can You Expect from Anti-Foundationalist Philosophers?: A Reply to Lynn Baker." *Virginia Law Review* 78, no. 3 (1992): 719–27.

Rosenberg, N., J. Pritchard, J. L. Weber, H. M. Cann, K. K. Kidd, L. A. Zhivotovsky, et al. "Genetic Structure of Human Populations." *Science* 298, no. 5602 (2002): 2381–85.

Rosenberg N., et al. "Clines, Clusters, and the Effect of Study Design on the Inference of Human Population Structure." *PLOS Genetics* 1, no. 6 (December 2005): 660–71.

Scheffler, Israel. *Science and Subjectivity*. Indianapolis: Bobbs-Merrill, 1967.

———. "Vision and Revolution: A Postscript on Kuhn." *Philosophy of Science* 39 (1972): 366–74.

Schopenhauer, Arthur. *The World as Will and Representation*, vol. 1., trans. E. F. J. Payne. New York: Dover, 1966.

Schwartz, Stephen, ed. *Naming, Necessity, and Natural Kinds*. Ithaca, NY: Cornell University Press, 1977.

Searle, John. "Proper Names." *Mind* 76 (1958): 166–73.

———. *Speech Acts*. Cambridge: Cambridge University Press, 1969.

Serre, David, and Svante Paabo. "Evidence for Gradients of Human Genetic Diversity Within and Among Continents." *Genome Research* 14, no. 9 (September 2004): 1679–85.

Shapere, Dudley. "The Structure of Scientific Revolutions." *Philosophical Review* 73 (1964): 383–94.

———. "Meaning and Scientific Change." In *Mind and Cosmos: Essays in Contemporary Science and Philosophy*, ed. R. Colodny, 41–85. Pittsburgh: University of Pittsburgh Press, 1966.

———. "The Paradigm Concept." *Science* 172 (1971): 706–9.

Sheldon, Sally, and Stephen Wilkinson. "Female Genital Mutilation and Cosmetic Surgery: Regulating Non-Therapeutic Body Modification." *Bioethics* 12 (1998): 263–85.

Simpson, Lorenzo C. "Marcuse, Time and Technique: Concerning the Rational Foundations of Critical Theory." *Philosophical Forum* 4 (1986): 245–70.

——. "On Habermas and Particularity: Is There Room for Race and Gender on the Glassy Plains of Ideal Discourse?" *Praxis International* 6 (1986): 328–40.

——. *Technology, Time and the Conversations of Modernity*. London: Routledge, 1995.

——. *The Unfinished Project: Toward a Postmetaphysical Humanism*. London: Routledge, 2001.

——. "Humanism and Cosmopolitanism after '68." *New Formations* 65 (Fall 2008): 54–66.

——. "Multiculturalism." In *Cambridge Habermas Lexicon*, ed. Amy Allen and Eduardo Mendieta, 279–82. Cambridge: Cambridge University Press, 2019.

Smedley, Audrey. *Race in North America: Origin and Evolution of a Worldview*. Boulder, CO: Westview, 1999.

Soames, Scott. *Philosophical Analysis in the Twentieth Century*, vol. 2. Princeton, NJ: Princeton University Press, 2003.

Spencer, Quayshawn. "A Radical Solution to the Race Problem." *Philosophy of Science* 81, no. 5 (2014): 1025–38.

——. "Philosophy of Race Meets Population Genetics." *Studies in History and Philosophy of Biological and Biomedical Sciences* 52 (2015): 46–55.

Strawson, P. F. *Individuals: An Essay in Descriptive Metaphysics*. London: Methuen, 1959.

Stroll, Avrum. "Proper Names, Names and Fictive Objects." *Journal of Philosophy* 95 (1998): 522–33.

——. *Twentieth-Century Analytic Philosophy*. New York: Columbia University Press, 2000.

Tamir, Yael. "Liberal Nationalism." *Philosophy and Public Policy* (Winter/Spring 1993): 1–7.

Taylor, Charles. "Interpretation and the Science of Man." *Review of Metaphysics* 25, no. 1 (1971): 3–51.

——. *Human Agency and Language*. Cambridge: Cambridge University Press, 1985.

——. *Philosophy and the Human Sciences*. Cambridge: Cambridge University Press, 1985.

Taylor, Charles, and Amy Gutmann, eds. *Multiculturalism: Examining the Politics of Recognition*. Princeton, NJ: Princeton University Press, 1994.

Thompson, Robert Ferris. "Esthetics in Traditional Africa." *Art News* 66 (1968): 44–45, 63–66.

Thornton, Russel. "Tribal Membership Requirements and the Demography of 'Old' and 'New' Native Americans." *Population Research and Policy Review* 16 (1997): 33–42.

UN Office of the High Commissioner for Human Rights. *Fact Sheet No. 23: Harmful Traditional Practices Affecting the Health of Women and Children.* Geneva: United Nations. August 1995.

United Nations Research Institute for Social Development. *Gender, Justice, Development and Rights: Substantiating Rights in a Disabling Environment* New York: UNRISD Workshop. June 3, 2000.

Van Fraassen, Bas. *The Scientific Image.* Oxford: Clarendon Press, 1980.

Villarosa, Linda. "Why America's Black Mothers and Babies Are in a Life-or-Death Crisis." *New York Times Magazine*, April 11, 2018. https://www.nytimes.com/2018/04/11/magazine/black-mothers-babies-death-maternal-mortality.html.

Vogel, Steven. *Against Nature: The Concept of Nature in Critical Theory.* Albany: State University of New York Press, 1996.

Waldenfels, Bernhard. "Der Andere und der Dritte in interkultureller Sicht." In *Ethik und Politik aus interkultureller Sicht*, ed. R. A. Mall and N. Schneider, 71–83. Amsterdam: Rodopi, 1996.

——. *The Question of the Other.* Hong Kong: Chinese University Press, 2007.

Waldman, Yedael Y., et al. "The Genetic History of Cochin Jews of India." *Human Genetics* 135, no. 10 (October 2016): 1127–43.

Wapner, Jessica. "Out of Africa." *Newsweek*, July 27–August 3, 2018.

Warnke, Georgia. "Race, Gender and Antiessentialist Politics." *Signs: Journal of Women in Culture and Society* 31, no.1 (Fall 2005): 93–116.

——, ed. *Inheriting Gadamer: New Directions in Philosophical Hermeneutics.* Edinburgh: Edinburgh University Press, 2016.

——. *After Identity: Rethinking Race, Sex and Gender.* Cambridge: Cambridge University Press, 2007.

Weiss, Kenneth M., and Jeffrey C. Long. "Non-Darwinian Estimation: My Ancestors, My Genes' Ancestors." *Genome Research* 19 (2009): 703–10.

Willett, Frank. *African Art.* New York: Thames and Hudson, 1971.

Wills, Christopher. "The Skin We're In." *Discover Magazine*, November 1, 1994. https://www.discovermagazine.com/health/the-skin-were-in.

Witherspoon, D. J., S. Wooding, A. R. Rogers, E. E. Marchani, W. S. Watkins, M. A. Batzer, and L. B. Jorde. "Genetic Similarities Within and

Between Human Populations." *Genetics* 176, no. 1 (2007): 351–59. 10.1534/genetics.106.067355.

Wolpoff, Milford H., John Hawks, and Racel Caspari. "Multiregional, Not Multiple Origins." *American Journal of Physical Anthropology* 112 (2000): 129–36.

Xie, Ming, ed. *The Agon of Interpretations: Towards a Critical Intercultural Hermeneutics*. Toronto: University of Toronto Press, 2014.

Zack, Naomi. *Philosophy of Science and Race*. New York: Routledge, 2002.

———. "Ethnicity, Race, and the Importance of Gender." In *Race or Ethnicity? On Black and Latino Identity*, ed. Jorge J. E. Gracia, 101–22. Ithaca, NY: Cornell University Press, 2007.

INDEX

act-descriptions, 86–87
actions, real meanings of, 57
adaptive preference, 21; of agents, 93–94
Adorno, Theodor, 144; negative dialectics of, 58; nonidentical concept of, 145; on primacy of object, 145; on real possibilities, 145–146
African American music, 137–138, 199nn102–103
agency: actualization of, 89–90; cognitive component of, 101–102; culpable lack of, 95; culture of poverty as deficit in, 84–85; enabling infrastructure of, 96–97; epistemic component of, 81–82, 91–92, 94–96, 101, 143; facilitation and impeding of, 81; first-order compromise, 89–92; mediation and, 144; normal conditions in, 98–100, 153, 184n25; unaided accomplishment and, 97–99; value deficit thesis, 18, 19, 85–89;

volitional component of, 81, 91–92, 94–95
agency deficit: culture of poverty thesis as, 84–85; poverty and, 23; values deficit in, 18, 19, 85–89; volitional deficit in, 18, 19
agential capacities: first-order, 19, 20, 81, 82, 89–92; second-order, 19, 58–60, 81–82, 90, 96, 180n29, 183n23
agents: adaptive preferences of, 93–94; cultural, 16, 72; first-person perspective of, 91, 128, 130–131; reasons approach, of Dray, 9; self-understanding of, 2, 23, 150, 202n17; text intelligibility to, 7, 62, 63; values, hermeneutic circle access, 18
algorithmically guided choice, for moral decisions, 159
Allen, Amy, 202n18
alterity: of others, 164; radical, 161–162; Waldenfels on ethics of, 56, 155, 161

ambivalence of alienness,
    Waldenfels on, 162–163
analogy, topics and, 64
analytic/continental distinction,
    24–26
Andreasen, R. O., 127
Appiah, Anthony, 130
application, of ethical rules, 158
arbitrariness objection, ordinary
    racial classification and, 121
Aristotle, 4
assertion, Heidegger on
    interpretation and, 39–40
assimilation, Waldenfels on, 163
attributive use, of descriptive
    phrases, 26
autonomous agency, 60, 76, 89,
    180nn36–37; competing values,
    77; internalist and externalist
    accounts of, 180n39; situated, 18,
    100–102

Bamshad, Michael, 117
behavior: racial identity and, 131–132;
    values relationship with, 18, 86,
    88
Being and Time (Heidegger), 40
being-in-the-world, Heidegger
    on, 27
Benhabib, Seyla, 203n27
Bilgrami, Akeel, 71
biological significance of race,
    Kitcher on, 105, 140–141;
    distinctive phenotypical
    differences component of,
    106–109, 186n14, 186n18;
heritability and, 106, 107;
    mechanism of reproductive
    isolation component of, 106,
    110–113, 188n29
biomedical significant phenotypes,
    124–125
Block, Ned, 170n44
blood type phenotype, 109, 186n14
bracketing of Being, consciousness
    and, 27
Brahe, Tycho, 35
Brooks, David, 85–86
Byron, Don, 138

Cavalli-Sforza, Luigi Luca, 115, 118,
    189n35
choice, 10; algorithmically
    guided, for moral decisions,
    159; distribution of social, 77;
    endorsement, 76, 78, 180n39;
    forced, 76; life-enhancing and
    person, 20; rational choice
    theory, 11, 55; scientific theory,
    55
civilization of work, Taylor on, 88
civil rights movement, 83
clinical genetics, racial classification
    and, 123, 192n60
cluster concept, of cultural identity,
    13, 15, 51, 59, 146
COFESFA Women's Association,
    female genital cutting and, 79
cognitive contexts: agency cognitive
    component, 101–102; in agency
    normal conditions, 184n25
Collingwood, R. G., 118

common language: common referents in, 48–49; Gadamer on conversation and, 47

common referents, reference determined by meaning and, 48–49

common sense conception, of race, 104–105

consciousness: bracketing of Being and, 27; fusion of horizons and, 6–7; historically-effected, 3; linguistic, 3; philosophy of, 26–27

consensus, on topics, 32–33, 167n9

"Conservation of Races, The" (DuBois), 139, 197n93

constitution of meaning, Lafont on, 32

context-invariant form, of rationality, 14–15

continental philosophy, *See* analytic/continental distinction

continuity, exhibited by successive scientific frameworks, 52, 171n45; fact of, race and, 114, 118

conversation: cross-cultural, 62–63; Gadamer on common language and, 47; topic, consensus for, 32–33, 167n9

conversational development practice, 17, 70–73

counterfactual dialogical critique, 14, 22, 58–60, 143, 146; conversational development practice in, 17, 70–73; as critical developmental practice, 17, 72–73; description of, 15; of female genital cutting, 16–17, 73, 74, 149, 179n33; interrogative framework of, 17

COVID-19 pandemic, racial disparities and, 195n78

criterion of reference, of Searle, 44

critical developmental practice, counterfactual dialogical critique as, 17, 72–73

critical fusions: cultural identity, 58–60, 68, 70, 177n25; intercultural understanding, 60–80, 174n7; second-order rationality, 14, 58–60, 68–69, 153

critical hermeneutics: emancipatory intent for, 9, 17, 60; Gadamer and, 8

critical hermeneutics, of intercultural understanding, 65, 68–69, 74–80; conversational development practice, 17, 70–73; on human rights, 66–67; intercultural encounters and humanity, 61, 174n7; promiscuous relativism and, 67; social practices and, 67

critical pluralism, in humanism, 55

Critical Race Theory, 22, 129

critical social theory, 8–9, 55

Critical Theory: formulation of, 143–144; of Horkheimer, Adorno, and Marcuse, 144

cross-cultural conversation, 62–63

cross-cultural understanding, 8, 14, 22

culpable lack of agency, 95

cultural agents, 16, 72

cultural appropriation, 199n101, 200n103
cultural difference, salience of, 7–8
cultural diversity, 134
cultural formations, non-question-begging critique on, 57, 75, 179n34
cultural identity, 58–60, 68, 70, 177n25; cluster concept of, 13, 15, 51, 59, 146; interest-based concerns of, 15, 72–74, 147; modality of, 148; racial identity compared to, 132; reified products of, 72; semantic resources for, 149; Tamir on, 71
cultural narratives, plurivocity of legitimate, 72, 77, 79, 146
cultural practices, non-question-begging critical posture toward, 153
cultural preservation, social practices for, 135–138, 197n92
cultural traditions, of Native Americans, 136
cultural transmission, Mendelian model of, 135, 196n91
culture of poverty thesis, 18–19, 151–152; as agency deficit, 84–85; McCarthy on, 182n5
cultures: interpretation process for, 70–71; theory choice in, 10

deconstruction, of Derrida, 58
deontological ethical theory, of Kant, 156–157
Derrida, Jacques, 163; deconstruction of, 58

descriptive ethical relativism: afterlife and, 87; protest demonstrations and, 88
descriptive phrases, 29–30; attributive and referential uses of, 26; Marcus on shared, 38; about objects, 33–34
destruction of metaphysics, of Heidegger, 58
dialogical humanism, 55
dialogical understanding, 7
differences, 5; distinctive phenotypical, 106–109, 186n14, 186n18; salience of cultural, 7–8; social and political discourse on, 56–57
Dilthey, Wilhelm, 1, 57; interpretive understanding analysis, 2
direct reference theory, 12, 50–51, 54, 173n52; common language, 47–49; continuity and, 52, 171n45; criticism of, 37, 168n19; fictive objects and, 168n19; indirect reference substitute program and, 37–38, 53; meaning determines reference and, 36; natural essences scientific accounts, 42–43; natural kind terms and, 21, 36, 41–45, 103–104, 113–114, 127; rejection of, 36–37
distinctions, salience and, 4
distinctive phenotypical differences component, of race, 106; of blood type, 109, 186n14; of skin color, 107–108; Zack on, 108, 186n18

division of linguistic labor, of Putnam, 43
"Does 'Race' Have a Future" (Kitcher), 133
double hermeneutic, Giddens on, 128
Dray, William, 9
DuBois, W. E. B., 138, 139, 197n93
Dupré, John, 41
dynamic nominalism, of Hacking, 130

emancipative self-reflection, 142
emancipatory intent, for critical hermeneutics, 9, 17, 60
emergent horizon, of intelligibility, 161
empirical science, Heidegger on, 34
eliminativism, racial, 112, 113, 134
enabling infrastructure, of agency, 96–97
endorsement, of choice, 76, 78, 180n39
Enlightenment: fundamentalism, 66; Habermas on self-reflection connection with, 142
environmental racism, 130
epigenetics, 195n78
epistemic component, of agency, 81–82, 91–92, 94–96, 143; interpretive agency, in social world, 101
epistemic injustice, 20
essentialism, postmodernism critique of, 57

ethical rules, judgment in, 158–160
ethical theory, Kant deontological, 156–157
ethics: of alterity, of Waldenfels, 56, 155, 161; of human rights, 66; of otherness, 164; responsive, of Waldenfels, 155–164
ethnicity and racial identity: behavior and, 131–132; interpretation of, 128; Kitcher on, 133–134, 139, 140; race, as social recognition category, 127–141; social construction of, 129; Taylor on, 131
ethnocentrism, 22, 59; Eurocentric, 13; transcendental, 64–65
Eurocentric ethnocentrism, 13
evolutionary medicine, 21
existing conditions, meaning-bearing properties of, 145–146
explanatory relevance, of science terms, 12
explanatory accounts, natural kind terms role in, 44
externalist accounts, of autonomy, 180n39
external norms, in situated autonomous agency, 100

facilitation, of agency, 81
fact of continuity, of race, 114, 118
fallacy: psychologizing the structural, 85; reading off values, 85
fallibilism, of Kripke-Putnam, 45, 173n52

female genital cutting, 15, 23, 70, 78, 181n43; COFESFA Women's Association and, 79; counterfactual dialogical critique of, 16–17, 73, 74, 149, 179n33; in Kenya and Senegal, 79; in West, 94–95
feminist theory, 94
Feyerabend, Paul, 46
fictive objects, 168n19
first-order agency, 19, 20, 81, 82; compromise of, 89–92; Locke example of, 90
first-person perspective, of agent, 91, 128, 130–131
Fish, Stanley, 57
fitting response, of intelligibility, 155, 157, 159, 174
forced choice, 76
foundationalism, 57–58, 60
Fraassen, Bas van, 52–53
fracturing of reason, in linguistic turn, 29
Frazer, James, 89
Fregean dimension, of linguistic turn, 29, 42; of meaning determining reference, 34, 36
Freud, Sigmund, 57
Freud and Philosophy (Ricoeur), 57
Freudian theory, 14, 59
Fricker, Miranda: on hermeneutic injustice, 129
fusion of horizons, 4, 54; consciousness and, 6–7; Gadamer on, 3, 52

Gadamer, Hans-Georg, 57; on conversation and common language, 47; critical hermeneutics and, 8; on fusion of horizons, 3, 52; on language constitutive view, 6; on language role, in understanding, 1–2; on language world, 28; on legitimate and illegitimate prejudices, 9, 17–18, 58, 148; on logic of question, 4, 5, 118–119; on self-withholding, 119; on text and interpreter tradition, 62; on text interpretation, 63; on tradition, 52, 171n48
Geertz, Clifford, 154
generalized model, of scientific theories, 52–53
genetic ancestry, 124–125, 135
genetic clustering, 116–121, 124–125, 191n53
genetics, population, 21
genomics, 21; of racial classification, 122
George, Stefan, 28
Giddens, Anthony, 128
Glasgow, Joshua, 115, 121, 191n52
global development theory, policy-informing claims in, 11
global injustice and inequality, 23, 81, 151
globalization, 18
global justice, 13, 18; McCarthy on, 82–83, 93
global multicultural societies, inclusiveness in, 54

Gooding-Williams, Robert, 130–131, 137, 140, 195n78

Habermas, Jürgen, 8, 150, 197n93, 201n4, 202n15; on Enlightenment and self-reflection connection, 142; on hermeneutics of suspicion conflict motivations, 74; on interest-based concerns, of cultural identity, 73–74, 147; Lafont on, 30–32; on linguistic turn, 31; multiculturalism and, 203n28; on mythical narratives, 88; on objectivism, 200n1; on relativism, 30–31; on social practices, 142; on social theory, 55; on universality conception of reason, 9
Hacking, Ian, 130
Hall, Stuart, 176n14
Hanson, Norwood, 10, 35
Hardimon, Michael, 122; minimalist concept of race, 109–110, 186n19
Harman, Gilbert, 170n44
Haslanger, Sally, 149–150
Hegel, G. W. F.: Adorno and Marcuse on, 144; real possibility conception of, 144–146
Heidegger, Martin, 1, 9, 52, 57; on assertion and interpretation, 39–40; being-in-the-world, 27; destruction of metaphysics, 58; on empirical science, 34; on language, 28, 41
heritability component, of race, 106, 107

hermeneutic circle, 2; agent values access in, 18
hermeneutic democracy, 152
hermeneutic injustice, Fricker on, 129
hermeneutic judgment, for moral decisions, 159
hermeneutics of suspicion, of Ricoeur, 54–56; Habermas on conflict motivations and, 74; intercultural understanding, 60–80, 174n7; on Nietzschean, Freudian, Marxian theory, 14; overt signs and, 73; real meaning of actions and, 57. *See also* cultural identity
"Hermeneutics of Suspicion" (Gadamer), 58
historically effected intelligibility, 3
"Hölderlin and the Essence of Poetry" (Heidegger), 28
holism, 49–51, 170n44; meaning, 29; semantic, 12, 137
Horkheimer, Max, 144; on real possibilities, 146
Hull, David, 42
humanism, 66–68; critical pluralism and, 55; dialogical, 55
humanity, intercultural encounters and, 61, 174n7
human rights, 67; ethics of, 66; McCarthy on, 93; violations of, 66
human sciences, objectivity of, 2
Husserl, Edmund, 200n1
hypotheses, of philosophy of science, 73–74

hysteretic effect, of racial discrimination, 84

identification: Appiah on, 130; intelligibility and topic, 62; Warnke on, 128
identity: Islamic, 71, 177n22; politics of, 66; social, 13–14, 65; social and political discourse on, 56–57; sociocultural, 147. *See also* cultural identity; ethnicity and racial identity
ideology, 15, 146, 148, 149
ideology critique, 152; Haslanger on, 149–150
illegitimate prejudices, 9, 17–18, 58, 148
illegitimate theory hope, 57–58
immanent critique, 66, 77, 144–146
immediate appearance, Marcuse on, 145
inclusiveness, in global multicultural societies, 54
incommensurability, 10, 11, 25–26, 50–51, 170n44; of language, 28, 34, 52
inequality, 23, 151
injustice: of epistemic sort, 20; Fricker on hermeneutic, 129; global inequality and, 23, 151; global social, 81
intelligibility, 2, 40, 176n14; emergent horizon of, 161; fitting response of, 155, 157, 159, 174; historically effected, 3; language as structure of, 4; matrix, meaning and, 12, 13, 78, 95, 160–162, 180n39; of other, for understanding, 61; prejudices and, 3; of text, to agent, 7; topic identification and, 62
intercultural encounters, humanity and, 61, 174n7
intercultural understanding, 60–64; critical hermeneutics of, 65–80, 174n7
interest-based concerns, of cultural identity, 15, 72; Habermas on, 73–74, 147
internalist accounts, of autonomy, 180n39
interpretation: Gadamer on text, 63; Heidegger on assertion and, 39–40; process, of cultures, 70–71; of racial identity, 128; reciprocity lacking in, 129; semantic authority for social, 101–102
interpreter, question and response equilibrium by, 6
interpretive agency, in social world, 101
interpretive understanding, 2
interracial diversity, 21
intertribal adoption, 198n96
intracultural hermeneutic dialogue, 71
intraracial diversity, 21
Islamic identity, 71, 177n22

judgment, in ethical rules, 158; hermeneutic, for moral decisions, 159; Waldenfels and, 159–160

justice: global, 13, 18, 82–83, 93; racial, 18; reparative, 81–102; social, 13, 59. *See also* injustice
Justice, John, 168n19

Kant, Immanuel, 27; deontological ethical theory of, 156–157; transcendental unity of apperception of, 28
Kenya, female genital cutting in, 79
Kepler, Johannes, 35, 173n52
Khader, Serene, 94
kinds, 24–25; natural, 21–22, 36, 41–42, 44–45, 103, 104–105, 113, 114, 127, 130, 189n33; social, 127, 129, 130, 140
Kitcher, Philip, 132; on cultural diversity, 134; on ethnicity, 133–134, 139, 140; on race and ethnicity harmony, 140; on race biological significance, 105–113, 140–141, 186n18, 187n24, 188n29; on transracial adoption, 134
knowledge, pre-judgments as condition of, 3
Kripke-Putnam position: on fallibilism, 45, 173n52; on natural kind terms, 44–45; on ordinary language, 42; Rory on, 46
Kuhn, Thomas, 10; postempiricist science accounts of, 34, 35

Lafont, Cristina: on constitution of meaning, 32; on fallibilism, 173n52; on Habermas, 30–32; on knowledge as progressive learning process, 30; on language incommensurability, 34, 52
language: descriptive phrases of, 26, 29–30, 33–34, 38; Gadamer on constitutive view of, 6; Gadamer on understanding and role of, 1–2; Gadamer on world of, 28; Heidegger on, 28, 41; incommensurability of, 28, 34, 52; inquiry through, 3–4; as intelligibility structure, 4; Lafont on constitution of meaning in, 32; ordinary, 42, 122–123; tagging in, 36, 39, 41; translatability between, 29; world-disclosing function of, 27
legitimate prejudices, 9, 17–18, 58, 148
"Letter on Humanism, The" (Heidegger), 28
linguistically mediated community formation, 62
linguistic consciousness, 3
linguistic turn, in hermeneutics, 26–28; conversation topic consensus, 32–33, 167n9; fracturing of reason in, 29; Fregean dimension of, 29, 34, 36, 42; Habermas on, 31; postempiricist philosophy of science and, 26; reservations about, 29–36
Locke, John, 90
Logic (Hegel), 144
logic of question, Gadamer on, 4, 5, 118–119
Lukács, Georg, 145

Marcus, Ruth Barcan, 36–37; on reference-fixing descriptions, 38–39
Marcuse, Herbert, 144; on immediate appearance, 145; on real possibilities, 145–146
Marx, Karl, 57
Marxian theory, 14, 59
McCarthy, Thomas, 84; on culture of poverty thesis, 182n5; on global justice, 82–83, 93; on human rights, 93; on neo-racism, 83
McPartland, Marian, 138
meaning: holism, 29; intelligibility matrix and, 12, 13, 78, 95, 160–162, 180n39; Lafont on constitution of, 32; observational concept of, 35, 173n52; radical meaning variance, of Feyerabend, 46; shared realm overlap and, 49–50; theoretical concept of, 34–35, 173n52
meaning-bearing properties, of existing conditions, 145–146
meaning determines reference, 12, 28–29, 35; common referents and, 48–49; direct reference theory and, 36; Fregean dimension of, 34, 36
"Meaning of 'Race,' The" (Andreasen), 127
mechanisms of reproductive isolation component, of race, 106, 110–113, 188n29
mediation, agency and, 144

Mendelian model of cultural transmission, 135, 196n91
metaphysical realism, of Putnam, 44
metric of similarity, in racial classifications, 116
mismatch objection, ordinary racial classification and, 121
"Modalities and Intentional Language" (Marcus), 37–38
monolithic, homogenous cultures, 13
moral decision modalities: algorithmically guided choice, 159; hermeneutic judgment, 159; normless relativeness, 159
moral discourse, topics and, 64
moral rationality, 158
Morphy, Howard, 175n13
multiculturalism, 13, 139; Habermas and, 203n28
mutual understanding: third-person position in, 56, 128–131, 161, 162; Waldenfels on, 56, 155, 161, 162
mythical narratives: Habermas on, 88; scientific narratives contrast with, 88–89

narrative representability, 144, 151; constraint of, 20, 23, 82
narratives: mythical, 88–89; plurivocity, of legitimate cultural, 72, 77, 79, 146
Native Americans, cultural traditions of, 136
natural essences scientific accounts, 42–43

natural kind terms, 21, 103–104, 127; direct reference theory and, 36; Dupré on, 41; in explanatory accounts, 44; Kripke-Putnam position on, 44–45; Marcus on, 36; on race, 113–114; species in, 42–43
natural sciences, 11
negative dialectics, of Adorno, 58
neo-pragmatism, of Rorty, 58
neo-racism, McCarthy on, 83
New Orleans: pre-Katrina, 83; public education system in, 83–84
Nietzschean theory, 14, 59
nonidentical concept, of Adorno, 145
nonintertranslatability, 50–51, 170n44
non-question-begging critique, 8, 17, 68; on cultural formations, 57, 75, 179n34; toward cultural practices, 153; Rorty on, 67
normal conditions, in agency, 98–100, 153; cognitive and intellectual contexts of, 184n25
normless relativism, for moral decisions, 159

Obama, Barack, 84
objectivism, 200n1
objectivity, of human sciences, 2
observational term, meaning of, 53, 173n52; Kepler and Brahe on, 35
Occupy Wall Street movement, 88
On the Way to Language (Heidegger), 28

oppression, 102, 185n28
ordinary language, 42; racial classification and, 122–123
others: alterity of, 164; intelligibility of, for understanding, 61; Waldenfels on, 160–162

partitioning, of species, 116–121, 126
phenotypes: biomedical significant, 124–125; blood type, 109, 186n14; distinctive phenotypical differences, 106–109, 186n14, 186n18; traits, of race, 21
philosophical hermeneutics: fusion of horizons, 3, 4, 6–7, 52, 54; Gadamer on, 1–2; intelligibility and, 2–3; logic of question, 4, 5, 118–119; salience in, 2–3
philosophy of consciousness, 26–27
philosophy of science, 22; hypotheses of, 73–74; postempiricist, 26, 34, 35, 173n52; on race, 105
plurivocity, of legitimate cultural narratives, 72, 77, 79, 146
police brutality, 102, 149, 152, 178n25
policy-informing claims, in global development theory, 11
political discourse, about difference and identity, 56
politics of identity, 66
population genetics, 21
positivists, 9–10
possibilities, Waldenfels and, 160
postcolonialism, 13, 139

postempiricist philosophy of science, 173n52; Hanson and, 35; Kuhn on, 34, 35; linguist turn and, 26
postmodernism, essentialism critique by, 57
poverty: agency deficit and, 23. *See also* culture of poverty thesis; social psychology of poor
power, 202n18; systematic distributive asymmetries, for social, 147–148
practical deliberation, 56
pre-judgments, as knowledge condition, 3
prejudices, 119; Gadamer on legitimate and illegitimate, 9, 17–18, 58, 148; intelligibility and, 3
primacy of object, Adorno on, 145
progressive learning processes, 11, 26, 30
protest demonstrations, descriptive ethical relativism and, 88
psychologizing the structural fallacy, 85
public acknowledgment, 101. *See also* social acknowledgment
public education system, in New Orleans, 83–84
Putnam, Hilary, 36; division of linguistic labor, 43; metaphysical realism of, 44; on reference, 45–46; twin earth scenario of, 41

Question of the Other, The (Waldenfels), 160

race: African American music, 137–138, 199nn102–103; biological significance of, 83; common sense conception of, 104–105; description of, 104–127; fact of continuity of, 114, 118; Hardimon minimalist concept of, 109–110, 186n19; heritability component of, 106, 107; hermeneutics of, 103–141; immediate gratification and, 86–87; Kitcher on biological significance of, 105–113, 140–141, 186n18, 187n24, 188n29; Kitcher on ethnicity harmony with, 140; natural kind terms on, 113–114; new biology of, 21; phenotype traits of, 21; philosophy of science on, 105; as social recognition category, 127–141. *See also* ethnicity and racial identity
"Race, Ethnicity, Biology, and Culture" (Kitcher), 132
racial classification, 21, 103, 186n9; Bamshad on, 117; biological justification for, 11; biomedical significant phenotypes and, 124–125; Cavalli-Sforza on, 115, 118, 189n35; clinical genetics and, 123, 192n60; genetic ancestry and, 124–125, 135; genetic clustering and, 116–121, 124–125, 191n53; genomic level of, 122; as interpretive phenomenon, 129;

medicine and, 123–126; metric of similarity in, 116; ordinary language practice and, 122–123
racial discourse, 21
racial discrimination, hysteretic effect of, 84
racial disparities, COVID-19 pandemic and, 195n78
racial identity. *See* ethnicity and racial identity
racial justice, 18
radical alterity, 161–162
radical meaning variance, of Feyerabend, 46
rational choice theory, 11, 55
rationality: context-invariant form of, 14–15; moral, 158; of scientific theory choice, 11, 55; technological, 7–8
rational motivation, of scientific change, 26
reading off values fallacy, 85
real possibility conception, of Hegel, 144; Adorno on, 145–146; Horkheimer on, 146; Marcuse on, 145–146; visibility of, 146
reason: approach, Dray on agent, 9; fracturing of, in linguistic turn, 29; Habermas on universalist conception of, 9
reference: descriptive phrases use of, 26; language and, 28; Marcus on shared descriptive language for, 38–39; determined by meaning, 12, 28–29, 34–36, 48–50; Putnam on, 45–46; sameness of, 47,

169n38. *See also* direct reference theory
reference-fixing descriptions, of Marcus, 38–39
reflective equilibrium, between topic and response, 63–64
reified products, of cultural identity, 72
relativism, 10, 18, 60; descriptive ethical, 87, 88; Habermas on, 30–31; normless, for moral decisions, 159; promiscuous, 67
reparative justice, 81–102
representativeness, of strategic self-images, 72–73
reproductive isolation, mechanism of, 106, 110–113, 188n29
responsive ethics, of Waldenfels, 155–164
Rethinking Race (Hardimon), 186n19
Ricoeur, Paul, 14, 57, 59–60
rights, human, 66, 93
Rorty, Richard, 30, 42, 46; on analytic and continental differences, 25; neo-pragmatism of, 58; non-question-begging critique of, 67

Sache. *See* topics
salience: of cultural difference, 7–8; distinctions and, 4; mutually acknowledged, 49–50; in philosophical hermeneutics, 2–3
sameness, of reference, 47, 169n38
Scheffler, Israel, 35
Schleiermacher, Friedrich, 1

Schopenhauer, Arthur, 156–157
science: natural, 11; objectivity of human, 2; philosophy of, 22, 73–74, 105; postempiricist philosophy of, 26, 34, 35, 173n52; terms, explanatorily relevance of, 12; theory choice in, 10; understanding of, 11
scientific change, rational motivation of, 26
scientific inquiry, 10
scientific narratives, mythical narratives contrast with, 88–89
scientific theories: generalized model of, 52–53; rationality of choice for, 55. 11
Searle, John, 51; criterion of reference of, 44
second-order agency, 19, 58–60, 81–82, 180n29; exercise of, 90; social privilege and, 96, 183n23
second-order rationality, 14, 58–60, 68–69, 153
self-critique, in understanding, 56
self-estrangement, in understanding, 56
self-images, representativeness of strategic, 72–73
self-reflection, Habermas on Enlightenment connection with, 142
self-understanding, 2; social legitimacy link to social, 150; sociocultural, 23, 202n17
self-withholding, Gadamer on, 119

semantic authority, 81, 179n34; for social interpretation, 101–102
semantic democracy, 152. *See also* hermeneutic democracy
semantic holism, 12, 137
semantic resources, for cultural identity, 149
"Semantics of Rigid Designation, The " (Justice), 168n19
Senegal, female genital cutting in, 79
sexual harassment, 102, 149, 152, 178n25
Shapere, Dudley, 35
shared realm overlap, meaning and, 49–50
situated autonomous agency, 18; agency cognitive component, 101–102; external norms in, 100
situated metalanguage, forging of, 3, 61–62, 174n7, 175n13
Snyder, Laurence, 105
social acknowledgment, 127. *See also* public acknowledgment
social agency, 143, 151; educational opportunity lack and, 19; interpretive agency, in social world, 101
social and cultural understanding: cluster concept of cultural identity, 13, 15, 51, 59, 146; monolithic cultures, 13
social choice, distribution of, 77
social construction, of racial identity, 129
social identity, 13–14, 65

social interpretation, semantic authority for, 101–102
social justice, 13, 59
social kinds term, 130
social legitimacy, 152; social self-understanding link to, 150
social pathologies, of underclass, 18
social possibilities, of cultural agents, 16, 72
social power, systematic distributive asymmetries for, 147–148
social practices, 67, 98–99, 152; for cultural preservation, 135–138, 197n92; Habermas on, 142
social privilege, second-order agency and, 96, 183n23
social psychology of poor: Brooks on, 85–86; on immediate gratification, 86–87
social recognition, of race, 127–141
social self-understanding, social legitimacy link to, 150
social theory, 10, 55
sociocultural identity, 147
sociocultural politics, 22
sociocultural self-understanding, 23, 202n17
sociopolitical prejudices, legitimate and illegitimate, 58
species: in natural kind terms, 42–43; partitioning of, 126
strategic generation, of interpretive horizons, 147–148
strategic self-images, representativeness of, 72–73, 178n28

suppressed interests, of cultural agents, 16
systematic distributive asymmetries, of social power, 147–148

tagging, in language, 36, 39, 41
Tamir, Yael, 71
Taylor, Charles: on civilization of work, 88; on racial identity, 131
technological rationality, 7–8
text: intelligibility, to agent, 7, 62, 63; interpretation, Gadamer on, 63
Thales effect, 148
theoretical term, meaning of, 34–35, 53; Kepler and Brahe and, 35, 173n52
theory: choice in, 10, 11; critical, 143–144; critical race, 22, 129; critical social, 8–9, 55; deontological ethical, of Kant, 156–157; feminist, 94; Freudian, Marxian, and Nietzschean, 14, 59; generalized model of scientific, 52–53; global development, 11; illegitimate theory hope, 57–58; meaning of terms in, 34–35, 173n52; rational choice, 11, 55; scientific, 55; social, 10, 55. *See also* direct reference theory
Theory of Communicative Action, The (Habermas), 201n4, 202n15
theory of direct reference. *See* direct reference theory
third-person position, in mutual understanding, 56, 128–129; Gooding-Williams and, 130–131; Waldenfels on, 161, 162

topics (*Sache*), 175n13; analogy and, 64; consensus on, 32–33, 167n9; identification, 52, 62; intelligibility and, 62; moral discourse and, 64; reflective equilibrium for response and, 63–64
Toulmin, Stephen, 10
"Toward a Responsive Ethics" (Waldenfels), 156
traditions: Gadamer on, 52, 62, 171n48; Native Americans cultural, 136
transcendental ethnocentrism, 64–65
transcendental intersubjectivism, 52, 171n46
transcendental self-reflection, 142
transcendental unity of apperception, of Kant, 28
translatability: between languages, 29; nonintertranslatability, 50–51, 170n44
transracial adoption, Kitcher on, 134
trust, Waldenfels analysis of, 163
Truth and Method (Gadamer), 28
twin earth scenario, of Putnam, 41

unaided accomplishment, agency and, 97–99
underclass, social pathologies of, 18
understanding: cross-cultural, 8, 14, 22; dialogical, 7; Gadamer on language role in, 1–2; Heidegger on, 1; of inquirer, 2; intelligibility of other for, 61; intercultural, 60–80, 174n7; internal feature of, 61; of science, 11; self-critique and self-estrangement in, 56; social and cultural, 13, 15, 51, 59, 146. *See also* mutual understanding; self-understanding
universal concepts, account of in Gadamer, 4–5
universality, Habermas conception of reason, 9

values: agent, 18; autonomous agency and competing, 77; behavior relationship with, 18, 86, 88; deficit, 18, 19, 85–89; reading off fallacy, 85
Verstehen method, 9
vocabularies, situated metalanguages of, 3, 61–62, 174n7, 175n13
Vogel, Steven, 173n52
volitional component, of agency, 81, 91–92; West female genital cutting example, 94–95
volitional deficit, 18, 19

Waldenfels, Bernhard: on ambivalence of alienness, 162–163; on assimilation, 163; ethics of alterity of, 56, 155, 161; judgment and, 159–160; on mutual understanding, 56, 155, 161, 162; on others, 160–162; possibilities and, 160; responsive ethics of, 155–164; on third-person position, 161, 162; trust analysis of, 163
Warnke, Georgia, 128
weathering hypothesis, 195n78

"White Mythology" (Derrida), 163
Winch, Peter, 89
within-group negotiation, 78–79.
 See also semantic authority

world-disclosing function, of
 language, 27

Zack, Naomi, 108, 112–113, 186n18

NEW DIRECTIONS IN CRITICAL THEORY

AMY ALLEN, GENERAL EDITOR

New Directions in Critical Theory presents outstanding classic and contemporary texts in the tradition of critical social theory, broadly construed. The series aims to renew and advance the program of critical social theory, with a particular focus on theorizing contemporary struggles around gender, race, sexuality, class, and globalization and their complex interconnections.

Narrating Evil: A Postmetaphysical Theory of Reflective Judgment,
María Pía Lara

The Politics of Our Selves: Power, Autonomy, and Gender in Contemporary Critical Theory, Amy Allen

Democracy and the Political Unconscious, Noëlle McAfee

The Force of the Example: Explorations in the Paradigm of Judgment,
Alessandro Ferrara

Horrorism: Naming Contemporary Violence, Adriana Cavarero

Scales of Justice: Reimagining Political Space in a Globalizing World,
Nancy Fraser

Pathologies of Reason: On the Legacy of Critical Theory, Axel Honneth

States Without Nations: Citizenship for Mortals, Jacqueline Stevens

The Racial Discourses of Life Philosophy: Négritude, Vitalism, and Modernity, Donna V. Jones

Democracy in What State?, Giorgio Agamben, Alain Badiou, Daniel Bensaïd, Wendy Brown, Jean-Luc Nancy, Jacques Rancière, Kristin Ross, Slavoj Žižek

Politics of Culture and the Spirit of Critique: Dialogues, edited by Gabriel Rockhill and Alfredo Gomez-Muller

Mute Speech: Literature, Critical Theory, and Politics, Jacques Rancière

The Right to Justification: Elements of Constructivist Theory of Justice,
Rainer Forst

The Scandal of Reason: A Critical Theory of Political Judgment, Albena Azmanova

The Wrath of Capital: Neoliberalism and Climate Change Politics, Adrian Parr

Media of Reason: A Theory of Rationality, Matthias Vogel

Social Acceleration: A New Theory of Modernity, Hartmut Rosa

The Disclosure of Politics: Struggles Over the Semantics of Secularization, María Pía Lara

Radical Cosmopolitics: The Ethics and Politics of Democratic Universalism, James Ingram

Freedom's Right: The Social Foundations of Democratic Life, Axel Honneth

Imaginal Politics: Images Beyond Imagination and the Imaginary, Chiara Bottici

Alienation, Rahel Jaeggi

The Power of Tolerance: A Debate, Wendy Brown and Rainer Forst, edited by Luca Di Blasi and Christoph F. E. Holzhey

Radical History and the Politics of Art, Gabriel Rockhill

Starve and Immolate: The Politics of Human Weapons, Banu Bargu

The Highway of Despair: Critical Theory After Hegel, Robyn Marasco

A Political Economy of the Senses: Neoliberalism, Reification, Critique, Anita Chari

The End of Progress: Decolonizing the Normative Foundations of Critical Theory, Amy Allen

Recognition or Disagreement: A Critical Encounter on the Politics of Freedom, Equality, and Identity, Axel Honneth and Jacques Rancière, edited by Katia Genel and Jean-Philippe Deranty

What Is a People?, Alain Badiou, Pierre Bourdieu, Judith Butler, Georges Didi-Huberman, Sadri Khiari, and Jacques Rancière

Death and Mastery: Psychoanalytic Drive Theory and the Subject of Late Capitalism, Benjamin Y. Fong

Left-Wing Melancholia: Marxism, History, and Memory, Enzo Traverso

Foucault/Derrida Fifty Years Later: The Futures of Genealogy, Deconstruction, and Politics, edited by Olivia Custer, Penelope Deutscher, and Samir Haddad

The Habermas Handbook, edited by Hauke Brunkhorst, Regina Kreide, and Cristina Lafont

Birth of a New Earth: The Radical Politics of Environmentalism, Adrian Parr

Genealogies of Terrorism: Revolution, State Violence, Empire, Verena Erlenbusch-Anderson

The Practice of Political Theory: Rorty and Continental Thought, Clayton Chin

Queer Terror: Life, Death, and Desire in the Settler Colony, C. Heike Schotten

Naming Violence: A Critical Theory of Genocide, Torture, and Terrorism, Mathias Thaler

Avicenna and the Aristotelian Left, Ernst Bloch

The Experience of Injustice: A Theory of Recognition, Emmanuel Renault

Fear of Breakdown: Politics and the Work of Psychoanalysis, Noëlle McAfee

Transitional Subjects: Critical Theory and Object Relations, edited by Amy Allen and Brian O'Connor

Capitalism on Edge: How Fighting Precarity Can Achieve Radical Change Without Crisis or Utopia, Albena Azmanova

GPSR Authorized Representative: Easy Access System Europe, Mustamäe tee 50, 10621 Tallinn, Estonia, gpsr.requests@easproject.com

www.ingramcontent.com/pod-product-compliance
Lightning Source LLC
Chambersburg PA
CBHW021941290426
44108CB00012B/918